**books**online

Read this book online today:

With SAP PRESS BooksOnline we offer you online access to knowledge from the leading SAP experts. Whether you use it as a beneficial supplement or as an alternative to the printed book, with SAP PRESS BooksOnline you can:

• Access your book anywhere, at any time. All you need is an Internet connection.
• Perform full text searches on your book and on the entire SAP PRESS library.
• Build your own personalized SAP library.

The SAP PRESS customer advantage:

Register this book today at *www.sap-press.com* and obtain exclusive free trial access to its online version. If you like it (and we think you will), you can choose to purchase permanent, unrestricted access to the online edition at a very special price!

Here's how to get started:

1. Visit *www.sap-press.com*.
2. Click on the link for SAP PRESS BooksOnline and login (or create an account).
3. Enter your free trial license key, shown below in the corner of the page.
4. Try out your online book with full, unrestricted access for a limited time!

Your personal free trial **license key** for this online book is:

72kd-inj3-g6a9-e4mc

100 Things You Should Know About Controlling with SAP®

 **PRESS**

SAP PRESS is a joint initiative of SAP and Galileo Press. The know-how offered by SAP specialists combined with the expertise of the Galileo Press publishing house offers the reader expert books in the field. SAP PRESS features first-hand information and expert advice, and provides useful skills for professional decision-making.

SAP PRESS offers a variety of books on technical and business related topics for the SAP user. For further information, please visit our website: *www.sap-press.com*.

John Jordan
Production Variance Analysis in SAP Controlling
2007, 120 pp.
978-1-59229-109-0

John Jordan
Product Cost Controlling with SAP
2009, 572 pp.
978-1-59229-167-0

Shivesh Sharma
Optimize Your SAP ERP Financials Controlling Implementation
2008, 465 pp.
978-1-59229-219-6

Marco Sisfontes-Monge
Controlling-Profitability Analysis (CO-PA) with SAP
2008, 407 pp.
978-1-59229-137-3

John Jordan

100 Things You Should Know About
Controlling with SAP®

Galileo Press

Bonn • Boston

Galileo Press is named after the Italian physicist, mathematician and philosopher Galileo Galilei (1564–1642). He is known as one of the founders of modern science and an advocate of our contemporary, heliocentric worldview. His words *Eppur se muove* (And yet it moves) have become legendary. The Galileo Press logo depicts Jupiter orbited by the four Galilean moons, which were discovered by Galileo in 1610.

Editor Meg Dunkerley
Copyeditor Mike Beady
Cover Design Graham Geary
Photo Credit iStockphoto.com/alonzo76ok
Layout Design Graham Geary
Production Manager Kelly O'Callaghan
Assistant Production Editor Graham Geary
Typesetting Publishers' Design and Production Services, Inc.
Printed and bound in Canada

ISBN 978-1-59229-341-4

© 2011 by Galileo Press Inc., Boston (MA)
1st Edition 2011

Library of Congress Cataloging-in-Publication Data
Jordan, John.
    100 things you should know about controlling with SAP/ John Jordan. — 1st ed.
       p. cm.
    ISBN-13: 978-1-59229-341-4
    ISBN-10: 1-59229-341-7
    1. SAP ERP. 2. Accounting—Computer programs. 3. Cost. 4. Pricing. I. Title. II. Title: One hundred things you should know about controlling with SAP. III. Title: A hundred things you should know about controlling with SAP.
       HF5679.J6357 2010
       657.0285'53—dc22
2010035940

Contents at a Glance

Dear Reader,

Have you ever spent days trying to figure out how to generate a report in Controlling in SAP ERP Financials only to find out you just needed to click a few buttons? If so, you'll be delighted with this book — it unlocks the secrets of an SAP Controlling expert for use by everyone. It provides users and super-users with 100 tips and workarounds you can use to increase productivity, save time, and improve the ease-of-use for your SAP system. The tips have been carefully selected to provide a collection of the best, most useful, and rarest information. And with these tips, your SAP user experience will be friendlier and easier, and you may even hear a few comments like, "I had no idea you could do that that way!" or "I wish I had known how to do that a long time ago!"

Thanks to the expertise of John Jordan, reading this book will put you in the best possible position to truly maximize your time and make your job easier. Throughout the course of writing his manuscript, John continually impressed me with his knowledge of this subject and dedication to his work. You are now the recipient of this knowledge and dedication, and I'm confident that you'll benefit greatly from both.

We appreciate your business, and welcome your feedback. Your comments and suggestions are the most useful tools to help us improve our books for you, the reader. We encourage you to visit our website at *www.sap-press.com* and share your feedback about this work.

Thank you for purchasing a book from SAP PRESS!

Meg Dunkerley
Editor, SAP PRESS

Galileo Press
100 Grossman Drive, Suite 205
Braintree, MA 02184

meg.dunkerley@galileo-press.com
www.sap-press.com

Contents

Acknowledgments

I'd like to acknowledge my brother Mark Jordan who left us in this world for a greater place while I was writing this book. Mark was part of the SAP implementation team for Work Clearance Management (WCM) and Permit To Work (PTW) at CS Energy power stations in Queensland. People's lives depend on work permit safety systems and Mark worked tirelessly at making a difference to other people's lives throughout his.

I'd also like to thank Jenifer Niles and Stephen Solomon for their help in creating this new series of SAP PRESS books, and Meg Dunkerley for her work in editing the manuscript.

I'd also like to thank Thomas Michael for living and sharing his vision that there is always a different and better way to do anything and to never stop looking.

Introduction

This book is the first of a new series of SAP ERP books based on 100 ideas for various SAP software components. It is designed to make reading and understanding SAP ERP more interesting and accessible for your day to day work. You can flip through this book and search for ideas on each page to see if any of the 100 topics catches your attention. If so, you can read through the idea in a matter of minutes and decide whether you'd like to research the topic further. Most ideas are two pages long so you can see the entire idea on each open page. Since its limited how much information can be placed on two pages, each idea generally references other materials where you can do further research and reading.

SAP OSS notes are a great way to research topics, though knowing the best search terms to find relevant notes takes practice. The OSS notes referenced in this book will take you to exactly the right place to carry out further research. In a way you, can use this book as an index to OSS notes and other resources.

This book is designed to be useful for users, managers, consultants, and anyone interested in gaining a greater understanding of the controlling process. It contains many ideas that are simply not documented anywhere else. Some are gleaned from techniques that consultants and clients have figured out by themselves and I've been fortunate enough to work with them.

It contains easy-to-understand process overviews and detailed master data and configuration setup requirements. You can use this book as a reference, referring to specific sections when needed. For example, during master data setup, you can refer to specific ideas on master data. Or you can refer to ideas on costing sheets when configuring overhead.

The screenshots and menu paths in this book are taken from an SAP ERP Central Component, Release 6.0 system. Manufacturing order is used as an umbrella term for production and process orders throughout.

Since the subject of controlling is vast in scope this book is divided into nine categories, each a sub-module within Controlling. Sometimes an idea spans across several sub-modules, so if you don't find an idea in a particular category, try looking in a related category and you might find either what you're looking for, or a useful idea on a related topic. Let's discuss in more detail the contents of this book and how it is structured.

There are ten ideas on Cost Center Accounting and two each on the closely related Internal Order and Profit Center Accounting modules. There are useful ideas on working with the standard hierarchy and account assignment. The standard hierarchy is guaranteed to contain all cost centers and should represent your organizational structure. Account assignments determine which general ledger accounts and cost and profit centers are determined automatically during a posting. You'll also find ideas on cost center, internal order and profit center planning, price calculation and advanced reporting.

The next fifty ideas belong to the Product Cost Planning and Cost Object controlling sub-modules which are part of Product Cost Controlling. This module takes up half the book because it's such a large part of Controlling and because it's integrated with so many other areas such as manufacturing, materials management, financial accounting and sales and distribution. In this module you have to for example move from configuring general ledger accounts and movement types to assigning purchasing condition types to origin groups for delivery costs. You need to have a good idea of how at least six other modules work at a detailed level to be able to know Product Cost Controlling well. In fact there is nearly always a discovery phase during any Controlling implementation when you learn how the detailed functions of another module work that are integrated with Controlling. This book is designed to provide you with a head start during the discovery phase since many of these ideas are based on integration with other modules.

While there is much information available in online help documentation on the material ledger and profitability analysis, the ten ideas in this book on each of these sub-modules provide an overview of how to work with common issues. Some of the material ledger ideas reference information available from several OSS notes which you can read for more information. By reading the ten ideas on each of these two modules you'll gain a good understanding how both modules work.

There are six ideas on general controlling such as working with controlling areas, and closing periods for accounting, controlling and materials management. You'll also find information on navigating the Implementation Guide (IMG).

Finally there are ten ideas on reporting. Several ideas describe the types of standard reports available, and discuss some useful standard reports you may not be aware of. Finally you'll find some handy ideas on finding information with the data browser and technical help.

For more information on Controlling with SAP, visit *www.sap-press.com*, where you can find additional resources and companions for further reading.

Part 1

Cost Center Accounting

Things You'll Learn in this Section

You use cost center accounting for controlling expenditure based on areas of responsibility within your organization. It allows you to post all primary expenses from financial accounting to cost centers. You are provided with many tools to analyze and control the costs. Cost center managers can run standard reports to analyze the costs they are responsible for and compare plan and actual expenditure. Documents are stored for all transactions allowing you to drill-down from cost items of interest to detailed line item reports and to source documents, such as purchase orders and material documents.

You can enter plan data at the cost element level for cost centers, and run standard reports comparing plan and actual values for each period. You can drill-down from the cost center report to line items and source documents. The standard hierarchy contains all cost centers since the hierarchy node is a mandatory cost center field. You set up the standard hierarchy based on your company structure. The standard hierarchy is easily maintainable so you can make adjustments based on changes to the actual company structure.

You are also provided with many methods to allocate overhead costs to production cost centers and then directly to production orders for inclusion in the cost of sales. Assessments allow you to allocate costs from high level overhead cost centers progressively to production cost centers. Production and overhead costs are assigned to products through activity confirmations and/or costing sheets. Activity-based costing is also available providing complete flexibility to allocate overhead costs based on any criteria.

If there is a balance left on production cost centers at period-end you can either revaluate the activity prices to absorb all the cost center costs, or you can assess the remaining costs directly to profitability analysis. In profitability analysis you can compare the cost of sales with revenue and sales deductions to provide detailed profitability information for each product or sales region, or any of the many other characteristics available in the standard system.

In this section of the book you will find ideas on working with the standard hierarchy, planning, price calculation and target cost and variance analysis.

Tip ① Standard and Alternate Hierarchies

A standard hierarchy represents your company structure while alternate hierarchies are for flexible reporting.

The cost center standard hierarchy should represent your company's structure and be what you use most often in your reporting. This is because the standard hierarchy, which is guaranteed to contain all of the cost centers in a controlling area, is easily maintainable. While alternative hierarchies offer more flexible reporting, you can only maintain them with a transaction with less functionality.

✔ Solution

You can maintain a cost center standard hierarchy with Transaction OKEON or via the following IMG menu path. The screen in Figure 1 is displayed.

> ACCOUNTING • CONTROLLING • COST CENTER ACCOUNTING • MASTER DATA • STANDARD HIERARCHY • CHANGE

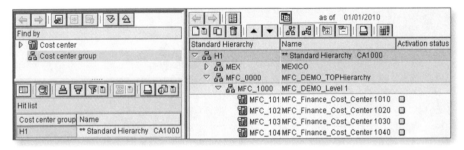

⌃ *Figure 1 Cost Center Standard Hierarchy*

You can drag and drop cost centers to different hierarchy nodes as your organizational structure changes. The standard hierarchy is really a special cost center group that contains all cost centers. The standard hierarchy also contains a hierarchy of cost center groups.

Any groups within the standard hierarchy can be maintained within the screen shown in Figure 1. Click on the COST CENTER GROUP in the top left of the screen and press [Enter] to display a list of all cost center groups in the standard hierarchy in the lower left of the screen. Double-click any cost center group and details of the group will be displayed on the right side of the screen.

Each time you run Transaction OKEON to maintain the standard hierarchy the system automatically displays the settings from the last time you ran the transaction. To ensure you are displaying the full standard hierarchy, continuing clicking the hierarchy and upward-pointing arrow icon. You can also determine the standard hierarchy for each controlling area with configuration Transaction OKKP.

You can only maintain the standard hierarchy or groups within the standard hierarchy with Transaction OKEON, as shown in Figure 1. You can create as many alternate hierarchies as you need for reporting purposes, however, you must maintain these with Transaction KSH2 or via the following menu path. Type in a cost center group and press [Enter] to display the screen shown in Figure 2.

> ACCOUNTING • CONTROLLING • COST CENTER ACCOUNTING • MASTER DATA •
> COST CENTER GROUP • CHANGE

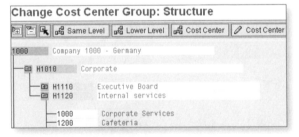

« *Figure 2*
Change Cost Center Group

You can maintain any cost center group with this transaction, however, you do not have the drag-and-drop functionality you have with Transaction OKEON. If you maintain a standard hierarchy with Transaction KSH2, the text at the top of the screen changes as shown in Figure 3.

« *Figure 3*
Change Standard Hierarchy with Transaction KSH2

You can change the structure of a standard hierarchy with this transaction, but you can't delete a cost center. ■

If you find you use an alternate hierarchy more than the standard hierarchy, you should consider swapping them.

The cost center standard hierarchy should represent your company's structure and be what you use most often in your reporting. The reason is that the standard hierarchy, which is guaranteed to contain all of the cost centers in a controlling area, is easily maintainable. You can only maintain an alternate hierarchy with Transaction KSH2, which has less functionality.

If you find you use an alternate hierarchy more often for reporting than the standard hierarchy, you should consider swapping hierarchies.

 Solution

You can determine the standard hierarchy with Transaction OKKP or via the following IMG menu path:

> CONTROLLING • GENERAL CONTROLLING • ORGANIZATION • MAINTAIN CONTROLLING AREA

Double-click the text Maintain Controlling Area, and then double-click on a controlling area. The screen in Figure 1 is displayed.

Chart of Accts	INT	Chart of accounts - international
Fiscal Year Variant	K4	Calendar year, 4 spec. periods
CCtr Std. Hierarchy	H1	** Standard Hierarchy CA1000

⌃ *Figure 1 Maintain Controlling Area*

If you attempt to change the STANDARD HIERARCHY you'll receive an error message stating that this can only be done if both the standard hierarchy assigned and the proposed hierarchy do not contain any cost centers.

Copying the alternate hierarchy as a node directly under the standard hierarchy and then deleting other existing nodes would be the simplest solution — if it were possible. This would also have the advantage that all existing reports using the alternate hierarchy would still run correctly. However, if you attempt to create the alternate hierarchy as a node directly under the existing standard hierarchy you'll receive an error message stating that the cost center group already exists.

Here's a procedure for streamlining the changeover:

1. **Copy the existing alternate hierarchy to another group:** Create a cost center group with Transaction KSH1 or via the following menu path:

> ACCOUNTING • CONTROLLING • COST CENTER ACCOUNTING • MASTER DATA • COST CENTER GROUP • CREATE

Create a new cost center group with a reference to your existing alternate hierarchy. Create it with a similar name by just adding a digit at the end.

2. **Delete the existing alternate hierarchy:** Delete a cost center group with Transaction KSH2 or via the following menu path:

> ACCOUNTING • CONTROLLING • COST CENTER ACCOUNTING • MASTER DATA • COST CENTER GROUP • CHANGE

Click the highest node, click the Select icon, and then click the Trash can icon to delete the alternate hierarchy.

3. **Create the deleted hierarchy as a node directly in the standard hierarchy:** Now that the alternate hierarchy doesn't exist, you can create it as a node directly under the existing standard hierarchy top node with Transaction OKEON or via the following menu path:

> ACCOUNTING • CONTROLLING • COST CENTER ACCOUNTING • MASTER DATA • STANDARD HIERARCHY • CHANGE

Click the New page icon and select Lower-Level Group to create the alternate hierarchy name directly under the standard hierarchy top node.

4. **Create alternate groups in the standard hierarchy:** Now create the alternate hierarchy structure within the standard hierarchy, duplicating any previous steps as necessary depending on which subnodes of the alternate hierarchy you need to continue reporting on with the same name.

5. **Reassign all cost centers into new groups:** Finally, reassign all cost centers to the new groups and delete all of the old groups. ▪

Tip Cost Element Default Account Assignment

You can quickly make a default account assignment by maintaining cost element master data.

You need to assign a cost object, such as a cost center or order, when posting to Controlling (CO). Usually, you assign a default object so that you don't have to make a manual entry for every expense posting.

✓ Solution

You can maintain cost elements with Transaction KA02 or via the following menu path:

> ACCOUNTING • CONTROLLING • COST CENTER ACCOUNTING • MASTER DATA • COST ELEMENT • INDIVIDUAL PROCESSING • CHANGE

Type in the cost element number, press [Enter], and navigate to the DEFAULT ACCT ASSGNMNT tab to display the screen in Figure 1.

« Figure 1
Cost Element Default Account Assignment

Enter a COST CENTER, ORDER, or both to maintain the default account assignment for any postings identified by this cost element per controlling area. If you make an entry in both fields, the posting to the ORDER is *real*, and the posting to the COST CENTER is *statistical* or for reporting purposes only. This means the cost center will keep a record of the posting, but the costs won't be included in cost center total costs. If you enter either a COST CENTER or ORDER, the posting will be real and included in the corresponding cost center or order total costs.

This method of setting up a default account assignment is relatively easy because it only requires a master data change. However, this may not be suitable if two plants in the same controlling area require different cost centers assigned to the same cost element. In this case, you'll need to assign cost objects with automatic account assignment configuration Transaction OKB9, which lets you enter a default cost center per cost element for each plant. *— PRIORITY TO COST ELEMENT M D ASSIGNMENT.*

A cost center entered in automatic account assignment takes priority over a cost center entered in cost element master data because it's more specific. Many plants can exist within a controlling area, whereas a cost element is defined for the entire controlling area. A posting identified by a cost element in a plant not defined in an automatic account assignment will post to a cost center in the cost element master data.

Some transactions, such as postings due to price differences, occur automatically, and you don't get the opportunity to enter the cost object manually. In these cases, you need to enter a default account assignment in either the cost element master data or via automatic account assignment configuration.

You can display a listing of all default account assignments in cost element master data with Transaction KA23 or via the following menu path:

> ACCOUNTING • CONTROLLING • COST CENTER ACCOUNTING • MASTER DATA •
> COST ELEMENT • COLLECTIVE PROCESSING • DISPLAY

Select All Cost Elements and Execute to display the screen shown in Figure 2.

Cost Element	Name	CElem category	Record Quantity	Unit of Meas.	Cost Center	Order
478000	Marketing/Sales Rep.	1				
479000	Bank Charges	1			2100	

⌃ *Figure 2 Cost Element List with Default Account Assignment*

The COST CENTER and ORDER columns list the default cost centers and orders. This list provides a quick check to see which cost elements have a default COST CENTER or ORDER entered in the cost element master data.

It's easier to keep track of default cost centers entered via *automatic* account assignment because they are maintained in one transaction and one screen. If you use this approach, the number of *default* cost centers entered in cost element master data should be kept to a minimum.

Only make default account assignment entries in cost elements when you need to make an account assignment quickly and don't have time to make the configuration change required for automatic account assignment. ◼

Tip 4 Automatic Account Assignment

You can make default cost center assignments per plant with automatic account assignment.

Automatic account assignment lets you enter a default cost center per primary cost element for each plant. Automatic assignment occurs during postings in external accounting modules, such as financial accounting, materials management, and sales and distribution, if you do not enter an automatic account assignment object, such as a cost center or order during a cost accounting relevant posting. You always need to enter an automatic account assignment entry for postings generated automatically by the system, for example, due to price and exchange rate differences.

 Solution

You can maintain automatic account assignments with Transaction OKB9 or via the following IMG menu path:

> CONTROLLING • COST CENTER ACCOUNTING • ACTUAL POSTINGS • MANUAL ACTUAL POSTINGS • EDIT AUTOMATIC ACCOUNT ASSIGNMENT

The screen in Figure 1 is displayed.

Dialog Structure		CoCd	Cost Elem.	BArIn	Cost Ctr	Order	PrfSeg	Profit Ctr	Acct assignmt detail	Acct assignmt detail
▽ 🗁 Default account assignment		1000	417000	☐	9030		☐	1		Valuation area is ma
🗁 Detail per business area/valuation		1000	473000	☐	1000		☐	1		Valuation area is ma

⌃ *Figure 1 Automatic Account Assignment Configuration*

Complete the following steps to proceed to the screen where you can assign cost centers per plant:

- ▶ Type "1" in the ACCT ASSIGNMENT DETAIL column
- ▶ Select the row of the required Cost Element (COST ELEM.)

▸ Double-click DETAIL PER BUSINESS AREA/VALUATION AREA on the left

▸ Click the New Entries button (not shown)

The screen shown in Figure 2 is displayed.

« *Figure 2*
Default Cost Center per Plant Configuration

Complete the Valuation Area (VALA) and Cost Center (COST CTR) fields and save your work to make cost center assignments. You can add more plants and assign cost centers, or you can delete rows as required.

A cost center entered in automatic account assignment takes priority over a cost center entered in cost element master data with Transaction KA02, because it's more specific. Many plants can exist within a controlling area, whereas a cost element is defined for an entire controlling area.

If you manually enter a cost object during a transaction, this will take priority over an automatic account assignment entry. If you do not want a user to manually enter a cost center, then you can suppress the cost center field. Let's look at an example of creating a goods issue (GI) to a cost center with Movement Type 201. When you carry out a manual GI with standard Transaction MB1A, the Cost center field is mandatory. You can suppress the Cost center field with Transaction OMBW or via the following IMG menu path:

> MATERIALS MANAGEMENT • INVENTORY MANAGEMENT AND PHYSICAL INVENTORY • GOODS ISSUE / TRANSFER POSTINGS • DEFINE SCREEN LAYOUT

Double-click Movement Type 201 and then Additional account assignments to display the screen shown in Figure 3.

« *Figure 3*
Maintain Field Status Groups

Select SUPPRESS next to the COST CENTER field and save your work. This will force the system to retrieve the cost center with automatic account assignment. ■

Plan Activity Price with Activity Type Groups

You can use activity type groups when entering plan activity prices to filter the price-planning screen to only display the activities you work with.

Activity type groups allow you to limit the list of activity types when planning activity prices with Transaction KP26. You enter an individual activity type, range, or group in the initial selection screen when planning activity prices:

▶ **Activity Type:** You need to manually enter all of your activity types

▶ **Range:** If your activity types are not named in logical ranges you may include activity prices you don't need

▶ **Group:** Groups filter your activity types on the plan activity price screen

Let's look at how to create and use activity type groups.

Solution

You can create an activity type group with Transaction KLH1 or via the following menu path:

> ACCOUNTING • CONTROLLING • COST CENTER ACCOUNTING • MASTER DATA • ACTIVITY TYPE GROUP • CREATE

Type in the name of your group and click the Execute icon to display the screen shown in Figure 1.

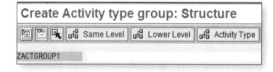

《 Figure 1
Create Activity Type Group — Structure Screen

Type in your group description, click the ACTIVITY TYPE button, and enter the activity types in your group to display the screen shown in Figure 2.

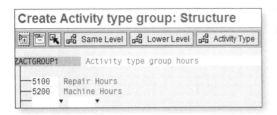

«   *Figure 2*
Add Activity Type to Create Activity Type Group Screen

After saving the details in Figure 2, you're ready to use your new activity type group during activity price planning. Enter your plan activity prices with Transaction KP26 or via the following menu path:

> ACCOUNTING • CONTROLLING • COST CENTER ACCOUNTING • PLANNING • ACTIVITY OUTPUT/PRICES • CHANGE

Enter the selection screen data (including your activity type group), click the Form-Based radio button at the bottom of the screen, and click the Overview (two peaks) icon to display the plan price screen, shown in Figure 3.

Activity type	Plan activity	Distribution key	Capacity	Distribution key	Unit	Fixed price	Variable price
5100		1		1	H		
5200		1		1	H		
*Activ							

⌃ *Figure 3 Change Activity Type Price Planning Overview Screen*

The screen is restricted to the activity types in your group and no new activity types can be entered. If you need to plan for more activities, you can either add activity types to your group, or click the Free Entry radio button at the bottom of the selection screen when you run Transaction KP26. Note that the system defaults to your last selection of either the Free or Form-based radio buttons. ■

Tip 6 Copy Cost Center Plan

You can copy cost center plans from year to year and version to version with a standard transaction.

When creating next year's cost center plan, you may want to copy the current-year's plan to next year and make the necessary adjustments. You can do this and copy and change actual data to plan data with standard transactions. Let's look at the details of these standard transactions.

 ## Solution

You can copy cost center data with Transaction KP97 or via the following menu path:

> ACCOUNTING • CONTROLLING • COST CENTER ACCOUNTING • PLANNING • PLAN-NING AIDS • COPY • COPY PLAN TO PLAN

The screen in Figure 1 is displayed.

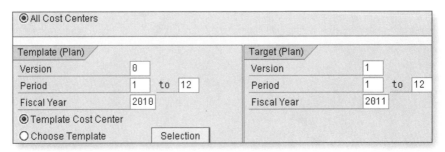

⌃ *Figure 1 Cost Center Copy Plan to Plan Selection Screen*

Select TEMPLATE COST CENTER to copy from a cost center on a 1:1 basis. If you'd like to copy from one cost center to multiple cost centers, select Choose TEMPLATE and click the SELECTION button to choose the Template cost center.

The selection screen settings in Figure 1 will copy all cost center plan data from Version 0 Fiscal Year 2010 to VERSION 1 FISCAL YEAR 2011. You can modify the plan data in VERSION 1 for FISCAL YEAR 2011 and, when finalized, you can copy from VERSION 1 FISCAL YEAR 2011 to VERSION 0 FISCAL YEAR 2011.

You can also create multiple versions that correspond to different scenarios, such as best and worst case for sales next year. You can maintain Versions with Transaction OKEQ or via the following IMG menu path:

> CONTROLLING • GENERAL CONTROLLING • ORGANIZATION • MAINTAIN VERSIONS

The screen in Figure 2 is displayed.

Dialog Structure						
▽ 🗁 General Version Definition		General Version Overview				
📁 Settings in Operating Concern		Version	Name	Plan	Actual	WIP/RA	Variance
📁 Settings for Profit Center Accounting		0	Plan/actual version	☑	☑	☑	☑
▽ 📁 Controlling Area Settings		1	Plan version: chang	☑	☐	☑	☑
📁 Settings for Each Fiscal Year		2	Plan version 2	☑	☐	☑	☑
		3	Plan version 3	☑	☐	☑	☐

⌃ **Figure 2** *General Version Definition*

Here, you can create and maintain the GENERAL VERSION. You maintain a VERSION for each fiscal year by selecting a VERSION on the right; double-clicking CONTROLLING AREA SETTINGS on the left, selecting the VERSION on the right and double-clicking SETTINGS FOR EACH FISCAL YEAR on the left to display the screen in Figure 3.

📁 Controlling Area Settings					
🗁 Settings for Each Fiscal Year		Year	Version Locked	Integrated Planning	Copying Allowed
📁 Delta Version: Bus. Transacti		2010	☐	☑	☑
📁 Settings for Progress Analysis (P		2011	☐	☑	☑

⌃ **Figure 3** *Version Settings for Each Fiscal Year*

Here, you can create and maintain versions for each fiscal year.

You can copy actual-to-plan cost center data with Transaction KP98 or via the following menu path:

> ACCOUNTING • CONTROLLING • COST CENTER ACCOUNTING • PLANNING • PLANNING AIDS • COPY • COPY ACTUAL TO PLAN

A selection screen similar to Figure 1 is displayed. In this screen, you enter the periods and fiscal year to access the actual data along with the plan version, periods, and fiscal year to copy the actual data to VERSION 0 FISCAL YEAR 2011. ■

Tip 7   Plan Cost Splitting

You can allocate cost center costs across activities.

During plan cost splitting, the system splits the activity-independent costs of a cost center among the activity types of that cost center. Plan costs are split automatically during plan price calculation. First, let's look at activity-dependent and activity-independent costs and then we'll move on to seeing how the costs are split.

✓ Solution

You can plan activity-independent and activity-dependent costs with Transaction KP06 or via the following menu path:

> Accounting • Controlling • Cost Center Accounting • Planning • Cost and Activity Inputs • Change

The screen in Figure 1 is displayed.

Cost Center	1000
to	
or group	
Activity Type	INST
to	
or group	
Cost Element	473000

« *Figure 1*
Cost Element Planning Selection Screen

In this screen, you have the option of entering an Activity Type:

▶ **Activity-Independent Planning**: If you do not enter an Activity Type, then the plan information you enter on the following planning screen is independent of an activity. All costs you enter are fixed.

▶ **Activity-Dependent Planning**: If you enter an Activity Type in Figure 1, then the plan cost information is directly associated with that activity. You have the choice of entering fixed and variable costs.

In order for the system to automatically calculate plan activity price, all activity-independent costs must be directly associated with activities. This functionality is called plan cost splitting. There are two methods of plan cost splitting: equivalence numbers and splitting structure.

You can define equivalence numbers when manually planning activity prices with Transaction KP26 or via the following menu path:

> ACCOUNTING • CONTROLLING • COST CENTER ACCOUNTING • PLANNING • ACTIVITY OUTPUT/PRICES • CHANGE

Click the Overview icon to display the screen in Figure 2.

Activity	Plan activity	Dist	Capacity	Dist	Unit	Fixed price	Variable price	Price unit	Pl	P	A	Alloc. cost	T	EquiNo
INST	1	1		1	DAY			00001	1	☐	☐	TRAINING	1	1

⌃ **Figure 2** *Planned Activity Price Entry Screen*

The equivalence number (EQUINO) in the last column defaults to one. You can change this to determine the ratio used to distribute costs across activities. If you need more flexibility to determine how costs are allocated across activities, you can maintain a splitting structure with Transaction OKES or via the following IMG menu path:

> CONTROLLING • COST CENTER ACCOUNTING • PLANNING • ALLOCATIONS • ACTIVITY ALLOCATION • SPLITTING • DEFINE SPLITTING STRUCTURE

The screen in Figure 3 is displayed.

Splitting Structures		Structure	Text
▽ ☐ Assignments		A1	IDES-ABC CCTR
☐ Selection for assignment		AC	
☐ Splitting rules		I1	IDES-OM CCTR 4276,4278,4280
☐ Selection for rules		I2	IDES-OM CCTR 4275,4277,4295

« **Figure 3**
Maintain Splitting Structures

SPLITTING STRUCTURES determine how and which selected activity-independent costs from a cost center are divided between the activity types. A splitting structure consists of one or more ASSIGNMENTS, which define the connection between the cost element(s) or cost element group to be split and the SPLITTING RULES used to divide the costs. Each splitting rule is based on a splitting method; for example, splitting costs based on statistical key figures.

After you define a splitting structure, you must assign it to the cost centers you want to split costs in according to the rules in Transaction OKEW. ▪

Tip (8) Actual Price Calculation

The system can automatically calculate your prices for activity types based on actual costs and actual activities.

Cost center under/over absorption can be allocated to products, if necessary, with an additional period-end process called *Revaluation at Actual Prices*. This process calculates the incremental planned activity price needed to allocate all cost center debits. Orders are then revalued with the incremental debits, and the cost center receives the corresponding credits. Following revaluation, the cost center's actual balance is zero.

There are two requirements for carrying out revaluation: a version configuration setting and an activity type setting. Let's discuss each in turn.

Solution

You can maintain version configuration with Transaction OKEQ or via the following IMG menu path:

> CONTROLLING • GENERAL CONTROLLING • ORGANIZATION • MAINTAIN VERSIONS

Navigate to the screen in Figure 1 using the following steps:

▶ Select Version 0

▶ Double-click Settings for Each Fiscal Year

▶ Double-click the current Fiscal Year

▶ Click the Price calculation tab

Actual	
Methods	1 Periodic price
Revaluation	1 Own business transaction
	1 Own business transaction

« *Figure 1*
Revaluation Settings in Version Configuration

Now that you've navigated to the correct tab, you can make the configuration setting by left-clicking on the REVALUATION field, choosing the OWN BUSINESS TRANSACTION, and saving.

Now that we've discussed the version configuration, let's look at activity type settings for actual price calculation. You can maintain activity types with Transaction KL02 or via the following menu path:

> ACCOUNTING • CONTROLLING • COST CENTER ACCOUNTING • MASTER DATA • ACTIVITY TYPE • INDIVIDUAL PROCESSING • CHANGE

This menu path brings you to the screen shown in Figure 2.

Variance Values for Actual Allocation		
Actl Acty Type Cat.		As in planning
Act. price indicator	5	Actual price, automatically based on activity

⌄ **Figure 2** *Actual Price Indicator in Activity Type*

Right-click on the ACT. PRICE INDICATOR field, select Possible Entries, then double-click ACTUAL PRICE AUTOMATICALLY BASED ON ACTIVITY, and save your work.

Now that we've ensured that the configuration and activity type settings are correct, let's examine how to carry out actual price calculation. Revaluation occurs automatically during actual price calculation. You carry out actual price calculation with Transaction KSII or via the following menu path:

> ACCOUNTING • CONTROLLING • COST CENTER ACCOUNTING • PERIOD-END CLOSING • SINGLE FUNCTIONS • PRICE CALCULATION

Complete the selection fields and click on the Execute icon to run the transaction. You can analyze the results of actual price calculation in the information system with Transaction KSBT or via the following menu path:

> ACCOUNTING • CONTROLLING • COST CENTER ACCOUNTING • INFORMATION SYSTEM • REPORTS FOR COST CENTER ACCOUNTING • PRICES • COST CENTERS: ACTIVITY PRICES

You can compare plan and actual activity prices with the resulting report. As long as you have set the revaluation indicator in the version as shown in Figure 1 and set the actual activity indicator in the activity type as shown in Figure 2, the revaluation automatically occurs during actual price calculation.

Actual price calculation and revaluation let you post cost center variances to product cost collectors and manufacturing orders. ■

You can use cost center target costs to allow for a more advanced analysis.

You can analyze cost center under/over absorption with the standard actual/plan cost center report S_ALR_87013611, and for most companies, this provides sufficient information for managing overhead costs. More advanced functionality is available to analyze cost center balance, if required, such as target cost and variance analysis.

✓ Solution

Cost center target costs are based on plan costs adjusted by activity quantity consumed. Target cost allows for a more detailed analysis of cost center balance, because an increase in actual costs may be due to an increase in activities consumed. Target costs can be higher than plan costs due to an increase in activity quantity. Target costs differ from plan costs when the following two conditions are met:

▶ **Activity-Dependent Planning**
You can carry out activity-dependent planning by entering an activity type in the selection screen of Transaction KP06 and entering fixed and variable costs during cost element planning. Let's follow an example to help illustrate how target costs work. Enter $10,000 fixed and $10,000 variable costs, and 100 hours variable quantity during activity-dependent primary cost planning.

▶ **Plan Activity Quantity and Prices**
You need to enter plan activity quantity and prices with Transaction KP26. Continuing with the same example, enter 100 hours plan activity, and $100 fixed and $100 variable during activity price planning.

10,000 FIX NOT ACTIVITY TYPE PRICE DEPENDENT

Before any activities are consumed, target costs equal only the fixed portion of plan costs. In this example, plan costs are $20,000, the sum of fixed and variable costs. Target costs, however, are only $10,000, calculated by adding fixed costs to the result of variable costs times the operating rate. The operating rate is defined as (actual activity / plan activity) × 100. Because actual activity quantity is zero the operating rate is zero and no variable costs are added to target costs.

When 50 hours of activity are consumed, target costs equal the fixed portion of plan costs plus 0.5 (50 actual hours/100 plan hours) times the variable costs. In the example, plan costs remain at $20,000. Meanwhile, target costs are $15,000, calculated by adding fixed costs of $10,000 to variable costs times the operating rate, or $5,000. If 140 hours of activity are consumed, target costs equal the fixed portion of plan costs plus 1.4 (140 actual hours/100 plan hours) times the variable costs. Plan costs remain at $20,000. Meanwhile, target costs are $24,000, calculated by adding fixed costs of $10,000 to variable costs times the operating rate, or $14,000.

Target costs are continuously calculated so that they can be reported on in real time. You can view the cost center actual/target report with Transaction S_ALR_87013625 or via the following menu path:

> ACCOUNTING • CONTROLLING • COST CENTER ACCOUNTING • INFORMATION SYSTEM • REPORTS FOR COST CENTER ACCOUNTING • TARGET/ACTUAL COMPARISONS • COST CENTERS: ACTUAL/TARGET/VAR.

Complete the selection fields and Execute to display a report similar to the screen shown in Figure 1.

Cost Elements	Actual Costs	Target Costs	Plan Costs	T/A-Var.(abs
415100 External activities	12.100,-	14.000,-	10.000,-	-1.900,-
404000 Spares	900,-			900,-
430000 Salaries	10.000,-	10.000,-	10.000,-	
* Debit	23.000,-	24.000,-	20.000,-	**-1.000,-**
619000 DIAA Production	-28.000,-	-28.000,-	-20.000,-	
* Credit	-28.000,-	-28.000,-	-20.000,-	
** Under/Overabsorption	-5.000,-	**-4.000,-**	0,-	-1.000,-

« *Figure 1*
Actual/Target Cost Center Report

ACTUAL and TARGET COSTS both increase with resource consumption, while PLAN COSTS remain constant. The PLAN COSTS are based on activity consumption resulting in a credit of -20,000. Actual activity consumption is greater than plan resulting in an actual credit of -28,000. The target DEBIT is more realistic than the plan DEBIT, because it is increased by rising variable costs due to increased activity consumption. There is only a 1,000 variance between actual and target in the UNDER/OVERABSORPTION row in Figure 1 compared with a 5,000 variance between total ACTUAL COSTS and PLAN COSTS. ■

Tip (10) Cost Center Variance Analysis

You can use automatic variance calculation to allocate cost center over/under absorption into variance categories.

Variances are caused by the difference between actual and target data. If you want to analyze the causes of cost center variances in detail, you can use automatic variance calculation. You may need to carry out variance analysis if target cost analysis does not provide enough information on the source of the variance or the responsible person. The two steps involved in variance analysis are examined in the following sections.

 Solution

The first step required to calculate variances is:

▶ **Actual Cost Splitting:** Actual costs are posted to a cost center in general, while variance calculation requires that activity-independent actual costs be distributed specifically to a cost center/activity type combination. During variance calculation, the actual cost of each activity is determined with *actual cost splitting*. The two steps involved during actual cost splitting per cost element are listed as follows:

  ▶ The cost center actual costs are allocated to activity types based on target costs per activity type for each cost element. If target costs don't exist for a cost element, costs are split according to the target costs of the cost element group assigned in customizing of the target version. If no target costs exist for the cost element group, the costs are split in the second step.

  ▶ This step is necessary if there are no target costs for the cost element or cost element group, or if activity-independent costs exist. In this step, actual costs are allocated to activity types according to splitting rules. If no splitting rules exist, costs are allocated based on equivalence numbers.

At the end of the actual cost splitting process, all actual costs per cost element are distributed to activity types. Actual cost splitting happens automatically during variance calculation.

▶ **Variance Calculation:** Variance calculation provides information on the reasons for variances, which are useful when analyzing the difference between actual and target costs. The cost center balance is assigned to input and output variance categories based on the source of the variance.

Configuration required for cost center variance calculation includes:

▶ Create target cost version — Transaction OKV5

▶ Create variance variant — Transaction OKVF

▶ Assign variance variant to a target a version — Transaction OKV5

You can calculate cost center variance with Transaction KSS1 or via the following menu path:

> ACCOUNTING • CONTROLLING • COST CENTER ACCOUNTING • PERIOD-END CLOSING • SINGLE FUNCTIONS • VARIANCES

Variances are saved automatically if you deselect the test run indicator.

You report on variance calculation in the information system with Transaction S_ALR_87013627 or by following menu path:

> ACCOUNTING • CONTROLLING • COST CENTER ACCOUNTING • INFORMATION SYSTEM • REPORTS FOR COST CENTER ACCOUNTING • TARGET/ACTUAL COMPARISONS • VARIANCE ANALYSIS • COST CENTERS VARIANCES

Variance calculation assigns the cost center balance to variance categories on both the input and output side:

▶ Input variances are based on actual costs minus target costs

▶ Output variances are based on target costs minus allocated actual costs

The sum of variances represents the total variance, or the cost center balance.

Input Variances
A report highlighting input variance is shown in Figure 1.

Cost Elements	Actual Costs	Target Costs	Plan Costs	T/A-Var (abs)
415100 External acty.	12,100	14,000	10,000	1,900
404000 Replacement	900			900
430000 Salaries	10,000	10,000	10,000	
* Debit	23,000	24,000	20,000	-1,000
619000 DILV Production	-28,000	-28,000	-20,000	
* Credit	-28,000	-28,000	-20,000	
** Under/Overabsorption	-5,000	-4,000	0	-1,000

« *Figure 1*

Input Variance Analysis —
Cost Center Debits

Highlighted input variance is based on *cost center Actual Debit — Target Debit*. In this example, the formula is 23,000 – 24,000 = (1,000). The four input variances are described as follows:

▶ **Input Price Variances:** These indicate changes in costs due to prices. The variances represent differences between target and actual costs due to differences in planned and actual prices of materials or services. The formula is: *Input price variance = (Actual price – Plan price) × Actual input quantity.* For example, if you plan 100 hours at \$100 per hour and post 110 actual hours at \$110 per hour, input price variance is (\$110 – \$100) × 110 h = \$1,100.

▶ **Input Quantity Variances:** These result from under/overconsumption for cost elements. The variances represent differences between target and actual costs caused by different quantities being consumed than planned. Input price variances include variances caused by both price and quantity differences. The formula is: *Input quantity variance = (Actual input quantity – Target input quantity) × Plan price.* For example, 100 hours are planned as a variable quantity for external services during activity-dependant cost planning with Transaction KP06, and 100 hours are entered as plan activity consumption with Transaction KP26. Actual activity consumption was 140 hours, so the target quantity for external services is 140 hours. Only 110 hours were actually consumed by entering the quantity with Transaction FB50 and by choosing a screen variant with cost center and quantity. Input quantity variance is: (110 h – 140 h) × \$100 = (\$3,000).

▶ **Resource-Usage Variance:** This indicates changes in the plan consumption of cost elements. It occurs if you post an actual cost against an unplanned cost element, or if no actualdata exists for a plan cost element. The formula is: *Resource-usage variance = Actual costs – Target costs – Input price variance.* For example, if there is \$900 of unplanned consumption of replacement parts, as shown in Figure 1, resource-usage variance is \$900.

▶ **Remaining Input Variance:** This includes all input variances that cannot be assigned to any other input variance category. This variance can occur if you planned cost elements and made actual postings but did not record consumption quantities.

Output Variances

An example report highlighting output variance is shown in Figure 2.

Cost Elements	Actual Costs	Target Costs	Plan Costs	T/A-Var (abs)
415100 External acty.	12,100	14,000	10,000	-1900
404000 Replacement	900			900
430000 Salaries	10,000	10,000	10,000	
* Debit	23,000	24,000	20,000	-1,000
619000 DILV Production	-28,000	-28,000	-20,000	
* Credit	-28,000	-28,000	-20,000	
** Under/Overabsorption	-5,000	**-4,000**	0	-1,000

« *Figure 2*
Output Variance Analysis — Cost Center Credits

Output variances are based on TARGET COSTS minus the sum of cost center CREDIT due to activity allocation. In this example the formula is 24,000 – 28,000 = (4,000). The four output variances are described as follows:

- **Output Price Variance:** This occurs if you use a price that differs from the plan price that is calculated iteratively each month based on planned activity. The target credit posting (*Plan price × Actual activity*) varies from the actual credit posting (*Allocation price × Actual activity*) on the cost center. Output price variance can result if you use average prices instead of period-based prices, if the capacity of the activity type is used as the basis of the price calculation, or if you set a price manually. The formula is: *Output price variance = Actual activity × (Plan price – Actual price)*.

- **Output Quantity Variance:** This is the difference between manually entered actual costs and allocated actual quantities. The formula is: *Output quantity variance = (Actual quantity – Manual actual quantity) × Plan price*. Variances arising from both price and quantity differences appear as output price variances.

- **Fixed Cost Variances:** These occur when the actual operating rate varies from the plan operating rate and some of the planned fixed costs are either underabsorbed or overabsorbed due to credit postings. The system only reports a fixed cost variance if the operating rate is not 100%.

- **Remaining Variance:** This includes all output variances that cannot be assigned to any other output variance category. This variance can occur if you deactivated calculation of variance categories on the output side, or if you deactivated all variance categories in the variance variant. ■

Part 2
Internal Orders

Things You'll Learn in this Section

Internal orders are designed to provide you with cost control and monitoring of short-term jobs and tasks. They are normally used to plan, collect, and settle the costs of internal jobs and tasks such as marketing campaigns and repairs. While cost centers are designed for long-term cost management, internal orders are for short to medium-term cost collection. You can monitor internal orders throughout their life cycle from creation, through the planning and posting of actual costs, to settlement and archiving.

The following different types of internal orders are available:

▶ **Overhead cost orders:** Used for short to medium-term monitoring of overhead costs or parts of overhead costs such as marketing campaigns

▶ **Investment orders:** Let you monitor investment costs to be capitalized and settled to fixed assets

▶ **Accrual orders:** Enable you to monitor period-related accrual calculation between expenses posted in financial accounting and controlling

▶ **Orders with revenues:** Let you monitor costs and revenues that are incurred for activities for external partners, or for internal activities. These can be used if you have not implemented the sales and distribution module.

Internal orders are created from order types which contain all the information necessary to create orders which are to be treated in the same manner for items such as period-end settlement. You can use the system supplied order types or create your own for your specific purposes. Different order types can be used to create internal orders with different levels of detailed input required and reporting functionality.

Status management determines the time that different business transactions are carried out. You can create user status structures using predefined system statuses, enabling you to specify more restrictions for allowed business transactions.

Statistical orders enable you to post costs to an order and a cost center at the same time. You can use the statistical posting of the order for reporting and evaluation purposes.

The ideas in this section of the book explain internal order planning and budgeting.

Tip Internal Order Planning

You can use internal order planning to enter plan costs, compare actual costs, and carry out variance analysis.

Cost planning is generally carried out on internal orders of long duration. Orders that exist for a short duration are not usually planned. You can carry out planning at an overall, an annual, or a detailed cost element level.

✓ Solution

You can maintain a planning profile with Transaction OKOS or via the following IMG menu path:

> CONTROLLING • INTERNAL ORDERS • PLANNING • MANUAL PLANNING • MAINTAIN PLANNING PROFILES FOR OVERALL PLANNING

Double-click a planning profile to display the screen in Figure 1.

« *Figure 1*
Internal Order Planning Profile

The PAST and FUTURE TIME FRAME fields define how many years in the past and future you can enter planning data. The TOTAL and ANNUAL VALUES checkboxes control whether you can plan with total and annual data. The Primary Cost Element group (PRIM.CELEM.GRP) defines the primary cost elements you can plan against.

You can assign the planning profile to an order type with Transaction KOAP or by following Menu Path 1.

You can carry out order planning with Transaction KO12 or via the following IMG menu path:

Accounting • Controlling • Internal Orders • Planning • Overall
Values • Change

The screen in Figure 2 is displayed.

Period	Plan	Tra	P	Planned total	Costing	Cost element plan
Overall	50,000.00	EUR		50,000.00		
2009		EUR				
2010		EUR	C	50,000.00		50,000.00

《 *Figure 2*

Maintain Annual Overview Plan Values

You can carry out Overall and annual planning in this screen. To enter a detailed cost element plan, click the year and then the Primary Costs button (not shown). The screen in Figure 3 is displayed:

Cost element	Text	Total plan costs	Dist	Total plan consumptn
420000	Direct labor costs	10,000.00	2	
421000	Indirect labor costs	40,000.00	2	
*Cost elem	Total	50,000.00		0.000

《 *Figure 3*

Maintain Primary Costs Planning

The primary cost element group you enter in the planning profile in Figure 1 determines the number of cost elements for planning. You can simplify this planning screen by minimizing the number of cost elements in the group.

You can run a standard report on these values with Transaction S_ALR_87012993 or via the following menu path:

Accounting • Controlling • Internal Orders • Information System •
Reports for Internal Orders • Plan/Actual Comparisons

The report is displayed as shown in Figure 4.

Cost elements	Actual	Plan	Abs. var.	Var. (%)
420000 Direct labor costs	12,000.00	10,000.00	2,000.00	20.00
421000 Indirect labor costs	35,000.00	40,000.00	5,000.00-	12.50-
* Costs	47,000.00	50,000.00	3,000.00-	6.00-
** Balance	47,000.00	50,000.00	3,000.00-	6.00-

☆ **Figure 4** *Actual/Plan/Variance Order Report*

There are many other standard reports for orders in the information system. ■

Tip **12**

Internal Order Budgeting

You can use internal order budgeting to control actual expenditures by activating availability control.

An internal order budget represents funds approved by management. A budget is maintained at either an overall or annual level. You can activate availability control, which can issue warning or error messages based on defined tolerances. Let's look at how to create an internal order budget and how to activate availability control.

Solution

You can maintain a budget profile with Transaction OKOB or via the following IMG menu path:

> CONTROLLING • INTERNAL ORDERS • BUDGETING AND AVAILABILITY CONTROL • MAINTAIN BUDGET PROFILE

Double-click a budget profile to display the screen in Figure 1.

Currency Translation: Overall Budget		Availability Control	
Exch. Rate Type	M	Activation Type	1 Usage
Value Date		☐ Overall	☐ Object Currency

⌃ *Figure 1 Internal Order Budget Profile*

ACTIVATION TYPE 1 indicates automatic activation of availability control during budget allocation. If the OVERALL checkbox is selected, availability control checks against the overall budget. If the OVERALL checkbox is not selected, availability control checks against the annual budget. Availability control works with controlling area currency unless you select the OBJECT CURRENCY checkbox. You can assign the budget profile to an order type with Transaction KOAB or via Menu Path 1.

You can maintain availability control tolerance limits via the following IMG menu path:

Left-click then right-click in an Action field and select Possible Entries to display the screen in Figure 2.

COAr	Prof.	Text	Tr.Grp	Act.	Usage in %	**Action**	**Short Descript.**
1000	000001	General Budget Profile	++	1	90.00	1	Warning
1000	000001	General Budget Profile	++	2	95.00	2	Warning with MAIL to person responsible
1000	000001	General Budget Profile	++	3	105.00	3	Error message

⌃ *Figure 2* *Availability Control Tolerance Limits*

The ACTION field defines the messages and emails the system will send at specific degrees of budget overrun. In this example, when the budget is nearly consumed at 95%, a warning is issued with an automatic email to the persons responsible. You need to specify a budget manager with Transaction OK14 or the system will issue an error message. With a budget overrun at 105%, an error message is issued and the document that caused the overrun cannot be posted.

You can enter an order budget with Transaction KO22 or via the following menu path:

ACCOUNTING • CONTROLLING • INTERNAL ORDERS • BUDGETING • ORIGINAL
BUDGET • CHANGE

You can enter the budget as shown in the example in Figure 3.

Period	Budget	Transaction currency	Current budget	Assigned	Planned total Version 0
Overall	100,000.00	EUR	120,000.00		100,000.00
2009	5,000.00	EUR	5,000.00		
2010	95,000.00	EUR	115,000.00	95,000.00	100,000.00

⌃ *Figure 3* *Change Original Budget Annual Overview*

The OVERALL BUDGET can be greater than the sum of the annual budgets, but cannot be smaller. The ASSIGNED amount of 95,000.00 is due to a manual journal entry and appears in an annual Budget row because the OVERALL checkbox in the budget profile in Figure 1 is not selected.

The PLANNED TOTAL VERSION 0 amount of 100,000.00 represents the original budget. The CURRENT BUDGET amount of 120,000.00 is greater because a budget supplement of 20,000.00 was posted with Transaction KO24. You can also post a budget return with Transaction KO26, if necessary. ▇

Part 3

Profit Center Accounting

Things You'll Learn in this Section

The main aim of profit center accounting is to determine profit for internal areas of responsibility. You determine profits and losses using either period accounting or the cost-of-sales approach. You assign a profit center manager who is responsible for costs and revenues. You also normally assign cost centers to profit centers. Cost centers in turn have a manager responsible for postings to each cost center.

Profit center accounting postings are collected in a separate parallel ledger for internal profit reporting purposes. Profit center postings are always in parallel with other postings and are statistical in nature, which means they can only be used for reporting and evaluation purposes. In other words profit centers are not a real cost object. Profit centers are considered part of the controlling module since they are used for internal reporting purposes. Financial accounting and business areas are designed for external reporting purposes.

You can guarantee all postings occur to profit center accounting in parallel with other postings by making the profit center a mandatory field in other master data such as cost centers, orders, and material masters.

Every profit center is assigned to a controlling area. Profit centers in a company code belong to a standard profit center hierarchy assigned to the controlling area. Goods movements between profit centers can be valuated either at external prices, group internal prices, or transfer prices.

The information system provides many user friendly reports for evaluating plan and actual data. Because results in profit centers are stored at the general ledger accounts level you can reconcile profit center postings with data in financial accounting.

The ideas in this section of the book cover profit center integrated planning, and the assignment monitor which checks if there are objects without a profit center assigned.

Tip 13 Profit Center Integrated Planning

You can automatically or manually transfer plan data from other modules to Profit Center Accounting (PCA).

Each profit center manager is responsible for planning their own revenues, assets, and expenses directly related to a facility. In addition, planned corporate overhead is allocated.

Overhead costs for each profit center are typically planned in the underlying cost centers. Let's look at the plan integration features for automatically transferring costs to the appropriate profit center.

Solution

You can allow profit center online transfer and integrated planning with Transaction OKEQ or via the following IMG menu path:

> CONTROLLING • GENERAL CONTROLLING • ORGANIZATION • MAINTAIN VERSIONS

Select a version and double-click SETTINGS FOR PROFIT CENTER ACCOUNTING to display the screen in Figure 1.

⮝ *Figure 1 General Version Definition — Online Transfer Checkbox*

Select the ONLINE TRANSFER checkbox to allow cost center plan line items to be automatically transferred to profit centers.

You also need to allow integrated planning for each fiscal YEAR version. To do this, double-click GENERAL VERSION DEFINITION in Figure 1, select a VERSION, double-click CONTROLLING AREA SETTINGS, select a VERSION, and then double-click SETTINGS FOR EACH FISCAL YEAR to display the screen in Figure 2.

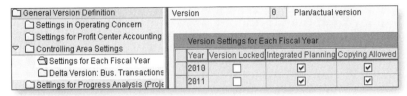

⌃ Figure 2 *General Version Definition — Integrated Planning Checkbox*

Select the INTEGRATED PLANNING checkbox to allow automatic online transfers of cost center plan data to profit centers per fiscal YEAR. Line item documents keep a record of every planning change. Manually setting or deleting the INTEGRATED PLANNING checkbox is only possible as long as no plan data exists.

If you don't allow automatic transfers of plan data to profit centers, or you cannot activate INTEGRATED PLANNING because plan data exists, you can transfer the plan data manually (Figure 3) with Transaction 1KE0 or via the following menu path:

> ACCOUNTING • CONTROLLING • PROFIT CENTER ACCOUNTING • PLANNING • PLAN DATA TRANSFER • CO PLAN DATA

Plan Version	0
Fiscal Year	2010

Objects

☑ Cost Centers	☐ General Cost Object
☐ Internal Orders	☐ Real Estate
☐ Projects	☐ Prof. Segments
☐ Networks	☐ SOP Orders
☐ Business Processes	☐ MRP Orders

Characteristic Values

Cost Centers	1000	to	
or	Cost Center Group		

« Figure 3
Transfer Plan Data to PCA

Enter the PLAN VERSION and FISCAL YEAR and COST CENTERS for the plan data to be transferred. You can transfer data from other modules in addition to cost center accounting. The existing profit center data will be deleted during the transfer. ■

Profit Center Assignment Monitor

The profit center Assignment Monitor allows you to analyze the assignment of profit centers to master data and objects.

A profit center receives postings made in parallel to a cost object, such as a cost center. Profit Center Accounting (EC-PCA) is a separate ledger that enables reporting from a profit center responsibility point of view. You normally create profit centers in areas that generate revenue and have a responsible manager assigned.

If the EC-PCA is active, you'll receive a warning message if you have not specified a profit center. All unassigned postings go to a dummy profit center. This ensures that internal and financial accounting data are reconciled.

The Assignment Monitor assists you in checking which objects are not assigned to a profit center to minimize postings to the dummy profit center. Let's follow a material master example. The profit center in the material master is copied to all financial documents generated by inventory movements.

 ## Solution

You can run Assignment Monitor with Transaction 1KE4 or via the following menu path:

> ACCOUNTING • CONTROLLING • PROFIT CENTER ACCOUNTING • MASTER DATA • ASSIGNMENT MONITOR

The screen in Figure 1 is displayed.

« *Figure 1*
Assignment Monitor

Click on ASSIGNMENT MONITOR in the menu bar to display a list of objects that contain profit centers. To display a list of unassigned materials select ASSIGNMENT MONITOR • MATERIAL • NONASSIGNED from the menu bar. Type in the material type and Execute to display the screen shown in Figure 2.

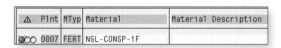

« *Figure 2*
Unassigned Material Numbers

You can drill down directly to each material master. There are two reasons why a material master may not be assigned to a profit center:

▶ The material master views containing the profit center are not created.

▶ The material master profit center field is not mandatory.

To make the profit center field mandatory, first determine which field selection group the profit center field is assigned to with Transaction OMSR or via the following IMG menu path:

> LOGISTICS - GENERAL • MATERIAL MASTER • FIELD SELECTION • ASSIGN FIELDS TO FIELD SELECTION GROUPS

The screen in Figure 3 is displayed.

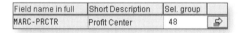

« *Figure 3*
Assign Profit Center to Field Selection Group

To quickly locate a field name, click the Position on Field Name button (not shown), type in the field name, and press ⸤Enter⸥.

Make the field mandatory with Transaction OMS9 or via the following IMG menu path:

> LOGISTICS - GENERAL • MATERIAL MASTER • FIELD SELECTION • MAINTAIN FIELD SELECTION FOR DATA SCREENS

Type in field selection group 48 in this case, press ⸤Enter⸥, change the radio button selection from Optional to Required, and save your work. ■

Part 4

Product Cost Planning

Things You'll Learn in this Section

Product cost planning allows you to automatically process large volumes of data in order to create cost estimates. It delivers cost-based data for material goods and intangible products and services, enabling you to make decisions such as:

▶ Inventory valuation

▶ Make or buy

▶ Lower price units

▶ Profitability analysis

Product cost planning supports the product throughout its life cycle, and ensures that the costing results are always available for analysis. Cost estimates are normally created automatically based on master data and configuration which you set up in the system:

▶ A bill of material (BOM) is a structured hierarchy of components necessary to build an assembly. BOM's together with purchasing info records or vendor quotations, provide cost estimates with the information necessary to calculate material costs of assemblies.

▶ A routing is a list of tasks containing standard activity times required to perform operations to build an assembly. Routings, together with planned activity prices, provide cost estimates with the information necessary to calculate labor and activity costs of products.

▶ A costing sheet summarizes the rules for allocating overhead from cost centers to cost estimates, product cost collectors and manufacturing orders. The components of a costing sheet include the calculation base (group of cost elements), overhead rate (percentage rate applied to base), and credit key (cost center receiving credit).

This section provides you with many useful and helpful techniques to optimize your setup of the above data as well as the setup and configuration of cost estimates. Because of the potentially large volume of data that cost estimates deal with, apparently small changes in configuration and/or master data can make large improvements to system performance and accuracy of the results.

Standard versus Moving Average Price

You have the choice of using standard or moving average price for purchased inventory valuation.

Many companies have to choose whether to use standard or moving average price control for inventory valuation. While you have complete flexibility in how you set this up, there are some best-practice guidelines.

Solution

First, let's look at how you set the price control for inventory and then discuss each method in detail. You can change the price control indicator with Transaction MM02 or via the following menu path:

> LOGISTICS • MATERIALS MANAGEMENT • MATERIAL MASTER • MATERIAL • CHANGE • IMMEDIATELY

Navigate to the Costing 2 view to display the screen shown in Figure 1.

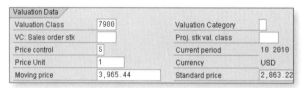

« **Figure 1**
Costing 2 View Valuation Data Section

The VALUATION DATA section contains the PRICE CONTROL field, which determines if a material is valuated by either standard or moving average price. You can change from standard (S) to moving average (V) price any time. The target field, in this case the moving average price, is overwritten with the standard price to ensure there is no change in inventory valuation for existing stock.

SAP suggests that you set a standard price control for all semifinished and finished products. Problems with moving average price control can occur if you consume more products than you produce during a period. There may not be enough stock coverage to absorb differences when settling production orders at period-end leading to an unrealistic moving average price. You can read more details of stock coverage and moving average price in OSS Note 81682.

SAP also suggests you use moving average price for purchased materials. This means inventory will be revalued during every goods and invoice receipt with a price different from the moving average price. While this provides real-time inventory valuation, it does not provide easy analysis of purchase price variance (PPV) postings.

If you set the price control to standard for purchased materials, all price differences will post to PPV general ledger accounts. These postings can be analyzed to help understand why the actual price differs from the planned purchase price. While this promotes more accountability for purchased materials, the inventory valuation may not be as accurate as with moving average price control.

The goal of setting purchased materials to standard price is to progressively reduce PPV postings by correcting issues that cause the postings. PPV postings become less significant over time as you gradually gain a better understanding of how the postings occur.

You can also activate the Material Ledger to analyze all of the different postings. You can activate the Material Ledger without the multiple valuation or actual costing components. In this case, you automatically generate a Material Ledger document for every inventory transaction. You can display a list of Material Ledger documents with Transaction CKM3 or by clicking the Material Price Analysis button in the material master Accounting 1 view, as shown in Figure 2.

Category	Quant	U	PrelimVal	Price d	Ex	Price	C
▷ ☐ Beginning Inventory	0	PC	0.00	0.00	0.00	0.00	MXN
▽ ☐ Receipts	1,000	PC	21,600.00	7,850.04	0.00	29.45	MXN
▽ ☐ Purchase order	200	PC	4,320.00	1,680.00	0.00	30.00	MXN
▽ ⚠ Vendor:0000001099 PurchOrg.:6000	200	PC	4,320.00	1,680.00	0.00	30.00	MXN
▤ 1000000112 GR goods receipt 4500015461/10	200	PC	4,320.00	1,680.00	0.00	30.00	MXN
▷ ☐ Production	800	PC	17,280.00	6,170.04	0.00	29.31	MXN
Cumulative Inventory	1,000	PC	21,600.00	7,850.04	0.00	29.45	MXN
▷ ☐ Consumption	700	PC	15,120.00	5,495.03	0.00	29.45	MXN
▷ ☐ Ending Inventory	300	PC	6,480.00	2,355.01	0.00	29.45	MXN

« Figure 2
Material Price Analysis Screen

To display an individual Material Ledger document, expand the hierarchy and double-click an individual document number.

The three possible options have their advantages. Standard price provides accountability for PPVs, moving average price provides real-time inventory accuracy, and the Material Ledger provides the ability to calculate actual cost by determining what portion of the variance is debited to the next-highest level using material consumption. ▪

Tip (16) Moving Average Historical Price

You can view historical moving average price at a summary level and calculate it at a detailed level

Finding historical values for moving average price is a question often asked when you have moving average price control for inventory valuation. You can view historical price at a summary level, and calculate it at a detailed level.

✓ Solution

As of Release 4.5 stock and valuation fields relating to the previous or earlier periods are stored in history table MBEWH, separate to table MBEW. History tables contain only one entry for each period. An entry in a history table is only created if stock or valuation relevant data changes occur in the current period.

Let's follow some example stock movements to see how this works:

▶ At the start of period 2 there are 10 pieces of a material.

▶ At time of goods receipt of 5 pieces in period 2, the system records a stock of 10 in the history table for period 1 and current stock is increased to 15.

▶ As 2 more pieces are received in period 2 the history table is unaffected since an entry already exists for period 1,current stock is increased to 17.

▶ As 4 pieces are withdrawn from stock in period 4 a stock of 17 pieces is recorded in the history table for period 3, current stock is reduced to 13.

▶ The history table does not contain an entry for period 2 because there were no goods movements in period 3.

You can display the data in table MBEWH with Transaction SE16N.

Material	ValA	Val. Type	Year	Pe	TotalStock	Total Val.	Pr.	MvAvgPrice	Std price	/	ValCl
100-110	1000		2004	1	272.000	1,389.93	V	5.11	5.11	1	3000
100-110	1000		2004	3	272.000	1,389.93	V	5.11	5.11	1	3000

⌃ *Figure 1 Material Valuation History Table*

The history table entries displayed for periods 1 and 3 indicate:

- There were no inventory movements during period 3
- The valuation data for period 2 is the same as for period 1
- Even though the price did not change in period 3, an entry was made in the history table due to goods movements in period 4

You can verify the above bullet points by displaying a list of goods movements with Transaction MB51 or by following menu path:

LOGISTICS • MATERIALS MANAGEMENT • INVENTORY MANAGEMENT • ENVIRON-
MENT • LIST DISPLAYS • MATERIAL DOCUMENTS

Type in the material, plant, and posting date and click Execute to display the screen shown in Figure 2.

```
100-110              Slug for spiral casing            1000 Production
0001 261   4900031691   1 04/07/2004        43- PC
0001 101   5000009983   1 04/06/2004        43  PC
0001 261   4900031314   1 02/06/2004        39- PC
0001 101   5000009831   1 02/05/2004        39  PC
```

⌃ *Figure 2 Material Document List*

The good movements in periods 2 and 4 resulted in entries in the history table in periods 1 and 3 as shown in Figure 1. Also, since there were no goods movements in period 3, there is no entry for period 2 in the history table.

Historical tables display one entry per period however there can be multiple changes to moving average price for multiple goods receipts. You can calculate the moving average price by displaying the accounting documents for a material with Transaction MR51 or by following menu path:

LOGISTICS • MATERIALS MANAGEMENT • INVENTORY MANAGEMENT • ENVIRON-
MENT • LIST DISPLAYS • ACCOUNTING DOCUMENT FOR MATERIAL

Enter material, plant, and posting date and Execute to display the screen in Figure 3.

```
100-110              Slug for spiral casing         1000 1000
WA   4900008919   1 04/07/2004        43- PC        219.73- EUR
WE   5000002936   1 04/06/2004        43  PC        219.73  EUR
WA   4900008779   1 02/06/2004        39- PC        199.29- EUR
WE   5000002883   1 02/05/2004        39  PC        199.29  EUR
```

⌃ *Figure 3 Accounting Documents for Material List*

Download the list of accounting documents to Excel and calculate the moving average price for every goods receipt for accounting document Type WE. ■

Tip **17** Changing Material Prices Manually

Transaction MR21 lets you change material prices manually.

Material prices are changed automatically with one of these three methods:

▶ Standard prices are updated by releasing cost estimates during a costing run

▶ Moving average prices are updated during goods and invoice receipt if the purchase order or invoice price varies from the moving average price

▶ During the material ledger period-end processing

Occasionally you may need to change material prices manually, for example if a goods receipt is carried out with an incorrect purchase order price for a moving average price material. You cannot change the price directly in the material master however there is a separate transaction available for this purpose which we'll now discuss.

Solution

You manually change material prices with Transaction MR21 or by going to:

LOGISTICS • MATERIALS MANAGEMENT • VALUATION • CHANGE IN MATERIAL PRICE • CHANGE MATERIAL PRICES

The selection screen shown in Figure 1 is displayed.

Posting Date	05/18/2010
Company Code	
Plant	1000
Reference	1234567890123456
Doc.Header Text	Example price change

« *Figure 1*
Price Change Overview Screen

You can either enter the COMPANY CODE or PLANT. The REFERENCE NUMBER can contain the document number of the customer or vendor.

The HEADER TEXT field contains explanations or notes which apply to the document as a whole, i.e., all line items. Press ⎡Enter⎤, type in the materials and press ⎡Enter⎤ to display the screen shown in Figure 2.

EUR Co.Code								
Variant		MR21_LAGERMATERIAL_BWKEY_C▣	Company code currency					
Material	V	Price control	Current valuation price	New price	Current price unit	New price unit	Current statistical price	New statistical price
P-100	S	6,903.70	6,903.70	10		10	4,755.50	4,755.50
100-100	V	135.98	135.98	1		1	135.98	135.98
100-110	V	7.00	7.00	1		1	5.11	5.11

⌃ **Figure 2** *Price Change Line Items*

The screen automatically populates the material PRICE CONTROL, CURRENT VALUATION PRICE, and other price-related fields. You can enter a NEW PRICE for Materials 100-100 and 100-110 in Figure 2 because they use moving average (V) PRICE CONTROL. You cannot change the NEW PRICE for MATERIAL P-100 since it uses standard (S) PRICE CONTROL and there is an existing current cost estimate. It would be inconsistent to have the material master standard price different to the current standard cost estimate. To change the standard price in this case you first need to delete the current standard cost estimate with Transaction CKR1.

The CURRENT STATISTICAL PRICE and NEW STATISTICAL PRICE in the last two columns of Figure 2 refer to a price that has no influence on the material valuation. For materials with PRICE CONTROL S the statistical price is the moving average price. For materials with PRICE CONTROL V the statistical price is the standard price.

When you first display the screen in Figure 2 there are twenty blank lines allowing you to copy and paste entries directly from Excel. This means you can easily change the price of hundreds of materials with this transaction if needed.

When you click the Save icon after entering materials and prices in Figure 2 you will generate a price change document recording details of the price change. If you revalue existing inventory with this transaction you will also generate accounting documents with document type PR recording the resulting postings to inventory accounts.

If the material ledger is active, a price change for a material with price determination 3 (single- and multilevel material price determination) is only possible if there have been no goods movements relevant to valuation and no incoming invoices for the material in the period. ▪

Tip **18** Price Unit versus Costing Lot Size

Price unit and costing lot size are different fields and you should use them based on price accuracy and procurement quantities.

There is often some confusion regarding the price unit and costing lot size fields in the material master costing views that can lead to less than ideal settings. Price unit is a factor that allows you to improve price accuracy because prices have a set number of decimal places. The unit price is easy to calculate if you make the price unit a factor of ten. Costing lot size should be set as close as possible to typical purchase and production quantities to reduce lot size and purchase price variance. These fields are based on different concepts, which we'll now discuss in detail.

Solution

Most currencies have a defined number of decimal places for price units, usually two as defined in Transaction OY04. For purchased materials with a low unit price, you can increase price accuracy by increasing the price unit.

For example, if the unit price of a material is $0.215, you can't enter this value as a price with a price unit of one because the material master price field will only accept a maximum of two values following the decimal point for U.S. dollars. Instead, you can enter the exact price by entering a price of $2.15 with a price unit of 10, or a price of $21.50 with a price unit of 100.

You can maintain price unit with Transaction MM02 or via the menu path:

> LOGISTICS • MATERIALS MANAGEMENT • MATERIAL MASTER • MATERIAL • CHANGE • IMMEDIATELY

Navigate to the Costing 2 view to display the screen shown in Figure 1.

In Figure 1, you calculate the unit standard price of 135.98 EUR by dividing the STANDARD PRICE by the PRICE UNIT. To keep this calculation simple, it's a good practice to make the PRICE UNIT 1, 10, 100, 1,000, or 10,000. The maximum price unit you can enter is 99,999. You can adjust the price unit at any time and the system will automatically adjust the price accordingly.

« *Figure 1*
Price Unit Field —
Costing 2 View

The price unit cannot be smaller than the costing lot size. If you change the price unit to a value larger than the costing lot size, then the system will automatically adjust the costing lot size to equal the price unit. This is necessary because a cost estimate is calculated based on the costing lot size. There would be rounding issues if you marked and released a cost estimate.

Now that we've discussed price unit, let's look at costing lot size. You maintain the costing lot size by navigating to the material master Costing 1 view. The screen shown in Figure 2 is displayed.

« *Figure 2*
Costing Lot Size Field —
Costing 1 View

The COSTING LOT SIZE determines the material quantity for cost estimate calculations. This is a mandatory field because a cost estimate must base cost calculations on a quantity. When a standard cost estimate is created, it uses the costing lot size value in the Costing 1 view by default. You have an opportunity to manually change the costing lot size defaulted from the Costing 1 view when creating a single cost estimate with Transaction CK11N. You don't get this opportunity when creating cost estimates collectively using costing run Transaction CK40N.

The costing lot size should be set as close as possible to typical purchase and production quantities to reduce purchase price and lot size variance. Unfavorable variances may result if a production order is created for a quantity less than the costing lot size. Setup time is needed to prepare equipment and machinery for assembly production, and is generally the same, regardless of the quantity produced. Setup time that is spread over a smaller production quantity increases the unit cost. This also applies to externally procured items, because vendors usually quote higher unit prices for smaller quantities, resulting in purchase price variances. ■

Tip (19) Optimize Costing Lot Size

Optimizing the costing lot size allows you to reduce production and purchase price variances.

A cost estimate uses the costing lot size to determine the quantity to base cost calculations on. This affects production variances because in many cases there are fixed costs, such as setup and teardown time, which do not change with different production lot sizes. This type of variance is known as an *output lot size variance*.

This also applies to externally procured items, because vendors usually quote higher unit prices for smaller quantities. You enter vendor quotes in the purchasing info record condition scales and the cost estimate determines the scale quantity and associated purchase price based on the costing lot size.

Solution

You can reduce production variances by using the costing lot size based on the quantity typically manufactured or purchased. Unfavorable production variances will occur if a production order is created for a quantity less than the costing lot size. Fixed production costs spread across a smaller production quantity increase unit costs.

A cost estimate determines the costing lot size from the corresponding field in the material master Costing 1 view. You can change this material master field with Transaction MM02 or via the following menu path:

> LOGISTICS • MATERIALS MANAGEMENT • MATERIAL MASTER • MATERIAL • CHANGE • IMMEDIATELY

Type in the material number, press [Enter], select Costing 1 view, type in the plant, and press [Enter] to display the screen shown in Figure 1.

⌃ **Figure 1** *Material Master Costing Lot Size Field in Costing 2 View*

In this example, the COSTING LOT SIZE is 100. You can manually override the costing lot size defaulted from the Costing 1 view while creating a single cost estimate with Transaction CK11N, as shown in Figure 2.

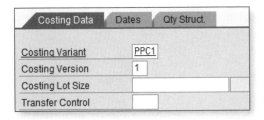

« **Figure 2**
Costing Lot Size Field When Creating a Single Cost Estimate

You can create a single cost estimate based on any COSTING LOT SIZE you enter in the initial screen as shown in Figure 2. If you don't make an entry in this field, the cost estimate takes the COSTING LOT SIZE from the Costing 2 view. This functionality is useful when carrying out scenario planning for individual products. You don't get the opportunity to enter the COSTING LOT SIZE when creating cost estimates collectively with costing run Transaction CK40N.

The costing lot size cannot be smaller than the price unit. Because costing is based on the costing lot size, this combination could result in rounding problems when determining a new price. You'll receive an error message if you attempt to enter this combination in the material master. ■

Tip Purchasing Info Record Prices

Purchasing info record prices are the preferred option for material valuation — although you may find the terminology confusing.

When implementing a search strategy to determine material prices for a cost estimate, you have the option of using purchasing data. There are many purchasing info record prices available. Let's examine each in detail.

✅ Solution

You can maintain material valuation search strategies with Transaction OKK4 or via the following IMG menu path:

> CONTROLLING • PRODUCT COST CONTROLLING • PRODUCT COST PLANNING • MATERIAL COST ESTIMATE WITH QUANTITY STRUCTURE • COSTING VARIANT: COMPONENTS • DEFINE VALUATION VARIANTS

Double-click a valuation variant to display the screen in Figure 1.

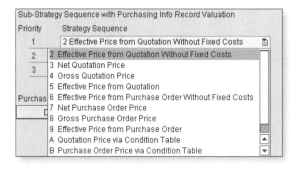

« *Figure 1*
Purchasing Info Record Valuation Possible Entries

If you've selected Price from Purchasing Info Record in the search strategy above this section of the Valuation variant screen, Purchasing Info Record Sub-Strategies will be available. Click any of the three SUB-STRATEGY SEQUENCE fields to display the list in Figure 1.

▶ **Prices from a Quotation (strategies 2 to 5)**
The purchasing info record quotation is the official quotation submitted by a vendor to supply a material. No discount or conditions are taken into account.

▶ **Prices from a Purchase Order (strategies 6 to 9)**
The system searches for the last purchase order or scheduling agreement defined in the purchasing info record. Select ENVIRONMENT • LAST DOCUMENT from the purchasing info record menu bar to display the document.

▶ **Gross prices (strategies 4 and 8)**
The gross price is the total vendor price without considering vendor discounts or surcharges, or adding on any other costs such as delivery charges. An example would be the purchase price without taking into account any discounts for purchasing large quantities or adding on any custom charges.

▶ **Net prices (strategies 3 and 7)**
The net price is the total vendor price after taking into account all vendor discounts and surcharges. You subtract quantity discounts, in addition to any other discounts, to calculate the net price.

▶ **Effective prices (strategies 5 and 9)**
The effective price is the price calculated after taking *all* pricing conditions into account. You first subtract vendor discounts and rebates to calculate the net price, then you add on other costs such as freight charges and customs and duty.

▶ **Price via condition table (strategies A and B)**
You can assign the purchasing condition type to an origin group. As of Release 4.6A, you can maintain this table via the DELIVERY COSTS button in Figure 1. In previous releases, you can access the table with Transaction OKYO or via the following IMG menu path:

> CONTROLLING • PRODUCT COST CONTROLLING • PRODUCT COST PLANNING •
> SELECTED FUNCTIONS IN MATERIAL COSTING • RAW MATERIAL COST ESTIMATE •
> ASSIGN CONDITION TYPES TO ORIGIN GROUPS

▶ **Effective prices without fixed costs (strategies 2 and 6)**
The effective price is calculated from all of the conditions contained in the assigned calculation schema with the exception of *fixed amount* conditions, (data element KRECH = B). All tax conditions (data element KOAID = D) are included in the price. ■

Tip 21 Purchasing Info Record Scales

Purchasing info record scales lets you store vendor quotes for different quantities.

Purchasing info record scales represent vendor quotes that contain reduced prices for purchasing large quantities. Scales assist you with the following:

► When you create a purchase order or requisition, the purchase quantity determines the proposed purchase price from the purchase info record scales

► When you create a cost estimate, the costing lot size determines the purchase price from purchase info record scales

Solution

You can display a purchasing info record with Transaction ME1M or by going to:

> LOGISTICS • MATERIALS MANAGEMENT • PURCHASING • MASTER DATA • INFO RECORD • LIST DISPLAYS • BY MATERIAL

Type in Material, Purchasing organization, and Plant in the selection screen and click the Execute icon. Double-click a purchasing info record, click the Conditions button, and double-click a condition type to display the screen shown in Figure 1.

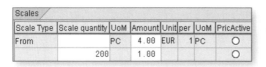

« *Figure 1*

Purchasing Info Record Scale

This scale indicates that the purchase price for a quantity between 1 and 199 is 4.00 EUR, which is discounted to 1.00 for a quantity of 200 or more.

Let's create two cost estimates with costing lot sizes of 10 and 200 and see how this works. You can create a cost estimate with Transaction CK11N or via the following menu path:

ACCOUNTING • CONTROLLING • PRODUCT COST CONTROLLING • PRODUCT COST
PLANNING • MATERIAL COSTING • MATERIAL COST ESTIMATE WITH QUANTITY
STRUCTURE • CREATE

In the selection screen type in Material, Plant, and Costing Variant and press
Enter twice to display the screen shown in Figure 2.

« **Figure 2**

*Cost Estimate Based on
Costing Lot Size of 10 —
Unit price 4 EUR*

The COSTING LOT SIZE 10 defaults from the material master Costing 1 view.
Because the COSTING LOT SIZE is less than 200, the cost estimate accesses the
first line of the purchasing info record scale in Figure 1. The system calculates the
cost estimate price of 40.00 EUR by multiplying the COSTING LOT SIZE of 10 by
the scale price of 4 EUR.

To create a cost estimate with a different costing lot size, run Transaction CK11N.
The selection screen shown in Figure 3 is displayed.

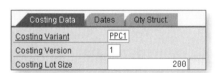

« **Figure 3**

Create Cost Estimate Selection Screen

The COST LOT SIZE field defaults as blank and the cost estimate accesses the
COSTING LOT SIZE from the material master Costing 1 view. If you manually type
in a COSTING LOT SIZE in the selection screen shown in Figure 3, the cost estimate uses this value. For example, enter 200 as the COSTING LOT SIZE and press
Enter twice to display the screen shown in Figure 4.

« **Figure 4**

*Cost Estimate Based on
Costing Lot Size of 200 —
Unit Price 1 EUR*

Because the COSTING LOT SIZE is 200 the cost estimate accesses the second line
of the purchasing info record scale in Figure 1. The system calculates the cost
estimate price of 200.00 EUR by multiplying the COSTING LOT SIZE of 200 by
the scale price of 1 EUR. ■

Tip 22

Plant-Specific Purchasing Info Records

When you need cost estimates to retrieve purchase prices per plant, you can set up plant-specific purchasing info records.

It's common practice to automatically create purchasing info records when a purchasing document is created. With some simple settings, you can specify automatically created purchasing info records as plant-specific. If you do not, a cost estimate may instead choose the lowest cost nonspecific plant info record.

Solution

You can display scheduling agreements, which are long-standing purchasing documents, with Transaction ME2M or via the following menu path:

> LOGISTICS • MATERIALS MANAGEMENT • PURCHASING • PURCHASE ORDER • LIST DISPLAYS • BY MATERIAL

Enter material, plant, scope of list, document type LP, and Execute to display a list of agreements. Double-click a line to display the screen in Figure 1.

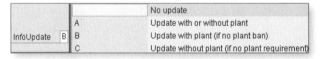

			No update
		A	Update with or without plant
InfoUpdate	B	B	Update with plant (if no plant ban)
		C	Update without plant (if no plant requirement)

« Figure 1
Purchasing Scheduling Agreement

You need option B to default to this field to ensure that plant-specific purchasing info records are created automatically. To display if the related purchasing info record is plant specific, select ENVIRONMENT • INFO RECORD from the menu bar and click the PURCH. ORG. DATA 1 button to display the screen in Figure 2.

Purchasing Org.	1000	Plant	1000	Standard

« Figure 2
Plant-Specific Purchasing Info Record

A PLANT entry means the info record is plant specific and a valuation variant will only search within the plant if all purchasing info records are plant specific.

There are two steps needed to make sure purchasing documents automatically create plant specific purchasing info records. The first is to configure default values for buyers with Transaction OMFI or via the following IMG menu path:

MATERIALS MANAGEMENT • PURCHASING • ENVIRONMENT DATA • DEFINE DEFAULT VALUES FOR BUYERS

Double-click the text Settings for Default Values and either change an existing default values setup or create your own. The screen in Figure 3 is displayed.

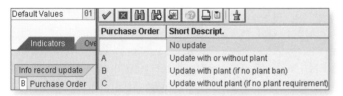

« **Figure 3**
Default Values for Buyers — Purchasing Info Record Update

Make sure B is entered for PURCHASE ORDER and save your entry. The next step is to assign this default value to buyers. You can do this either as a collective update with Transaction SU10 or by assigning the Default Values to your own profile by selecting SYSTEM • USER PROFILE • OWN DATA from the menu bar from any screen. Click the Parameters tab and enter the Default Values profile you just created for PARAMETER ID EVO as shown in Figure 4.

Parameter ID	Parameter value	Short Description
EVO	01	Default Values for Purchasing

« **Figure 4**
Parameter ID for Default Values for Purchasing

While you can set a specific info record update for each scheduling agreement, selecting the purchase order update info record checkbox in the MATERIAL DATA tab causes the following:

▶ If two info records exist, the info record with a plant is updated.

▶ If just one info record exists, with or without a plant, it is updated.

▶ If no info record exists, and B is specified as a buyer default, an info record with a plant is created. Otherwise, an info record without a plant is created.

OSS Note 569885 contains more details about the purchase order info record update checkbox (EKPO-SPINF). ∎

Tip (23) Cost Estimates and Procurement Type

A cost estimate obtains data on how a material is sourced based on your procurement type setting.

Cost estimates utilize the procurement type field setting to determine how materials are procured. The cost estimate searches for either in-house production information (bill of material (BOM), routing, or production version) or purchasing information (purchasing info record). The special procurement type can be used to override the procurement type, if required. Material requirements planning (MRP) guarantees material availability by monitoring stocks and requirements and by generating planned orders for procurement and production. A cost estimate needs data on how the material is procured as the first step in determining material cost. Let's see how to display procurement types, and then take a look at how cost estimates utilize this information.

✓ Solution

The procurement type field is located in the material master MRP 2 view, which you can access with Transaction MM02 or via the following menu path:

> LOGISTICS • MATERIALS MANAGEMENT • MATERIAL MASTER • MATERIAL • CHANGE • IMMEDIATELY

Navigate to the MRP 2 tab to display the screen shown in Figure 1.

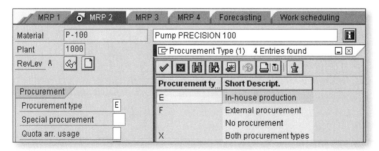

⌃ *Figure 1 Procurement Type Field in MRP 2 View*

To display a list of possible entries for PROCUREMENT TYPE, right-click in the field and select Possible Entries. A list of possible procurement types is displayed as shown in Figure 1. Let's discuss each in detail:

▶ **In-house Production (E):** This entry means the cost estimate will search for production information, such as BOM and a routing. A BOM is a structured hierarchy of components necessary to build an assembly. A routing is a list of tasks containing the standard activity times required to build an assembly.

▶ **External Procurement (F):** This entry means the cost estimate will search for purchasing information, usually from a purchasing info record containing vendor quotes for the material.

▶ **Both Procurement Types (X):** This entry means a planned (proposed) order generated by MRP can be converted into either a production order or purchase requisition. A cost estimate will be based on a BOM and routing if they are available; that is, the procurement type will behave as an in-house production. You can make the cost estimate treat the material as though it's externally procured with an entry in the special procurement type field, as discussed next.

The SPECIAL PROCUREMENT field found immediately below the PROCUREMENT TYPE field shown in Figure 1 more closely defines the procurement type. For example, it can indicate if the item was produced in another plant and transferred to the plant you are looking at. A cost estimate normally follows the MRP special procurement type when determining costs. However, an entry in the special procurement type for the costing field in the Costing 1 view, as shown in Figure 2, will be used by costing instead of the MRP setting.

⌃ *Figure 2 Special Procurement Type for the Costing Field*

The special procurement type can be used to override the procurement type. For example, if you enter a special procurement type that contains an external procurement type (F) in configuration Transaction OMD9, the material will behave as if it's externally procured, regardless of the procurement type setting. ▪

Tip 24 Costing Sheets Allocate Overhead

Costing sheets offer you flexibility in allocating overhead across individual products or product groups.

There are three methods for distributing overhead costs to cost of goods sold. In increasing level of flexibility and complexity, they are:

▶ **Activity Rate:** You can either increase the planned activity price to include overhead or you can create separate overhead activity types. Manufacturing orders are debited and the production cost center is credited during activity confirmation.

▶ **Costing Sheets:** Costing sheets offer more flexibility in allocating overhead across individual products or product groups based on cost elements and origin groups. Manufacturing orders are debited and production cost centers are credited during overhead calculation.

▶ **Templates:** In addition to cost elements, templates give you more options to base your overhead costs on.

Because costing sheets offer sufficient flexibility to allocate overhead costs in most cases, let's discuss how these work in more detail.

Solution

You can view the configuration of the costing sheet settings with Transaction KZS2 or via the following IMG menu path:

> CONTROLLING • PRODUCT COST CONTROLLING • PRODUCT COST PLANNING • BASIC SETTINGS FOR MATERIAL COSTING • OVERHEAD • DEFINE COSTING SHEETS

The screen shown in Figure 1 is displayed.

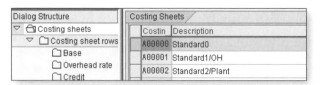

《 *Figure 1*
Costing Sheet Overview

Available COSTING SHEETS are listed on the right of this Overview screen. Select the first costing sheet, A00000, and double-click COSTING SHEET ROWS on the left to display the screen shown in Figure 2.

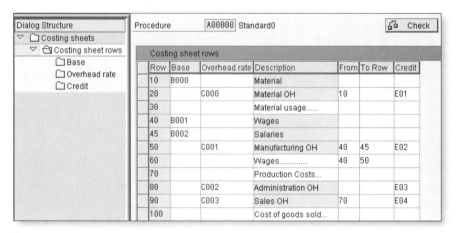

≋ **Figure 2** *Costing Sheet Rows Overview*

You can view the details of the three costing sheet components by:

► **Calculation Base:** Select any row with an entry in the BASE column and double-click BASE at the left to display a screen that lets you enter cost elements and origin groups. Each cost element identifies unique cost types within a cost estimate, such as raw materials or machining costs. Costs indentified by the base are multiplied by an overhead rate to determine the overhead value in the cost estimate.

► **Overhead Rate:** Select any row with an entry in the OVERHEAD RATE column and double-click OVERHEAD RATE at the left to display a screen that lets you enter date-dependent overhead rate percentages.

► **Credit Key:** Select any row with an entry in the CREDIT column and double-click CREDIT at the left to display a screen that lets you enter the cost center to receive the overhead credit during overhead calculation.

Costing sheets require an overhead calculation that debits manufacturing orders and credits cost centers. ■

Tip 25

Template Alternative to Costing Sheets

Templates provide you with a flexible alternative to costing sheets for distributing overhead costs.

While you typically allocate overhead costs during activity type confirmations or with costing sheets, templates offer an alternative with more flexibility. Although setting up templates is more complex, they are set out logically and are worth considering as a flexible alternative.

Activity type confirmations and costing sheets determine overhead allocation based on either cost elements or activity quantity. While this works fine in most situations, templates allow you to allocate overhead based on most table fields available in the system, and also on formulas. Let's follow a simple example of how a beverage manufacturer can allocate plan overhead based on volume.

 Solution

There are three basic steps involved in setting up templates for plan allocation.

Environments determine the columns available in the template. You can define an environment with Transaction CTU6 or via the following IMG menu path:

> CONTROLLING • PRODUCT COST CONTROLLING • PRODUCT COST PLANNING • BASIC SETTINGS FOR MATERIAL COSTING • TEMPLATES

Expand the Environment 001 hierarchy to display the screen in Figure 1.

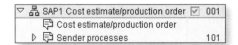

« *Figure 1*

Maintain Environment and Function Hierarchies

There are many environments already available in the standard system. You can maintain templates with Transaction CPT1 or via the following IMG menu path:

> CONTROLLING • PRODUCT COST CONTROLLING • PRODUCT COST PLANNING •
> BASIC SETTINGS FOR MATERIAL COSTING • TEMPLATES • MAINTAIN TEMPLATES

Enter the name and environment, and press Enter to display the screen in Figure 2.

Template overview : change						
Type	Description	Object	Unit	Plan quantity	Plan fix	Plan activation
Cost Center/Activity Type	Corporate Services	1000 / 1000	D			

⌃ *Figure 2 Maintain Template Sender Fields*

Click the down arrow in the first TYPE row and choose COST CENTER/ACTIVITY TYPE. Then click the down arrow in the OBJECT field to choose the actual sender cost center and activity type, 1000 / 1000 in this example.

Next, double-click the PLAN QUANTITY field, double-click the MATERIALVOLUME function below, and click the PLAN QUANTITY button. Click the down arrow in the PLAN ACTIVATION field and choose ACTIVE to display the screen in Figure 3.

Template overview : change						
Type	Description	Object	Unit	Plan quantity	Plan fix	Plan activation
Cost Center/Activity Type	Corporate Services	1000 / 1000	D	MaterialVolume		ACTIVE

⌃ *Figure 3 Maintain Template Plan Quantity and Activation*

Save your entries in this screen. The next step is to assign the template you just created with Transaction KTPF or via the following IMG menu path:

> CONTROLLING • PRODUCT COST CONTROLLING • PRODUCT COST PLANNING •
> BASIC SETTINGS FOR MATERIAL COSTING • TEMPLATES • ASSIGN TEMPLATES

Assign the template to a costing sheet (COSTSH) and overhead key (OH KEY) as displayed in Figure 4.

COAr	CostSh	OH key	Environ.	Template	Name
1000	COGM	SAP12	001	Z_VOLUME	Process Order Volume

« *Figure 4*

Assign Template to Costing Sheet and Overhead Key

The template is selected through a costing sheet and an overhead key. The costing sheet determines the conditions for calculating overhead rates, and is selected through the valuation variant. The overhead key is selected through the overhead group specified in the material master Costing 1 view. You can assign overhead keys to overhead groups with Transaction OKZ2. ■

Tip 26 Copying Costing Variants

Leaving system-supplied costing variants unchanged is a good practice. If you need different settings, you can create your own costing variants.

If you need different costing variants aside from the system-supplied ones, it's a good practice to create your own and leave the system-supplied variants unchanged for future reference. You should create your own costing variants starting with X, Y, or Z so they will not be overwritten during an upgrade.

 ## Solution

You can maintain costing variants with Transaction OKKN or via the following the IMG menu path:

> CONTROLLING • PRODUCT COST CONTROLLING • PRODUCT COST PLANNING • MATERIAL COST ESTIMATE WITH QUANTITY STRUCTURE • DEFINE COSTING VARIANTS

Double-click costing variant PPC1 to display the screen shown in Figure 1.

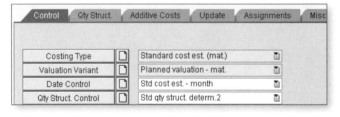

« **Figure 1**
Costing Variant Details Screen

If you copy this system-supplied costing variant you cannot change the costing type or valuation variant components. If you create your own costing variant, then you can enter your own components.

PPC1 is the system-supplied costing variant for standard cost estimates. You can create your own costing variant, for example, ZPC1, and make changes while referring back to system-supplied PPC1. You know from the numbering logic that ZPC1 was copied from PPC1 settings.

If your changes involve settings to either the costing type or valuation variant components, you should first copy the system-supplied components and then make the changes to your own costing variant components. You can then create your own costing variant that includes your own components.

A typical scenario is when you need a different strategy sequence for material valuation than contained in the valuation variant for costing variant PPC1. You can maintain valuation variants with Transaction OKK4 or via the following IMG menu path:

CONTROLLING • PRODUCT COST CONTROLLING • PRODUCT COST PLANNING • MATERIAL COST ESTIMATE WITH QUANTITY STRUCTURE • COSTING VARIANT: COMPONENTS • DEFINE VALUATION VARIANTS

Select valuation variant 001 – Planned valuation and click the Copy icon to display the screen shown in Figure 2.

≪ Figure 2
Valuation Variant Details Screen

You may need a different STRATEGY SEQUENCE if, for example, you need PLANNED PRICE 1 to take precedence over PRICE FROM PURCHASING INFO RECORD. In this case, you can swap the two PRIORITIES and if there is no entry in the material master PLANNED PRICE 1 field, the system will search for a purchasing info record price. This change allows you to manually override the purchasing info record price.

Make your required changes to the STRATEGY SEQUENCE, change the valuation variant name from 001 to Z01, and save. Create your own costing variant without copying an existing costing variant and you can enter and save your new valuation variant as a component in your new costing variant. ■

Tip 27 — Cost Estimate User Exits

User exits allow you to add your own functionality in a structured way within the standard program.

There are five user exits available for cost estimates. A user exit is a point in the standard program where you call your own program. User exits use *includes* which are criteria used to group fields and insert them in a table or structure.

Since product costing is integrated with other modules you should use standard functionality whenever possible, however, the following five cost estimate user exits are available:

- Cross-company costing: *COPCP001*
- Costing production resources/tools: *COPCP003*
- Costing Bulk Materials: *COPCP004*
- Valuation Strategy U: *COPCP005*
- Costing Reports: *SAPLXCKA*

Let's look at how to configure a user exit and then examine each of the cost estimate user exits in detail.

Solution

You access cost estimate user exits with Transaction CMOD or by following IMG menu path:

> CONTROLLING • PRODUCT COST CONTROLLING • PRODUCT COST PLANNING • SELECTED FUNCTIONS IN MATERIAL COSTING • DEVELOP ENHANCEMENTS FOR MATERIAL COSTING

Type in the name of your user exit, click the Create button, type in the short text, click the Enhancement Assignments button, and click the Local Object button to display the screen shown in Figure 1.

COPCP001	User exit for cross-company code costing
COPCP003	User exit for production resource/tool costing
COPCP004	Customer enhancement bulk material
COPCP005	User exit for material valuation (strategy U)
SAPLXCKA	Exits for product costing

« *Figure 1*
Cost Estimate User Exits

Normally you work with one user exit at a time. Click a user exit and click the Components button to access details of the *include* and your ABAP program. Below are details of the five standard cost estimate user exits and components:

▶ **Cross-Company Code Costing**

Enhancement COPCP001 allows you to define prices for materials transferred between company codes where cross-company code costing is not activated. Let's compare this with cross-company code costing activated with Transaction OKYV or by following IMG menu path:

> Controlling • Product Cost Controlling • Product Cost Planning • Selected Functions in Material Costing • Activate Cross-Company Costing

The screen shown in Figure 2 is displayed.

Controlling Area	Costing Type	Valuation Variant	Cost Across Company Codes
WR01	01	601	☑

« *Figure 2*
Activate Cross-Company Costing

The Cost Across Company Codes checkbox allows a material to be costed and released in more than one company code within a Controlling Area. If you enter a special procurement type with transfer from another plant proceed as follows:

▶ If you want to re-cost the materials in another company code or transfer an existing cost estimate using transfer control, select the checkbox in Figure 2.

▶ If you want the system to transfer the current valuation price from the material master with the valuation strategy, do not select the checkbox. The material is treated as if it were externally procured.

You can develop enhancement COPCP001 to define a price if costing across company codes is not active. In include LXCKAF you can find example program code, however this cannot be directly copied and used.

▶ **Production Resource/Tool Costing**

A production resource or tool is a moveable operating resource used in production or plant maintenance. The function module is called if you have activated enhancement COPCP003.

The costs for production resources and tools are calculated as a flat rate within production overhead. This enhancement enables you to plan the costs for production resources as separate cost components.

This enhancement contains component EXIT_SAPLCK01_001 which contains example program code that you can modify or use as is.

▶ **Bulk Material Costing**

Bulk materials such as washers and grease are normally charged directly to a cost center and included in overhead cost components. If you attempt to make an entry in the RELEVANT TO COSTING field in a BOM item for a bulk material you receive an error message. Enhancement COPCP004 allows you to include bulk materials in the material cost component and itemization.

▶ **Material Valuation**

Enhancement COPCP005 allows you to specify prices for valuation of materials with valuation strategy U in a valuation variant. You display a valuation variant with Transaction OKK4 or by following IMG menu path:

> CONTROLLING • PRODUCT COST CONTROLLING • PRODUCT COST PLANNING • MATERIAL COST ESTIMATE WITH QUANTITY STRUCTURE • COSTING VARIANT: COMPONENTS • DEFINE VALUATION VARIANTS

Double-click a costing variant to display the screen shown in Figure 3.

⌃ *Figure 3 Valuation Variant with Valuation Strategy U*

You use this user exit to determine a valuation price such as a fixed price which is not available with any of the standard valuation strategies.

▶ **Costing Reports**

Itemization and cost component reports are displayed directly when you view a cost estimate. You can add columns to these reports using standard layouts. If you need to display a non-standard or calculated column you can create your own custom report and add it to the costing report user exit with enhancement SAPLXCKA. You can run the reports directly from the cost estimate menu bar.

Display a cost estimate with Transaction CK13N or by following menu path:

ACCOUNTING • CONTROLLING • PRODUCT COST CONTROLLING • PRODUCT COST
PLANNING • MATERIAL COSTING • COST ESTIMATE WITH QUANTITY STRUCTURE
• DISPLAY

The screen shown in Figure 4 is displayed.

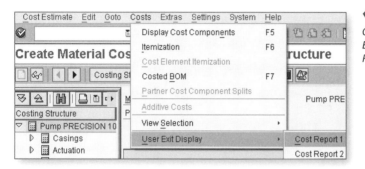

<< **Figure 4**

Cost Estimate User Exit Report Menu Path

Select COSTS • USER EXIT DISPLAY • COST REPORT 1 from the menu bar to
display the example report shown in Figure 5.

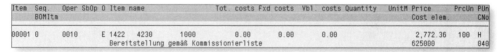

⭡ **Figure 5** *Cost Estimate Report with User Exit*

You can design this itemization report to display columns not available in standard reports. Cost estimate user exit *SAPLXCKA* contains the components:

▸ EXIT_SAPLCKAZ_001 Display/print itemization. This enhancement contains
  example program code that you can modify or activate directly.

▸ EXIT_SAPLCKAZ_002 Display/print cost components. This enhancement
  contains example program code that you can modify or activate directly.

▸ EXIT_SAPLCKAZ_003 Display/print cost components and itemization. This
  enhancement does not contain example program code. ■

Tip 28

Purchased Material Delivery Costs

You can report on inbound freight costs as a separate cost component in cost estimates.

Cost estimates can automatically calculate and report on purchased material delivery costs, such as freight and duty, as cost components. To set this up, create a link between purchasing condition types, origin groups, and cost components with the following steps:

- ▶ Identify the purchased material consumption accounts
- ▶ Configure a costing variant to analyze the delivery costs table
- ▶ Assign condition types to origin groups
- ▶ Assign condition types to purchasing info records
- ▶ Assign origin groups to the cost component structure

In the following solution, we'll review each of these steps in detail.

Solution

You need to determine purchased material consumption accounts because you will assign an origin group, together with the consumption accounts, to basic material costs in a later step.

▶ **Purchased Material Consumption Account**

You can identify purchased material consumption accounts by first determining the valuation class of the purchased materials. Run Transaction MM03 and navigate to the Costing 2 view of a material master for a purchased material. Right-click in the VALUATION CLASS field and select POSSIBLE ENTRIES to display a list of purchased material valuation classes.

You can analyze general ledger accounts assigned to each valuation class with Transaction SE16N (Data Browser). Type in table T030, press [Enter], and in the selection screen, enter your chart of accounts, Transaction GBB, account modifier VBR, and the valuation class to display the screen shown in Figure 1.

Chart of Accounts	Transaction	Valuation Grpg Code	Acct modif	Val. Class	G/L Account	G/L Account
INT	GBB	0001	VBR	3000	400000	400000
INT	GBB	B101	VBR	3000	400000	400000

⌃ *Figure 1* Data Browser Listing of General Ledger Accounts in Table T030

Now that we've determined the purchased material consumption account, the next step is to configure the costing variant.

▶ **Configure the Costing Variant**

To configure a costing variant, select the IMG menu path:

> CONTROLLING • PRODUCT COST CONTROLLING • PRODUCT COST PLANNING • MATERIAL COST ESTIMATE WITH QUANTITY STRUCTURE • DEFINE COSTING VARIANTS

Double-click a costing variant and click the VALUATION VARIANT button to display the screen shown in Figure 2.

« *Figure 2* Valuation Variant Material Strategy Sequence

Because the first PRIORITY in the STRATEGY SEQUENCE searches for PRICE FROM PURCHASING INFO RECORD, the system must then search the SUB-STRATEGY SEQUENCE to determine which purchasing info record price to search for. The QUOTATION PRICE represents the material vendor quote, which is stored in the purchasing info record. In Figure 2, we are directing the cost estimate to search the purchasing info record for Condition types and then access the CONDITION TABLE to determine the origin group.

You can obtain more information about valuation variant strategy sequences from OSS Note 351835 — Valuation variant with purchasing info record strategies. Next, let's look at the link between condition types and origin groups.

▶ **Assign Condition Types to Origin Groups**

You can create origin groups with Transaction OKZ1. To assign condition types to origin groups, click the conveniently located DELIVERY COSTS button in Figure 2 to display the screen shown in Figure 3.

Condition type	V	Valuation Variant	Controlling Area	Company Code	Valuation Area	Origin group
FRA1	0	001	0001	0002	0021	FRA1
PB00	0	001	0001	0002	0021	PB00

⌃ **Figure 3** *Assign Condition Types to Origin Group*

In this screen, you can assign the purchasing CONDITION TYPE to an ORIGIN GROUP. If your entry is for all COMPANY CODES or VALUATION AREAS, you can leave these fields blank. You can also leave the ORIGIN GROUP blank to exclude all cost components with an origin group assigned.

Now let's assign condition types to purchasing info records.

▶ **Assign Condition Types to Purchasing Info Records**

In Figure 2, we instructed the cost estimate to search for a purchasing info record. You can display a purchasing info record with Transaction ME1M or via the following menu path:

> LOGISTICS • MATERIALS MANAGEMENT • PURCHASING • MASTER DATA • INFO RECORD • LIST DISPLAYS • BY MATERIAL

Type in the Material, Purchasing organization, and Plant in the selection screen and click the Execute icon. Double-click a Purchasing Info Record and click the Conditions button to display the screen shown in Figure 4.

CnTy	Name	Amount	Unit	per	UoM	DeletionID	Scales	Texts
PB00	Gross Price	10.00	USD	1	EA		☐	☐
FRA1	Freight %	10.000	%				☐	☐

« **Figure 4**
Purchasing Info Record Condition Types

We assigned Condition types PB00 (GROSS PRICE) and FRA1 (FREIGHT %) to origin groups in Figure 3. The FREIGHT % condition type calculates freight as a percentage of the GROSS PRICE. You can obtain more information about assigning origin groups to both condition types and material masters with OSS Note 1445940 — Raw material cost estimate: origin group for delivery costs.

Now we need to assign origin groups to cost components and then create a cost estimate.

▶ **Assign Origin Groups to Cost Components**

To determine which main cost component structure to access, display a cost estimate, click the COSTING DATA tab, double-click the underlined COSTING VARIANT, select the ASSIGNMENTS tab, and click the COST COMPONENT STRUCTURE button to display the screen shown in Figure 5.

Company Code	Cost Comp. Str.	Name	Cost Comp. Str.	Name
0001	01	Cost Comp Struct. (Main Cost Comp Split)		Product Costing: Prim
0005	01	Product Costing	02	Product Costing: Prim

⌃ *Figure 5 Assignment of Cost Component Structures to Company Codes*

This screen displays the assignment of the main and auxiliary cost component splits to company codes. You can hover your mouse over the column headings to display more details of each column as shown in Figure 5.

You can assign origin groups to cost components with Transaction OKTZ or via the following IMG menu path:

CONTROLLING • PRODUCT COST CONTROLLING • PRODUCT COST PLANNING • BASIC SETTINGS FOR MATERIAL COSTING • DEFINE COST COMPONENT STRUCTURE

Select your cost component structure; double-click COST COMPONENTS WITH ATTRIBUTES at the left, create a new FREIGHT COST COMPONENT, and assign the FREIGHT ORIGIN GROUP to the purchased material consumption accounts, as shown in Figure 6.

Cost Comp. Str.	Chart of Accts	From cost el.	Origin group	To cost elem.	Cost Component	Name of Cost Comp.
MB	CAUK	500000	FRA1	500100	2	Freight

⌃ *Figure 6 Assign Freight Origin Group to Freight Cost Component*

After you save the new FREIGHT COST COMPONENT, new cost estimates will list FREIGHT as a separate cost component. ■

Tip 29

Activity Type Search Strategies

You can set more than one search strategy for activity types.

The valuation variant is a component of the costing variant that determines how a cost estimate searches for prices. You can assign different strategies for materials, activity types and processes, subcontracting, and external processing prices. Let's follow a detailed example of how you can benefit from adding an additional search strategy for activity prices.

✓ Solution

While there is a costing variant for creating standard cost estimates, there are also other costing variants for creating planned and actual manufacturing order costs. Manufacturing orders typically use costing variant PPP1 with valuation variant 006, which determines order plan costs. You can display a manufacturing order valuation variant with Transaction OPN2 or via the following IMG menu path:

> CONTROLLING • PRODUCT COST CONTROLLING • COST OBJECT CONTROLLING
> • PRODUCT COST BY ORDER • MANUFACTURING ORDERS • CHECK VALUATION
> VARIANTS FOR MANUFACTURING ORDERS (PP)

Double-click valuation variant 006 and click the ACTIVITYTYPES/PROCESSES tab to display the screen shown in Figure 1.

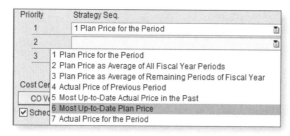

« *Figure 1*
Activity Type Valuation Strategy — Possible Entries

The system supplied valuation variant 006 contains 1 PLAN PRICE FOR THE PERIOD as the only activity type price strategy by default. You can enter up to three search strategies from the possible entries list, shown in Figure 1.

Production may need to create manufacturing orders for the next fiscal year before reaching the end of the current one. If you have not yet calculated and entered the planned activity rate for the next fiscal year, error messages will be generated when you attempt to calculate the manufacturing order plan costs.

However, if you include MOST UP-TO-DATE PLAN PRICE as PRIORITY 2 in the strategy sequence as highlighted in Figure 1, then the plan activity price for the current fiscal year will be successfully accessed even though there is no plan price in the period in the next fiscal year for which the manufacturing order is scheduled to begin production.

While the activity plan price may not be the same as the plan price you eventually plan for the next fiscal year, you'll still be able to create manufacturing orders without error. You can recost the production order after the plan activity price is entered for the next fiscal year and before any confirmations take place. You can recost a production order with Transaction CO02 or by going to:

> LOGISTICS • PRODUCTION • SHOP FLOOR CONTROL • ORDER • CHANGE

The screen shown in Figure 2 is displayed.

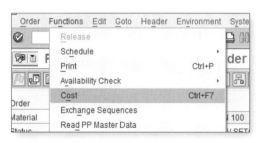

《 *Figure 2*
Recost Production Order

Choose FUNCTIONS • COST from the menu bar to *recalculate* the production order costs based on the new activity price. Choose GOTO • COSTS • ANALYSIS from the menu bar to *display* the production order costs. You can also reread the master data before any confirmations are carried out by choosing FUNCTIONS • READ PP MASTER DATA from the menu bar. This will copy any bill of material (BOM) and routing changes to the production order.

OSS Notes 399305, 590181, and 460587 contain more information on using valuation variant strategy 6, MOST UP-TO-DATE PLAN PRICE, for activity price. ∎

Tip (30)

Cost Estimate Default Dates

You can use date control to determine cost estimate default dates.

When you create cost estimates, you are presented with four default dates. Unless you have previously created and used cost estimates, it's not immediately clear what effect these dates have. We'll first look at the cost estimate date fields, see how the dates default, and then explain them.

Solution

You can create a single cost estimate with Transaction CK11N or via the following menu path:

> ACCOUNTING • CONTROLLING • PRODUCT COST CONTROLLING • PRODUCT COST PLANNING • MATERIAL COSTING • COST ESTIMATE WITH QUANTITY STRUCTURE

Enter the material, plant, and costing variant in the COSTING DATA tab and press ⌨Enter to display the screen shown in Figure 1.

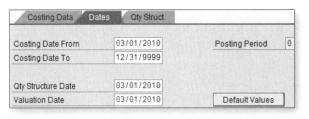

« *Figure 1*
Cost Estimate Dates Screen

The four DATES default into the fields and are modifiable in this example. If you do change the dates, you can revert to the original entries by clicking the DEFAULT VALUES button.

The default dates are determined by the date control which is a component of the costing variant. To display the configuration behind these dates, click the COSTING

DATA tab in Figure 1, double-click the underlined costing variant, and click the Date Control button to display the screen shown in Figure 2.

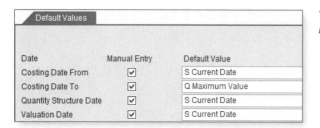

« *Figure 2*
Date Control Details Screen

You select the MANUAL ENTRY indicators to make the default dates modifiable when creating a cost estimate. The default date configuration shown in Figure 2 is associated with the system-supplied costing variant PPC1, which you can use to create standard cost estimates. Let's examine each of the four dates in detail:

▶ **Costing Date From**
 This field determines the valid start date of the cost estimate. The cost estimate cannot be released, for example, to adjust inventory valuation, until the start date has been reached. The start date can be changed to a previous date and the cost estimate can be created. However, a standard cost estimate cannot be saved, marked, or released with a start date in the past.

▶ **Costing Date To**
 This field determines the valid finish date of the cost estimate. Variance calculation requires a standard cost estimate that is valid for the entire fiscal year. This date is typically set to the maximum possible date. If you encounter difficulties when creating a costing run for the next fiscal year, setting this date to the maximum date lets you calculate variance in the new fiscal year until you release the new costing run.

▶ **Quantity Structure Date**
 This field determines which bill of material (BOM) and routing are selected for the cost estimate. Because these can change over time, it is useful for scenario testing to select a particular BOM or routing by date.

▶ **Valuation Date**
 This field determines which material and activity prices are selected for the cost estimate. Activity prices are planned for each fiscal year, while purchasing info records can contain different vendor-quoted prices for different dates.

You can display default dates when creating multiple cost estimates with a costing run with in the DATES tab of the general data section. ▪

Tip 31 Transfer Control Uses Existing Cost Estimates

Transfer control requires a higher-level cost estimate to use existing standard cost estimates for lower-level materials.

The costing variant transfer control component lets you transfer existing cost estimates for subassemblies and components to a higher-level cost estimate when developing new products during a fiscal year. It also lets you create new cost estimates in one plant while transferring existing cost estimates from other plants.

When you create a finished goods cost estimate, the system first creates cost estimates for all of the lowest-level components, and then works progressively up, level-by-level, through the bill of material (BOM) hierarchy.

During a yearly costing run, you typically create and release new cost estimates for all components and assemblies. During the year, if a new product contains all new components, a new standard price is needed for all of the components. However, some of the components may already exist and are shared with other existing products. Changing the existing standard price for these components could lead to a planned variance on production orders for existing products.

Solution

Transfer control allows for the transfer of existing component and subassembly cost estimates to new product cost estimates. You can maintain transfer control either by clicking the Transfer Control button on the CONTROL tab of a costing variant with Transaction OKKM, or via the following the IMG menu path:

> CONTROLLING • PRODUCT COST CONTROLLING • PRODUCT COST PLANNING • MATERIAL COST ESTIMATE WITH QUANTITY STRUCTURE • COSTING VARIANT: COMPONENTS • DEFINE TRANSFER CONTROL

Double-click on transfer control PC02 to display the screen shown in Figure 1.

This screen indicates the sequence that the system uses to search for existing cost estimates for subassemblies and components in a single plant. If an existing cost estimate is found, it is transferred to the new product cost estimate. This lets you avoid recosting existing materials between main costing runs. The screen in Figure 1 also shows a list of possible entries for the transfer control strategy sequence.

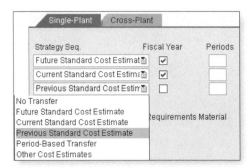

« Figure 1
Transfer Control PP02 Details Screen

If you select the FISCAL YEAR checkbox the system will search for a cost estimate with a start date within the current year. An entry in the PERIODS field for CURRENT, PREVIOUS, and OTHER COST ESTIMATES refers to the number of periods before the start date of the cost estimate. For a FUTURE STANDARD COST ESTIMATE, the PERIODS field refers to the number of periods after and before the cost estimate START DATE.

If you select PERIOD-BASED TRANSFER, an entry in the PERIODS field has no effect because the system searches for cost estimates with exactly the same costing type, valuation variant, costing version and, if applicable, period.

For an example of how you may use cross-plant transfer control, run Transaction OKKM and double-click TRANSFER CONTROL PP01 to display the screen shown in Figure 2.

« Figure 2
Transfer Control PP01 Details Screen

Costing runs using transfer control PC01 create and release new cost estimates within a single plant without using any existing cost estimates. The costing run, however, uses existing cost estimates from other plants, if available, because the cross-plant transfer control strategy is the same, as shown in Figure 1. This strategy lets cost accountants create and release new cost estimates only in their own plants. ▪

Tip 32

Marking Allowance for Valuation Variants

Marking allowance is needed for you to mark standard cost estimates for each period, company code, and valuation variant.

Marking allowance provides you with an extra control over the releasing of standard cost estimates. You can use marking allowance for one valuation variant and costing version per period. There are three basic steps you must take before you can update inventory valuation with a standard cost estimate: create, mark, and release. To further control the process of updating inventory valuation, you need to carry out an extra step called marking allowance, which we'll now discuss in detail.

✓ Solution

When you mark a cost estimate, the saved standard price is copied to the future column in the material master Costing 2 view, as shown in Figure 1.

« **Figure 1**
Marked Cost Estimate Price in Future Column

The marked value remains in the FUTURE column until either the COST ESTIMATE is marked again or released. You can mark a cost estimate many times, but you can only release it once per period.

If you mark a standard cost estimate and then create and save another standard cost estimate, the value in the FUTURE column does not reflect the value of the last saved cost estimate. In this case, you cannot release the value displayed in the FUTURE column because the related cost estimate has since been overwritten.

You can access marking allowance from the Padlock icon on the marking step of a costing run, with Transaction CK24, or via the following menu path:

> ACCOUNTING • CONTROLLING • PRODUCT COST CONTROLLING • PRODUCT COST PLANNING • MATERIAL COSTING • PRICE UPDATE

Click the Marking Allowance button to display the screen shown in Figure 2.

Posting Period/Fiscal Year		3	2010		

Executed	Company Code	Valuation View	Costing Version	Released
☐	0008	Legal Valuation	1	
☐	1000	Legal Valuation	1	
☀	2000	Legal Valuation		

« **Figure 2**
Marking Allowance Screen

The authorization for marking specifies the COMPANY CODE and POSTING PERIOD you can mark a standard cost estimate in with a given valuation variant. You cannot mark cost estimates with different valuation variants in this period. To create a marking allowance, click a COMPANY CODE next to a red traffic light icon in Figure 2. The dialog box shown in Figure 3 is displayed.

☞ Permitted std cost est variant	⊠
Costing Variant	PPC1
Costing Version	01

« **Figure 3**
Create Marking Allowance Dialog Box

Type in the COSTING VARIANT and COSTING VERSION and press ⌗Enter⌗ to create the marking allowance. A green traffic light icon appears next to the COMPANY CODE and the COSTING VERSION column is populated, as shown in Figure 2. If you click a COMPANY CODE with a green traffic light icon or a marking allowance already created, you will see the dialog box, shown in Figure 4.

Cstg Vrnt	Name
PPC1	Standard Cost Est. (Mat.)
ZJJ1	Same Valuation Variant

« **Figure 4**
Permitted Costing Variants

The reason you may see more permitted costing variants than entered in the dialog box in Figure 3 is that marking allowance is based on valuation variant, which is a component of the permitted costing variant. There may be more than one costing variant that contains the permitted valuation variant. ◼

Tip 33 — Mixed Cost Estimates

Mixed cost estimates let you combine the costs of different procurement alternatives into an inventory value.

When you have procurement alternatives for the same material, such as two production lines or two vendors, you can use mixed cost estimates when you need inventory valuation to reflect the mixed procurement costs.

✓ Solution

Let's examine each of the four steps required to create mixed cost estimates.

▶ **Create Quantity Structure Type and Assign Costing Version**
You can display quantity structure types with Transaction OMXA or via the following IMG menu path, which brings you to the screen in Figure 1:

> CONTROLLING • PRODUCT COST CONTROLLING • PRODUCT COST PLANNING •
> SELECTED FUNCTIONS IN MATERIAL COSTING • MIXED COSTING • DEFINE QUANTITY
> STRUCTURE TYPES

QtStT	Time dependency	Perc.valid	Name
MIX	1	☑	Mixed Costing

《 Figure 1
Change Quantity Structure Types for Mixed Costing

The quantity structure type (QTSTT) controls how mixed costing is applied. Next, assign the costing version with Transaction OKYD or via the following IMG menu path, which brings you to the screen in Figure 2.

> CONTROLLING • PRODUCT COST CONTROLLING • PRODUCT COST PLANNING •
> SELECTED FUNCTIONS IN MATERIAL COSTING • MIXED COSTING • DEFINE COSTING
> VERSIONS

Costing Version	Costing Type	Valuation Variant	Variant for Transfer	Exch. Rate Type	Qty Str. Type 1
30	01	001			MIX

⌃ *Figure 2 Costing Version Configuration*

Mixed cost estimates are created with reference to a costing version. This lets you create more than one mixed cost estimate for the same material.

▶ **Create Procurement Alternative**

You can create procurement alternatives with Transaction CK91N or via the menu path:

> ACCOUNTING • CONTROLLING • PRODUCT COST CONTROLLING • PRODUCT COST PLANNING • MATERIAL COSTING • MASTER DATA FOR MIXED COST ESTIMATE • EDIT PROCUREMENT ALTERNATIVES

Enter material and plant, and click the New page icon. Choose the process category from the drop-down list shown in Figure 3.

BB	Purchase order
BBV	Procurement (change involving stocks)
BF	Production
BL	Subcontracting
BU	Stock transfer

« Figure 3
Procurement Alternative Process Category —
Possible Entries

The process category you select will determine the fields that appear below the drop-down list. Enter the purchasing or production information and save.

▶ **Define Mixing Ratios for Procurement Alternatives**

You can create mixing ratios with Transaction CK94 or by going to:

> ACCOUNTING • CONTROLLING • PRODUCT COST CONTROLLING • PRODUCT COST PLANNING • MATERIAL COSTING • MASTER DATA FOR MIXED COST ESTIMATE • MIXING RATIOS • CREATE/CHANGE

Enter your material, plant, fiscal year, and quantity structure type and press Enter.

PCat	Changeable name	Lot Size	V	QtyStrDate	MR	Mixing Ratio
BF	Procurement alternative 01	100	PC		☑	50.000

⌃ Figure 4 *Change Mixing Ratios*

Enter the MIXING RATIO for each procurement alternative and save.

▶ **Create Cost Estimate with Quantity Structure**

When you create a cost estimate for the material with the costing version you configured in Figure 2 with Transaction CK11N, a mixed cost estimate will be created. ■

Optimize Costing Runs

Changing some costing variant default settings allows you to streamline costing run and cost estimate processing.

Adjusting certain default costing variant settings in your SAP system can save you time when processing costing run and cost estimate messages.

The first entry you make when creating individual or collective cost estimates with a costing run is the costing variant, which instructs the system on how to determine the standard price.

When first setting up costing variants, you have a choice of copying system-supplied variants to create your own variants or creating your own variants without referencing existing variants. If you choose to create your own costing variants, you should consider changing some of the default settings.

✓ Solution

You can maintain costing variants with Transaction OKKN or via the following IMG menu path:

> CONTROLLING • PRODUCT COST CONTROLLING • PRODUCT COST PLANNING • MATERIAL COST ESTIMATE WITH QUANTITY STRUCTURE • DEFINE COSTING VARIANTS

Click the New Entries button and then the MISC. tab to display the screen in Figure 1.

« *Figure 1*
Costing Variant Error Management Field

The default MESSAGES ONLINE setting means the costing run will stop processing at the first message encountered. You need to correct the individual error message and rerun the costing run, which will then stop processing again at the next error message.

To streamline the costing run error message processing, click the ERROR MANAGEMENT field in Figure 1 to display a list of possible entries and select LOG AND SAVE MESSAGES, MAIL INACTIVE. This will allow the costing run to create cost estimates for all selected materials and save messages in a log that can be accessed at any time following the costing run. You can correct all of the messages before running the costing run again.

Other default settings that should typically be changed are update parameters. Click on the UPDATE tab to display the screen shown in Figure 2.

《 Figure 2
Costing Variant Update Parameters Tab

When you create a new costing variant without referring to an existing costing variant, all indicators in this tab are deselected. The following settings are recommended:

▶ The SAVING ALLOWED checkbox determines whether you can save cost estimates created with this costing variant. If you intend to update prices in the material master, such as the standard price, you'll need to select this checkbox.

▶ The SAVE ERROR LOG checkbox together with the recommended LOG AND SAVE MESSAGES in Figure 1 lets you save error messages, and analyze and take corrective action on the completion of a costing run.

▶ The DEFAULTS CAN BE CHANGED BY USER checkbox determines whether a dialog box will appear when saving an individual cost estimate. This allows the user to decide not to save the cost estimate log and itemization. You're typically interested in saving this information so leaving this indicator deselected saves you time because the update parameters dialog box does not appear when saving an individual cost estimate.

▶ The ITEMIZATION checkbox determines whether you can save cost estimate itemization. This is useful information, so you should select this checkbox. ▉

Tip 35 Material Status Reduces Costing Messages

Material status provides you with an efficient method to eliminate redundant costing run messages.

Many messages can result following a costing run. Problems usually include logistics master data issues that need correction, such as a missing bill of material (BOM) or routing (task list) for an in-house-produced assembly.

However, the system can also generate unnecessary error messages. Obsolete or discontinued materials may not require cost estimates, but a costing run may still select them and generate messages. Material master status can eliminate unnecessary costing messages and provide benefits to other departments, such as purchasing and production.

Solution

Material status can be used for two purposes:

► Cross-plant material status restricts usability for all plants (Basic data 1)
► Plant-specific material status restricts usability for individual plants

Because costing is generally plant-specific, we are concerned with the plant-specific material status field located in the material master Costing 1 view. You can maintain material status with Transaction MM02 or via the following menu path:

> LOGISTICS • MATERIALS MANAGEMENT • MATERIAL MASTER • MATERIAL • CHANGE • IMMEDIATELY

Navigate to the COSTING 1 view, right-click on the plant-specific status field, and choose POSSIBLE ENTRIES to display, as shown in Figure 1.

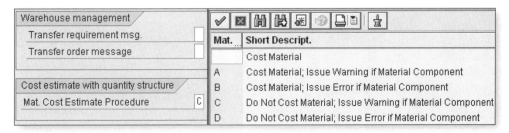

General data			MS	Description
Base Unit of Measure	PC		01	Blocked for Procmnt/Whse
☐ Do Not Cost			02	Blocked for task list/BOM
			BP	Blocked for Purchasing
Origin group			ED	Eng. detailed design
Overhead Group	SAP10		KA	Blocked for Costing
Plant-sp.matl status	KA		OB	Obsolete Materials

《 *Figure 1*
Plant-Specific Material Status Possible Entries

You can maintain the configuration for material status with Transaction OMS4 or via the following IMG menu path:

> CONTROLLING • PRODUCT COST CONTROLLING • PRODUCT COST PLANNING • MATERIAL COST ESTIMATE WITH QUANTITY STRUCTURE • SETTINGS FOR QUANTITY STRUCTURE CONTROL • MATERIAL DATA • CHECK MATERIAL STATUS

Double-click a material status, right-click the MATERIAL COST ESTIMATE PROCEDURE field, and select POSSIBLE ENTRIES to display the screen in Figure 2.

Warehouse management			Mat.	Short Descript.
Transfer requirement msg.				Cost Material
Transfer order message			A	Cost Material; Issue Warning if Material Component
			B	Cost Material; Issue Error if Material Component
Cost estimate with quantity structure			C	Do Not Cost Material; Issue Warning if Material Component
Mat. Cost Estimate Procedure	C		D	Do Not Cost Material; Issue Error if Material Component

ʌ *Figure 2 Define Material Status Cost Estimate Possible Entries*

- ▶ Option C ensures that the material will not be selected during a costing run. You will receive a warning message if the material is included in an active bill of material (BOM).

- ▶ Option D ensures the material will not be selected during a costing run, however, an error message results if the material is included in an active BOM.

Plant-specific material status can also be used for purposes other than costing, such as to issue a warning or error message when a purchase or production order is created for discontinued materials, or to restrict the use of new parts during different stages of product development. ▪

Tip 36

Reduce the Clutter in Cost Estimate Screens

You can simplify cost estimate screens by reducing the number of cost component views.

Although five cost component views are listed by default when displaying a cost estimate, you may not need to display them all. Continuing to list redundant cost component views clutters the cost estimate screen, which already contains a lot of information. You can easily control the number and order of cost component views listed in the COST ESTIMATE screen with the following procedure.

Solution

You can display a cost estimate with Transaction CK13N or via the following menu path:

> ACCOUNTING • CONTROLLING • PRODUCT COST CONTROLLING • PRODUCT COST PLANNING • MATERIAL COSTING • COST ESTIMATE WITH QUANTITY STRUCTURE • DISPLAY

Type in the Material, Plant, and Costing Variant and press Enter to display the screen shown in Figure 1.

Cost Component View	Total Costs	Fixed	Variable	Currency
Cost of goods manufactured	15,551.10	7,940.99	7,610.11	USD
Cost of goods sold	17,813.05	9,091.27	8,721.78	USD
Sales and administration costs	2,261.95	1,150.28	1,111.67	USD
Inventory (commercial)	15,551.10	7,940.99	7,610.11	USD
Inventory (tax-based)	15,551.10	7,940.99	7,610.11	USD

« Figure 1
Cost Component View List in the Cost Estimate Screen

Double-click a COST COMPONENT VIEW to see the corresponding cost components and costs listed in the lower section of the COST ESTIMATE screen (not shown). Cost components group together costs of similar type, such as materials, labor, and overhead, by cost elements.

Note that in Figure 1 the INVENTORY (COMMERCIAL) and INVENTORY (TAX-BASED) cost component views appear by default. The distinction between tax valuation and commercial valuation is not observed in the U.S. and in some European countries. If these are not relevant for your company, you can remove them from your COST ESTIMATE screen by selecting SETTINGS • COST DISPLAY from the menu bar. The dialog box shown in Figure 2 is displayed.

Costs for View	
1	Cost of goods manufactured
2	Cost of goods sold
3	Sales and administration costs
4	Inventory (commercial)
5	Inventory (tax-based)

« *Figure 2*

Choose the Cost Component Views to List in a Cost Estimate

Entries you make in this screen determine the number and order of the cost component views listed in the COST ESTIMATE screen. If you leave an entry blank, the corresponding cost component view will not appear in the cost estimate. In this example, let's delete entries 4 and 5 and press ⌐Enter⌐ to return to the cost estimate, shown in Figure 3.

Cost Component View	Total Costs	Fixed	Variable	Currency
Cost of goods manufactured	15,551.10	7,940.99	7,610.11	USD
Cost of goods sold	17,813.05	9,091.27	8,721.78	USD
Sales and administration costs	2,261.95	1,150.28	1,111.67	USD

⌃ *Figure 3 Simplified Cost Component View List in Cost Estimate*

Only the cost component views you selected in Figure 2 are now displayed in the COST ESTIMATE screen.

If you click the Note button (not shown) at the bottom of the dialog box in Figure 2, you have the option of saving these settings for only this cost estimate independent of the costing variant, or for all cost estimates dependent on the costing variant. ■

Tip (37) Unit Cost Estimate — Base Planning Object

A unit cost estimate lets you calculate the planned costs for base planning objects without a bill of material (BOM) or routing.

When you develop a new product, or modify an existing one, there are several stages:

▶ If you haven't yet developed any master data in the system, you can carry out initial cost planning by creating a base planning object.

▶ When you've created a material master you can create a cost estimate without a quantity structure to manually plan costs for the new material.

▶ After you've created the necessary BOM and routing, you can create a material cost estimate with a quantity structure.

✓ Solution

You can maintain a base planning object with Transaction KKE2 or via the following menu path:

> ACCOUNTING • CONTROLLING • PRODUCT COST CONTROLLING • PRODUCT COST PLANNING • REFERENCE AND SIMULATION COSTING • CHANGE BASE PLANNING OBJECT

Enter a base planning object and press ⌜Enter⌝ to display a header information screen. You can create a basic structure and valuation in the Cost estimate section by clicking the Calculator icon to display the screen in Figure 1.

This screen is in a spreadsheet format, and it's easy to make modifications and analyze the resulting changes in total value. Let's examine the relevant columns.

▶ ITEM: You can modify existing items or add new items by clicking the green Plus sign icon. You can easily explore the functionality of the other icons in this screen by clicking them.

	M	Item	C	Resource	Plant/Activity	Purc	Quantity	U	L	Value - Total	Description	Price - Total	Price Unit	Cost Elem
Base Planning Obj		R-1110			CPU-66									
Costing Items - Basic View														
	4	M	R-1220	1200		1	PC			51.13	MEMORY, 8 MB	51.13	1	410000
	5	E	4275	1423		4	H			28.41	Burn-in Hours	7.10	1	623000
	6	M	R-1230	1200		1	PC			3.07	BIOS	3.07	1	410000
	7	G								21.55	OS - Raw Material			655100
	8	S								195.98	Grand total			

≫ *Figure 1* Unit Cost Estimate for Base Planning Object

▶ C (Category): Right-click the C field and click POSSIBLE ENTRIES to display a list of item categories. The item category you enter in this field influences the entries you can make in the following fields for each item.

▶ RESOURCE: The resource you enter in this field corresponds to the item category entered in the C column. For example, if you enter item category M, you will be restricted to entering an existing material in the corresponding field in the RESOURCE column. Some item categories, such as V, do not require an entry in the RESOURCE column.

▶ PLANT/ACTIVITY: An entry you make in this field corresponds to the entries you made in the C and RESOURCE columns.

▶ QUANTITY: This entry refers to the quantity of resources required for this estimate. You can easily change quantities and see how this affects the total value of the base planning object.

▶ VALUE – TOTAL: The total value for each item is calculated by multiplying the quantity by the entry in the PRICE – TOTAL column. You should be aware of the value in the PRICE UNIT column when considering base planning object prices. Divide the PRICE – TOTAL entry by the PRICE UNIT entry to calculate the unit cost. You increase the price unit to increase the accuracy of the price.

▶ COST ELEM (Cost Element): The cost element identifies the type of cost in cost reports. You can see standard base planning object detailed reports via the following menu path:

> ACCOUNTING • CONTROLLING • PRODUCT COST CONTROLLING • PRODUCT COST PLANNING • INFORMATION SYSTEM • DETAILED REPORTS • FOR BASE PLANNING OBJECT

Material Cost Estimate without Quantity Structure

A material cost estimate without quantity structure lets you calculate the planned costs for materials without a bill of material (BOM) or routing.

After you've carried out initial research on the cost of items in new products with base planning objects, you can create a material master to continue the development process. You can also take an existing material, copy the existing quantity structure, and manually make adjustments to carry out cost analysis.

✓ Solution

You can create a material cost estimate without quantity structure for a new or modified product with Transaction KKPAN or via the following menu path:

> ACCOUNTING • CONTROLLING • PRODUCT COST CONTROLLING • PRODUCT COST PLANNING • MATERIAL COSTING • COST ESTIMATE WITHOUT QUANTITY STRUCTURE • CREATE

To create a cost estimate without the quantity structure, enter a Material, Plant, and Costing Variant, and press [Enter] to display the screen in Figure 1.

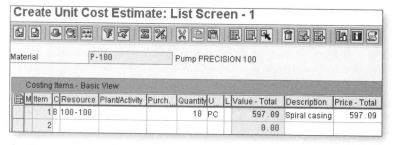

Create Unit Cost Estimate: List Screen - 1

| Material | P-100 | Pump PRECISION 100 |

Costing Items - Basic View

M	Item	C	Resource	Plant/Activity	Purch.	Quantity	U	L	Value - Total	Description	Price - Total
	1	B	100-100			10	PC		597.09	Spiral casing	597.09
	2								0.00		

⌃ *Figure 1 Create a Cost Estimate without Quantity Structure*

This screen is similar to the unit cost estimate screen for a base planning object. Let's follow an example of how to copy existing structures and master data into a unit cost estimate. A base planning object 100-100 with a quantity of 10 has been entered and ITEM 1 selected. Select FUNCTIONS • EXPLODE BASE PLANNING OBJECT from the menu bar to display the dialogue box shown in Figure 2.

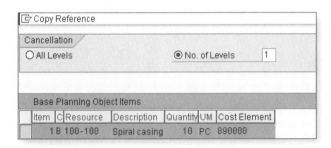

《   Figure 2

Copy Base Planning Object with Reference

In this example, we'll explode the existing base planning object by selecting NO. OF LEVELS and entering 1, and then by selecting the base planning object item and clicking the Explode button, which brings you to the screen in Figure 3.

Material	P-100			Pump PRECISION 100					

	M	Item	C	Resource	Plant/Activity	Purc	Quantity	U	L	Value - Total	Description	Price - Total
		1	E	4230	1422		0.500	H		13.86	Setup Hours	2,772.36
		2	M	100-110	1000		10	PC		51.10	Slug for spiral casing	5.11
		3	M	100-120	1000		10	PC		230.00	Flat gasket	23.00
		4	M	100-130	1000		80	PC		80.00	Hexagon head screw	100.00
		5	E	4230	1420		0.833	H		22.18	Machine hours	2,662.54
		6	E	4230	1420		1.667	H		44.38	Machine hours	2,662.54
		7	E	4230	1420		0.833	H		22.18	Machine hours	2,662.54
		8	E	4230	1422		0.167	H		4.63	Setup Hours	2,772.36

Costing Items - Basic View

∧ *Figure 3 Base Planning Object Copied to Unit Cost Estimate*

You can copy the existing quantity structures, or modify, add, or delete existing individual items to a unit cost estimate.

Once you've developed a unit cost estimate and are ready to progress to the production phase, you can develop BOMs and routings, and create cost estimates with quantity structure and standard cost estimates. ■

Tip **39** Searching for Cost Estimates

There are several standard methods available for you to search for cost estimates.

Because cost estimates contain useful historical information, such as the setup of bill of materials (BOMs) and routings, you don't routinely delete them. However, you can archive cost estimates with Transaction CKR3, which generally allows you to access the data on another server. Let's examine the three options you have for locating cost estimates before they are archived.

Solution

When you mark and release standard cost estimates, you update the material master price fields. Buttons are available as a link between material masters and corresponding cost estimates. You can view these fields and buttons with Transaction MM03 or via the following menu path:

> LOGISTICS • MATERIALS MANAGEMENT • MATERIAL MASTER • MATERIAL • DISPLAY • DISPLAY CURRENT

Navigate to the Costing 2 view to display the fields shown in Figure 1.

« Figure 1
Material Master Standard Cost Estimate Buttons

To display the current standard cost estimate, click the CURRENT button. Click the FUTURE and PREVIOUS buttons to display the respective cost estimates. You will most often need to display one of these three cost estimates, so the quickest way to do this is to go to the Costing 2 view of the material master with Transaction MM03 and click the relevant button.

You can create and mark a standard cost estimate multiple times during a period. Each time you create a standard cost estimate within the same period, a previous cost estimate created in the same period is overwritten. This means that the cost estimate referred to in the FUTURE column may no longer exist because it may have been overwritten by a more recent cost estimate not yet marked.

You can also search for a cost estimate with Transaction S_P99_41000111 or via the following menu path:

ACCOUNTING • CONTROLLING • PRODUCT COST CONTROLLING • PRODUCT COST PLANNING • INFORMATION SYSTEM • OBJECT LIST • FOR MATERIAL • ANALYZE/ COMPARE MATERIAL COST ESTIMATES

Type in the plant and material, and click the Execute icon to see a list of all cost estimates for the material, as shown in Figure 2.

Material	Material Description	Plant	Status	Costing Result	Lot Size	Base Unit	Valid from
P-100	Pump PRECISION 100	1000	KA	58,199.66	100	PC	04/24/2010
P-100	Pump PRECISION 100	1000	FR	52,840.10	100	PC	01/03/2008
P-100	Pump PRECISION 100	1000	FR	52,840.10	100	PC	01/08/2007

⌃ *Figure 2 Material Cost Estimate List*

Double-click any line to display the corresponding cost estimate details. To assist in finding a particular cost estimate, you can add the VALID FROM column to the layout and sort the list in descending order on this column as shown in Figure 2. You can also restrict the list of cost estimates displayed by entering the VALID FROM costing date on the initial selection screen.

A third method to search for a cost estimate is by running Transaction CK13N or via the following menu path:

ACCOUNTING • CONTROLLING • PRODUCT COST CONTROLLING • PRODUCT COST PLANNING • MATERIAL COSTING • COST ESTIMATE WITH QUANTITY STRUCTURE • DISPLAY

Enter the parameters for your cost estimate. If more than one cost estimate meets your criteria, you can double-click on a line to display the cost estimate. ▪

Part 5

Cost Object Controlling

Things You'll Learn in this Section

Cost object controlling enables you to determine the cost of goods manufactured and the cost of goods sold. You can assign the costs incurred in the production of assemblies, individual orders, or intangible goods to those activities. Cost object controlling enables you to determine the cost of goods manufactured and the cost of goods sold. You can:

▸ Establish planned costs

▸ Record actual costs for the orders

▸ Compare actual costs with target and planned costs and analyze variances

▸ Determine price floors for products or individual orders

Actual and plan costs are collected on manufacturing orders for lot size production, and product cost collectors for period based production. Plan costs are determined by master data such as bill of material (BOM) and routings which are copied to the order. Target costs are determined by plan data adjusted for quantity output to inventory.

During simultaneous costing actual costs are collected on the order in real time as goods are issued from inventory to the order and as activities provided by cost centers are confirmed against the order. You can include overhead in activity prices or use costing sheets for period-end allocation of overhead costs. As manufactured goods are delivered to inventory, the manufacturing order receives a credit based on the standard price of the product.

A balance may be left on the order due to the difference between the order debits incurred during production activities and credits from production output to inventory. You can analyze the order balance with variance analysis. The system automatically determines the reasons for the variance and divides the order balance into four possible input and four possible output variances. The variance categories can be displayed and analyzed in cost element level detailed reports. You can drill down through the detailed reports to line item reports and to the source document such as material documents and activity confirmations.

You settle the order balance to profitability analysis and financial accounting at period-end. You can map the eight possible variance categories to separate value fields in profitability analysis for detailed analysis.

Tip (40) Valuation Class and Material Type

Only allow one valuation class when you are creating a material master.

The material type contains attributes that are referenced when you create a material master. One of these attributes is the account category reference field that represents a group of valuation classes allowed for a material master. A valuation class is a material master field that determines the general ledger account postings during an inventory transaction.

When configuring material masters, it is good practice to limit the number of valuation classes to one per material type. A default valuation class can be manually changed during material master creation. The problem is if you enter the wrong valuation class it is difficult to correct after there's stock in inventory. In this case you need to remove existing stock with a scrap movement type, correct the valuation class, and then reverse the scrap transaction. It is not always possible to scrap stock, particularly in validated and controlled environments.

Solution

Let's first look at how to define the account category reference and then find out how to assign it to a material type. You can define the account category reference with Transaction OMSK or via the following IMG menu path:

> MATERIALS MANAGEMENT • VALUATION AND ACCOUNT ASSIGNMENT • ACCOUNT DETERMINATION • ACCOUNT DETERMINATION WITHOUT WIZARD • DEFINE VALUATION CLASSES

The screen shown in Figure 1 is displayed.

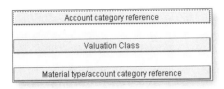

« **Figure 1**

Account Category Reference Overview Screen

Click the ACCOUNT CATEGORY REFERENCE button to display the screen shown in Figure 2.

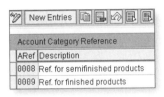

« **Figure 2**

Define Account Category Reference

Click the NEW ENTRIES button to create a new ACCOUNT CATEGORY REFERENCE. To assign valuation classes to an account category reference, click the VALUATION CLASS button in Figure 1. The screen shown in Figure 3 is displayed.

Valuation Classes			
ValCl	ARef	Description	Description
7910	0008	Semi-finished (external)	Ref. for semifinished products
7920	0009	Finished products	Ref. for finished products

« **Figure 3**

Assign a Valuation Class to an Account Category Reference

You can see in Figure 3 that AREF 0009 is only assigned to VALCL 7920. You can assign more than one account category reference to a single valuation class, however, there is a risk that the wrong valuation class will be assigned when creating a material master.

The last step is to assign the account category reference to a material type by clicking the MATERIAL TYPE/ACCOUNT CATEGORY REFERENCE button in Figure 1. The screen shown in Figure 4 is displayed.

Account Category Reference/Material Type			
MTyp	Material type descr.	ARef	Description
ERSA	Spare parts	0003	Reference for spare parts
FERT	Finished product	0009	Ref. for finished products

« **Figure 4**

Material Type Account Category Reference Field

You can assign more than one MATERIAL TYPE to an ACCOUNT CATEGORY REFERENCE and still have only one valuation class available when creating a material master. ■

Tip (41)

Display Automatic Account Assignment Entries

In this tip, you'll learn how to easily display automatic general ledger account entries.

Transaction OBYC lets you maintain or view SAP General Ledger (G/L) accounts that are posted to automatically during goods movements. You can only view the details of this transaction if you have authorization to configuration transactions, which is not normally available to end users. If you have authorization, you need to understand a lot of codes and navigate through several configuration screens to maintain or display the G/L accounts.

Instead, you can view the contents of the table that stores these configuration settings with the general table display Transaction SE16N. It's quicker and easier to view these settings with Transaction SE16N than with the customizing Transaction OBYC.

Solution

You can run the Data Browser with Transaction SE16N or via the following menu path:

> TOOLS • ABAP WORKBENCH • OVERVIEW • DATA BROWSER

Type in Table T030 and press ⌈Enter⌉ to display the screen in Figure 1.

Selection Criteria						
Fld name	O	Fr.Value	To value	More	Output	Technical name
Client						MANDT
Chart of Accts	🔁	INT		⇨	☑	KTOPL
Transaction	🔁	GBB		⇨	☑	KTOSL
Val.Grpg Code	🔁	0001		⇨	☑	BWMOD
Acct modif	🔁	VBR		⇨	☑	KOMOK
Valuation Class	🔁			⇨	☑	BKLAS

《 Figure 1
Table T030 Selection Screen

You can restrict the table entries displayed on the subsequent results screen by making entries in the SELECTION CRITERIA section. To display accounts posted to during goods issues to production orders, make the following entries:

- **Chart of accounts:** Restrict your selection by chart of accounts
- **Transaction:** Display inventory movement entries with Transaction GBB
- **Valuation grouping code:** Assign company codes to grouping codes with Transaction OMWD
- **Account modifier:** VBR relates to goods issued to production orders
- **Valuation class:** In the material master Costing 2 view, you can assign a valuation class to each material and material type

After you've made entries in the SELECTION CRITERIA field, click the Execute icon to display the screen shown in Figure 2.

Chart of Accounts	Transaction	Valuation Grpg Code	Acct modification	Valuation Class	G/L Account	G/L Account
INT	GBB	0001	VBR		400000	400000
INT	GBB	0001	VBR	0010	476000	476000
INT	GBB	0001	VBR	1210	400000	400000
INT	GBB	0001	VBR	3000	400000	400000

⌃ **Figure 2** *Table T030 Entries*

This screen displays the G/L ACCOUNTS debited or credited during goods issued to production orders.

For more information on entries in Table T030 follow IMG menu path:

> MATERIALS MANAGEMENT • VALUATION AND ACCOUNT ASSIGNMENT • ACCOUNT DETERMINATION • ACCOUNT DETERMINATION WITHOUT WIZARD • CONFIGURE AUTOMATIC POSTINGS

Figure 3 displays this menu path.

« **Figure 3**
Configure Automatic Postings Menu Path

Click the Paper and glasses icon to the left of CONFIGURE AUTOMATIC POSTINGS to display the standard documentation on setting up automatic postings. ▪

Tip 42 Valuation Grouping Code Message

You can eliminate valuation grouping code warning messages when initially running Transaction OMWB.

Have you ever entered a transaction to update automatic postings for account determination only to have to wade through messages that state that a valuation grouping code is not defined for a valuation area, just to get to your plant? Let's look at what the message means and how to stop it from appearing for good.

Solution

You can update automatic postings for account determination with Transaction OMWB or via the following IMG menu path:

> MATERIALS MANAGEMENT • VALUATION AND ACCOUNT ASSIGNMENT • ACCOUNT DETERMINATION • ACCOUNT DETERMINATION WITHOUT WIZARD • CONFIGURE AUTOMATIC POSTINGS

A valuation grouping code dialog box may appear as shown in Figure 1.

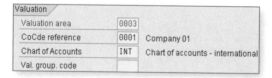

« **Figure 1**
Valuation Grouping Code Not Defined Message

If you click the Next Entry button, you can continue to scroll through the messages or you can click the Cancel button to skip them. The message appears because, in this example, VALUATION AREA, or plant 0003, has been defined in Transaction OX10 and assigned to a company code in Transaction OX18, but has not been assigned entries in automatic postings for account determination. The plant exists and is assigned to a company code, however, no inventory postings can occur, because there are no assigned general ledger (G/L) accounts.

There are two ways to prevent the messages from appearing. You can either delete the plant-to-company code assignment or assign a grouping code to the plant.

You can assign a plant to a company code with Transaction OX18 or via the following IMG menu path:

> ENTERPRISE STRUCTURE • ASSIGNMENT • LOGISTICS – GENERAL • ASSIGN PLANT TO COMPANY CODE

The screen in Figure 2 is displayed.

Assignment Plant - Company Code				
CoCd	Plnt	Name of Plant	Company Name	Status
0001	0003	Production 03	Company 01	

« **Figure 2**
Assignment of Plant to Company Code

If you delete the assignment line from this screen, then the missing valuation grouping code message in Figure 1 will stop appearing. However, if you do not wish to delete the assignment of the Plant (PLNT) to the Company Code (COCD), then you need to assign the plant to a valuation grouping code with Transaction OMWD or via the following IMG menu path:

> MATERIALS MANAGEMENT • VALUATION AND ACCOUNT ASSIGNMENT • ACCOUNT DETERMINATION • ACCOUNT DETERMINATION WITHOUT WIZARD • GROUP TOGETHER VALUATION AREAS

The screen in Figure 3 is displayed.

Val. Area	CoCode	Company Name	Chrt/Accts	Val.Grpg Code
0003	0001	Company 01	INT	
0005	0005	Company 05	INT	0001

« **Figure 3**
Assign Valuation Grouping Code to Valuation Area

The Valuation Grouping Code (VAL. GRPG CODE) lets you assign the same G/L account assignments across several plants to minimize your work. The grouping code can represent one or a group of plants. After you enter and save any freely definable alphanumeric up to four characters long in this field, the pop-up warning dialog box shown in Figure 1 will stop appearing for the corresponding plant. You can enter a new grouping code or use an existing one. When you run Transaction OBYC, and double-click any procedure, the grouping code corresponds to the valuation modifier in the first column. ■

Purchasing Account Assignment Categories

You can assign default general ledger accounts when you create purchase orders for nonstock items.

When you create a purchase order with Transaction ME21N you enter either:

- A material number — the system determines the G/L account from automatic posting table T030 configured with Transaction OBYC, or
- An account assignment category — the system accesses table T163K configured with Transaction OME9.

Let's look at how you can configure account assignment categories to default the correct G/L account into a purchase order for nonstock items.

Solution

You can maintain account assignment categories with Transaction OME9 or via the following IMG menu path:

> MATERIALS MANAGEMENT • PURCHASING • ACCOUNT ASSIGNMENT • MAINTAIN
> ACCOUNT ASSIGNMENT CATEGORIES

Double-click account assignment category K to display Figure 1.

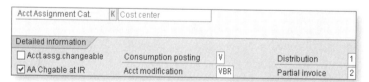

⌃ *Figure 1 Maintain Account Assignment Category*

Account assignment category (ACCT ASSIGNMENT CAT.) K lets you expense the purchase to an expense G/L account and cost center. In this example, you determine the default G/L account by ACCT MODIFICATION VBR. In this transaction, you can also maintain fields such as cost center as hidden, optional, mandatory, or for display only. You can see an overview of account assignment category settings by displaying table T163K entries with Transaction SE16N.

You can maintain the G/L accounts for ACCT MODIFICATION VBR with Transaction OBYC or via the following IMG menu path:

> MATERIALS MANAGEMENT • VALUATION AND ACCOUNT ASSIGNMENT • ACCOUNT DETERMINATION • ACCOUNT DETERMINATION WITHOUT WIZARD • CONFIGURE AUTOMATIC POSTINGS

Click the Account assignment button, double-click Transaction GBB, enter your chart of accounts, and navigate to GENERAL MODIFICATION VBR to display the screen in Figure 2.

Valuation modif.	General modification	Valuation class	Debit	Credit
0001	VBR		400000	400000
0001	VBR	0010	476000	476000

« *Figure 2*
Configure Automatic G/L Postings

If the item you are purchasing does not have a material master, it may not have a VALUATION CLASS assigned. In this example, the purchase order item will default with G/L account 400000 next to the blank VALUATION CLASS.

You can assign a VALUATION CLASS to a material group entered in the purchase order to determine a different G/L account. You can assign a valuation class to a material group with Transaction OMQW or via the following IMG menu path:

> MATERIALS MANAGEMENT • PURCHASING • MATERIAL MASTER • ENTRY AIDS FOR ITEMS WITHOUT A MATERIAL MASTER

The screen in Figure 3 is displayed.

Mat. Grp	Mat. Grp Descr.	ValCl
001	Metal processing	0010
00101	Steels	

« *Figure 3*
Assign Valuation Class to Material Group

When you create a purchase order for a nonstock item with Material Group (MAT. GRP) 001 METAL PROCESSING in this example, the system will default with G/L account 476000 next to VALUATION CLASS 0010 in Figure 2.

You can manually change the purchase order default G/L account. ▨

Tip 44 — Post Purchase Price Variance to Purchasing

You can post purchase price variance (PPV) to the purchasing cost center so that purchasing can analyze the variances.

The standard price for purchased materials is typically retrieved from purchasing info records during a costing run. Purchasing info records store vendor quotes per material and represent an estimate of a planned purchase price.

When purchased materials are valued at a standard price, there will be a PPV posting during goods and invoice receipt if the actual purchase price is different from the material standard price.

Because PPV postings represent the difference between the planned and actual purchase price, they can be used as a measure of the purchasing department's performance. An increase in unfavorable PPV postings may need to be analyzed and reported on by purchasing at period-end. You can readily examine PPV postings if you make the purchasing cost center the receiving cost object in controlling for PPV expense account postings and then run a standard cost center report.

✓ Solution

You can make the purchasing cost center the default cost center for PPV postings with Transaction OKB9 or via the following IMG menu path:

> CONTROLLING • COST CENTER ACCOUNTING • ACTUAL POSTINGS • MANUAL ACTUAL POSTINGS • EDIT AUTOMATIC ACCOUNT ASSIGNMENT

The screen shown in Figure 1 is displayed.

You will be presented with a list of existing cost center assignments to cost elements, which in this case equate to general ledger accounts. To assign a default cost center to the PPV cost element, click the NEW ENTRIES button and enter the company code, cost element, and cost center, and click the Save icon. To enter a different default cost center per plant, select the cost element in Figure 1 and double-click the DETAIL PER BUSINESS AREA/VALUATION AREA text.

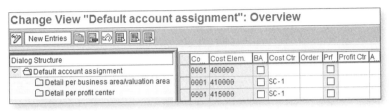

Change View "Default account assignment": Overview

New Entries

Dialog Structure		Co	Cost Elem.	BA	Cost Ctr	Order	Prf	Profit Ctr	A
▽ 🗀 Default account assignment		0001	400000	☐			☐		
	🗀 Detail per business area/valuation area	0001	410000	☐	SC-1		☐		
	🗀 Detail per profit center	0001	415000	☐	SC-1		☐		

✿ *Figure 1 Default Account Assignment Configuration*

You can view the standard actual/plan cost center report with Transaction S_ALR_87013611 or via the following menu path:

> ACCOUNTING • CONTROLLING • COST CENTER ACCOUNTING • INFORMATION SYSTEM • REPORTS FOR COST CENTER ACCOUNTING • PLAN/ACTUAL COMPARISONS • COST CENTERS: ACTUAL/PLAN/VARIANCE

Enter the selection screen information and click the Execute icon to display the screen shown in Figure 2.

Cost Center/Group	1700		Purchasing
Person responsible:	John Jordan		
Reporting period:	1 to 12 2009		

Cost Elements	Act. Costs	Plan Costs
500200 PPV - Favourable	1,983,544.39-	972,720.84-
500210 PPV - Unfavourable	1,581,617.33	869,630.61
* Debit	401,927.06-	103,090.23-

《 *Figure 2*

Cost Center Report Results Screen

You can assign PPV postings to separate FAVORABLE and UNFAVORABLE accounts with Transaction OBYC to have more transparency for the PPV postings in this report than if you just display the total DEBIT balance in one account. Double-click a PPV cost element in Figure 2 and press ⎡Enter⎤ to display a line item report of individual postings to this account, as shown in Figure 3.

Cost Elem.	Cost element name	∑ Val.in RC	Material
500210	PPV - Unfavourable	108,922.14	MBEU14
500210	PPV - Unfavourable	53,977.02	MBEU18

《 *Figure 3*

Cost Center — Actual Line Items Report

You can sort the VAL.IN RC (value in reporting currency) column to provide visibility to the largest PPV postings. By double-clicking any line shown in Figure 3 you can drill down and analyze the transaction that caused the PPV posting. ∎

Tip 45

Default Values for Product Cost Collectors

Order-type default values are transferred into product cost collectors as you create them.

Product cost collectors are orders of order type category 05. You set up default values in customizing for order types. Default values for an order type are transferred into product cost collectors as they are created.

✓ Solution

You can set up default values for product cost collector order types with Transaction OKZ3 or via the following IMG menu path:

> CONTROLLING • PRODUCT COST CONTROLLING • COST OBJECT CONTROLLING
> • PRODUCT COST BY PERIOD • PRODUCT COST COLLECTORS • DEFINE COST-
> ACCOUNTING-RELEVANT DEFAULT VALUES FOR ORDER TYPES AND PLANTS

Double-click a plant and order type to display the screen in Figure 1.

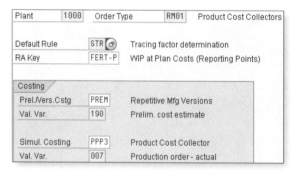

« Figure 1
Default Values for Product Cost Collector Order Type

DEFAULT RULE STR (with strategy for tracing factor determination) is specified in order types for product cost collectors. This default rule ensures that the settlement rules for product cost collectors are automatically created with settlement type PER. Default rules are predefined and cannot be changed.

DEFAULT RULE STR also ensures that the values settled from a product cost collector can be distributed. This is necessary for example when a product cost collector collects the costs of materials with different valuation types, such as special batch inventories, or that are part of valuated sales order inventory. When the product cost collector is settled the balance is apportioned among different inventories in accordance with the delivery values for the period. Distribution rules are generated automatically during settlement on the basis of the delivery values. System created equivalence numbers are transferred into the dynamic distribution rule based on the delivery values.

A results analysis key (RA KEY) must be specified in all product cost collectors to determine work in process (WIP).

You can also enter costing variants for Preliminary (PREL./VERS.CSTG) and Simultaneous Costing (SIMUL. COSTING) in the order type in Figure 1. Valuation Variants are determined by the costing variants. These define the valuation for materials, internal activities, external activities, and business processes, and also how overhead is calculated.

You can define default values for production order types linked to product cost collectors with Transaction OKZ3 or via the following IMG menu path:

> CONTROLLING • PRODUCT COST CONTROLLING • COST OBJECT CONTROLLING •
> PRODUCT COST BY ORDER • MANUFACTURING ORDERS • DEFINE COST-ACCOUNTING-
> RELEVANT DEFAULT VALUES FOR ORDER TYPES AND PLANTS

Double-click a plant and order type PP08 to display the screen in Figure 2.

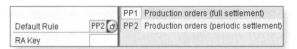

« Figure 2
Default Values for Production Order Type

DEFAULT RULE PP2 (PERIODIC SETTLEMENT) must be specified for production order types linked to product cost collectors. No RA KEY is specified in this order type because WIP is calculated on the product cost collector. The costing variant specified in this order type is used to create the production order preliminary cost estimate, which is for informational use only and cannot be saved. Selecting the PRODUCT COST COLLECTOR checkbox (not shown) ensures that production orders are automatically connected to a product cost collector when they are created. ■

Tip **46**

Process versus Production Orders

Process orders provide you with extra functionality, such as phases and process instructions for process industries.

If you use production orders, the system transfers a routing and a bill of material (BOM) into the master data of the order header. If you are manufacturing on the basis of process orders, the system uses the master recipe and associated materials list. The difference occurs because process industries manufacture in phases, converting initial liquid batches into consumable batches, which are then bottled and packaged.

While there are no costing differences between process and production orders, there are differences in terminology and production functionality. Let's discuss the differences between process and production orders.

✅ Solution

You can display a process order with Transaction COR3 or by going to:

> LOGISTICS • PRODUCTION - PROCESS • PROCESS ORDER • PROCESS ORDER • DISPLAY

Click the Operations button to display the screen shown in Figure 1.

Operation/Activity	Phase	Superordinate Operation	Ctrl Rec.Destination	Resource	Control key
0100				T-MT100	PI01
0110	☑	0100	FE	T-MT100	PI01

⌃ *Figure 1 Process Order Operation Overview*

A process order contains OPERATIONS that are divided into PHASES. A *phase* is a self-contained work step that defines the detail of one part of the production process using the primary RESOURCE of the operation. A *resource* is equivalent in concept to a work center, and is assigned to a cost center. The cost center assigns activity types to the resource.

In process manufacturing, only phases are costed, not operations. A phase is assigned to a SUPERORDINATE OPERATION as shown in Figure 1, and contains standard values for activities, which are used to determine dates, capacity requirements, and costs. The RELEVANT TO COSTING indicator in the phase must be selected.

For each operation or phase you plan, one or more materials are required for the execution of each step. Raw materials and semi-finished products that enter the production process debit the manufacturing order as they are withdrawn from inventory.

▶ Intra materials (material type INTR) are temporary and only exist between production phases. Intra materials appear in the material list as items of category M, but are not costed. If the process is interrupted because of a malfunction, however, an intra material may have to be put into inventory. In this case, it is valuated with a price in the material master that is selected through the valuation variant for the valuation of goods received.

▶ Remaining materials are represented as by-products. A *by-product* is an incidental output of a joint process. You enter a by-product with a negative quantity in the materials list of a primary product or process material. For by-products, you do not select the CO-PRODUCT indicator in the material master or in the bill of material (BOM).

▶ Circulating materials (such as catalysts) can be both a process input and a process output. You can specify in the material list whether the costs for a circulating material should be taken into account. The system selects a price for the circulating material from the material master. If the circulating material is flagged as relevant to costing, the material costs appear in the itemization twice: once with a plus sign and once with a minus sign. The balance is the material input cost.

If the materials list contains co-products, you can add additional co-products. You cannot, however, delete co-products from the materials list. To check to see if a material component is relevant to costing, go from the materials list to the detail screen for the material. All co-products (both leading co-products and non-leading co-products) are items with a negative quantity. Leading co-products are called *primary products*. For primary products, you can also select the co-product indicator in the BOM.

You can maintain process instructions (PI) for phases by clicking the Operations button in the header screen of a process order, selecting a phase, and choosing OPERATION • PROCESS INSTRUCTION OVERVIEW from the menu bar. ■

Tip 47 Valuated Sales Order Stock

Valuated sales order stock allows related inventory postings to occur in real time with no period-end processing.

Sales order costing scenarios involve special or custom customer orders. This sometimes involves configurable materials, where the customer can choose between component or assembly options when placing an order. Because the customer sales order involves special requirements, costing of sales orders needs to be treated on an individual basis.

There are two options for valuated sales order stock scenarios:

▶ Sales orders without Controlling (CO) and valuated inventory
▶ Sales orders with CO and valuated inventory

Let's examine the scenario without CO, because it is used most often.

Solution

The first indication that sales order controlling is involved in a process is the requirements type, which is displayed in the PROCUREMENT tab of a sales order line item. The requirements type field maintained in the sales order is mapped to the requirements class with configuration Transaction OVZH.

You can maintain the configuration settings for a requirements class with Transaction OVZG or via the following IMG menu path:

> CONTROLLING • PRODUCT COST CONTROLLING • COST OBJECT CONTROLLING • PRODUCT COST BY SALES ORDER • CONTROL OF SALES-ORDER-RELATED PRODUCTION/PRODUCT COST BY SALES ORDER • CHECK REQUIREMENTS CLASSES

The screen in Figure 1 is displayed.

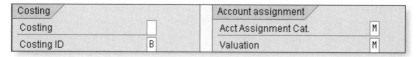

⤊ *Figure 1 Requirements Class Account Assignment*

The Account Assignment Cat. field determines if costs are maintained on the sales order line item with sales order controlling as follows:

▶ **E:** Sales order controlling is active. So, revenues and costs are maintained on the sales order line item, and there is an associated settlement process at period-end.

▶ **M:** Sales order controlling is not active. No costs are maintained on the sales order, and there is no associated settlement process. This is the setting you normally choose for sales order costing because it is the simplest, and no period-end process is involved.

The Valuation field determines if sales order stock is managed on a valuated or nonvaluated basis as follows:

▶ **Blank:** Sales order stock is not valuated. With this option, you need to choose sales order controlling as active in the previous field. You also need to run period-end results analysis to determine revenue and cost of sales (COS) and then settle the values to general ledger (G/L) accounts or Profitability Analysis (CO-PA).

▶ **M:** Sales order stock is valuated based on either the sales order line item cost estimate or the manufacturing order preliminary cost estimate at the time of first goods receipt into inventory. You can display valuated special stocks using report RM07MBWS and Transaction SA38.

Valuated sales order inventory has been available since R/3 version 4.0. This is the preferred scenario because it's the simplest. COS and revenue postings occur in real time because sales order stock is valuated. The sales order stock standard price is based on either the sales order line item cost estimate or the manufacturing order preliminary cost estimate, based on the sales order costing checkbox (not shown in Figure 1). Period-end processing, including work in process (WIP) and variance analysis, is based on manufacturing orders and not the sales order because no costs reside on the sales order. ■

Tip 48 — Valuation of Sales Order Stock

You can valuate sales order stock with a sales order cost estimate or production order preliminary cost estimate.

Valuated sales order inventory has been available since SAP R/3, version 4.0. Cost of sales (COS) and revenue postings occur in real time because sales order stock is valuated. No period-end process is required to calculate and settle COS and revenue. Let's look at the procedure for implementing valuated sales order stock.

The sales order stock standard price is based on either the sales order line item cost estimate or the manufacturing order preliminary cost estimate, as determined by the SALES ORDER COSTING checkbox in the requirements class.

Solution

You can maintain the requirements class with Transaction OVZG or via the following IMG menu path:

> CONTROLLING • PRODUCT COST CONTROLLING • COST OBJECT CONTROLLING • PRODUCT COST BY SALES ORDER • CONTROL OF SALES-ORDER-RELATED PRODUCTION/PRODUCT COST BY SALES ORDER • CHECK REQUIREMENTS CLASSES

Double-click a REQUIREMENTS CLASS to display the screen in Figure 1.

Assembly / Requirements		Assembly type	Short Descript.
Assembly type	2	0	No assembly order processing
Sales order costing	✔	1	Planned order ("static" processing)
		2	Production order, network or service (static processing)
Automatic plnng	☐	3	Production order (dynamic processing)
		4	Planned order (dynamic processing)

⌃ *Figure 1 Requirements Class Sales Order Costing*

Right-click the ASSEMBLY TYPE field and select POSSIBLE ENTRIES to display the list of ASSEMBLY TYPES shown in Figure 1. Assembly processing involves generating a manufacturing order together with the sales order. There are two methods of assembly processing:

▶ **Static:** A single manufacturing or planned order is generated for a sales order line item

▶ **Dynamic:** Multiple manufacturing or planned orders are generated for a sales order line item

The SALES ORDER COSTING indicator is only relevant if you are using ASSEMBLY TYPE 2 — PRODUCTION ORDER, NETWORK OR SERVICE (STATIC PROCESSING).

If you don't select SALES ORDER COSTING, the system copies the planned costs, which are calculated using the production order preliminary cost estimate, to the Sales and Distribution (SD) conditions. You can't create a sales order cost estimate for the sales order line item.

If you do select SALES ORDER COSTING, you can create a sales order cost estimate for the sales order line item, which is then copied to the SD conditions. The planned order costs, created using the production order preliminary cost estimate, are not copied to the SD conditions.

If the VALUATION field in the requirements class is set to M, indicating sales order stock is valuated, a standard price for the customer segment stock is created at the time of first goods receipt into inventory from the production order. The goods receipt is valuated using the following predefined strategy sequence:

▶ **Already-Existing Price in Sales Order Stock Segment:** A standard price selected through one of the subsequent strategies is copied and serves as the valuation basis from this point on.

▶ **Customer Exit:** The standard price is calculated on the basis of customer exit COPCP002 — Material valuation for valuated sales order stock.

▶ **Sales Order Costing:** The system calculates the standard price in a sales order cost estimate. This sales order cost estimate can be based on a unit cost estimate or on a product cost estimate or a combination of the two.

▶ **Production Order Planned Costs:** The system determines the standard price using the production order cost estimate or the planned costs for the Work Breakdown Structure (WBS) element. If there are multiple production orders for the same sales order item, the system uses the standard price that results from the production order that delivers first (see strategy 1).

▶ **Standard Cost (Standard Cost Estimate):** If you created the same material as a collective requirements material, the system reads the material master of the collective requirements material. The standard price in the master record of the collective requirements material may have been calculated in different ways, such as in a standard cost estimate. ▪

Tip 49 Target Cost Versions

Target cost versions let you determine the basis for calculating target costs.

Target cost version 0 calculates total variance and explains the difference between order debits and credits. You settle target cost version 0 data.

You may be familiar with total variance calculated with target cost version 0. Production and planning variance are less well known standard calculations.

✓ Solution 1 – Total Variance

You configure target cost versions with Transaction OKV6 or by following IMG menu path:

> CONTROLLING • PRODUCT COST CONTROLLING • COST OBJECT CONTROLLING • PRODUCT COST BY PERIOD • PERIOD-END CLOSING • VARIANCE CALCULATION • VARIANCE CALCULATION FOR PRODUCT COST COLLECTORS • DEFINE TARGET COST VERSIONS.

Double-click TARGET COST VERSION 0 to display the screen shown in Figure 1.

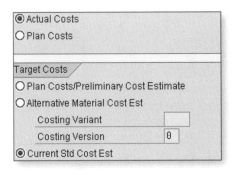

« Figure 1
Target Cost Version 0 Details Screen

CONTROL COSTS are based on ACTUAL COSTS while TARGET COSTS are based on actual credits determined by the current standard cost estimate (CURRENT STD COST EST).

Solution 2 – Production Variance

Production variance excludes variances due to a different bill of material (BOM) and/or routing used for production compared to the standard cost estimate.

You configure production variance with Transaction OKV6. Double-click target cost version 1 to display the screen shown in Figure 2.

«   Figure 2
Target Cost Version 1 Details Screen

Production variance is the difference between net ACTUAL COSTS debited to the order and TARGET COSTS based on the PRELIMINARY COST ESTIMATE and delivered quantity. You can calculate production variances with target cost version 1. Production variances are for informational purposes only and not relevant for settlement.

Solution 3 – Planning Variance

Planning variance helps you decide which BOM and routing to manufacture with. This target cost version is for information only and cannot be settled.

You configure planning variance with Transaction OKV6. Double-click target cost version 2 to display the screen shown in Figure 3.

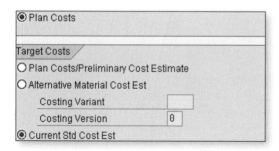

«   Figure 3
Target Cost Version 2 Details Screen

Planning variance is the difference between the order preliminary cost estimate and target costs based on the standard cost estimate and planned order quantity. You calculate planning variances with target cost version 2. Planning variances are for information only and are not relevant for settlement. ◼

Tip 50 Work in Process and Product Cost Collectors

Work in process at target allows you to select the cost estimate to calculate work in process and scrap

Work in process (WIP) at target for product cost collectors is calculated based on a cost estimate. Any differences between calculated and actual WIP are posted each period-end as production variance. WIP at target provides some advantages over WIP at actual based on manufacturing orders such as:

▶ You can easily reconcile Controlling (CO) and Financial Accounting (FI) postings since WIP and variance are posted each period-end

▶ Variance analysis based on products instead of manufacturing orders makes efficiency and profitability analysis more intuitive

▶ WIP at target allows you change routings and still calculate WIP

Let's discuss WIP at target in detail and look at the configuration settings.

✓ Solution

Product cost collectors are available for use with production orders since SAP R/3 Release 4.5. Product cost collectors allow you to calculate WIP at target.

WIP at actual involves moving the balance of incomplete production orders to general ledger accounts at period-end. When production order status changes to either fully delivered (DLV) or technically complete (TECO) WIP is canceled and order balance is posted as production variance. If production orders remain open for several periods, production variance can relate to FI postings in earlier periods making reconciliation between CO and FI difficult.

WIP at target involves calculating WIP based on a cost estimate. Production variance is the difference between calculated and actual costs.

The valuation variant for WIP allows you to choose which cost estimate will value WIP for product cost collectors and repetitive manufacturing. The setting can be accessed with the following IMG menu path:

CONTROLLING • PRODUCT COST CONTROLLING • COST OBJECT CONTROLLING • PRODUCT COST BY PERIOD • PERIOD-END CLOSING • WORK IN PROCESS • DEFINE VALUATION VARIANT FOR WIP AND SCRAP

The screen shown in Figure 1 is displayed.

« Figure 1
Valuation Variant Cost Estimate Strategy

The valuation strategies indicate that WIP calculation first searches for a PRELIMINARY COST ESTIMATE and if unsuccessful it will search for a CURRENT STANDARD COST ESTIMATE. With this strategy, if a preliminary cost estimate is not created, the current standard cost estimate can be used to valuate WIP.

WIP at target can be successfully calculated based on a preliminary cost estimate even if the routing structure is changed. If WIP is calculated based on a standard cost estimate after a routing structure change, error messages will result and the WIP will be posted as variance. This has an unnecessarily unfavorable impact on profitability since the variance posting is actually WIP.

Define WIP at target with Transaction OKGD or by following IMG menu path:

CONTROLLING • PRODUCT COST CONTROLLING • COST OBJECT CONTROLLING • PRODUCT COST BY PERIOD • PERIOD-END CLOSING • WORK IN PROCESS • DEFINE VALUATION METHOD (TARGET COSTS)

Click the New Entries button to display the dialog box shown in Figure 2.

« Figure 2
Valuation Methods for WIP

Click the relevant button to display the dialog box shown in Figure 3.

CO Area	1000
RA Version	0
RA Key	000003

« Figure 3
WIP Valuation Method Dialog Box

Fill in the fields, press ⌈Enter⌋, and required entries will be made automatically. ▪

Tip 51 Results Analysis Involves Revenue

Results analysis lets you calculate cost of sales and revenue postings at period-end.

Ever wonder why manufacturing orders contain a results analysis (RA) key in the Control tab when you want to calculate work in process (WIP). WIP is a simplified version of RA, because there is no revenue on a manufacturing order. RA calculates cost of sales (COS) and revenue postings on a sales order line item, work breakdown structure (WBS) element or an internal order. Let's look at some of the basic settings for RA.

✓ Solution

You can create and maintain RA methods with Transaction OKG3 or via the following IMG menu path:

> CONTROLLING • PRODUCT COST CONTROLLING • COST OBJECT CONTROLLING •
> PRODUCT COST BY SALES ORDER • PERIOD-END CLOSING • RESULTS ANALYSIS •
> DEFINE VALUATION METHODS FOR RESULTS ANALYSIS

Double-click an RA version and RA key to display the screen in Figure 1.

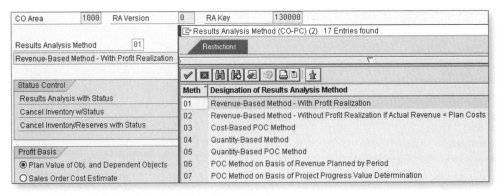

| CO Area | 1000 | RA Version | 0 | RA Key | 130000 |

Results Analysis Method: 01
Revenue-Based Method - With Profit Realization

Status Control
- Results Analysis with Status
- Cancel Inventory w/Status
- Cancel Inventory/Reserves with Status

Profit Basis
- ⦿ Plan Value of Obj. and Dependent Objects
- ○ Sales Order Cost Estimate

Results Analysis Method (CO-PC) (2) 17 Entries found

Meth	Designation of Results Analysis Method
01	Revenue-Based Method - With Profit Realization
02	Revenue-Based Method - Without Profit Realization if Actual Revenue < Plan Costs
03	Cost-Based POC Method
04	Quantity-Based Method
05	Quantity-Based POC Method
06	POC Method on Basis of Revenue Planned by Period
07	POC Method on Basis of Project Progress Value Determination

≽ *Figure 1 Results Analysis Valuation Methods*

The standard system contains 17 predefined RA valuation methods. You also have the option of creating your own methods. Let's analyze the predefined RA valuation method 01 as an example of how RA calculation works.

The REVENUE-BASED METHOD — WITH PROFIT REALIZATION calculates the percentage of completion (POC) based on actual revenue divided by plan revenue. You determine costs relevant to profit by multiplying plan costs by POC. The following bullet points work through an example scenario with plan revenues of 3,000 and costs of 2,000 for a sales order:

▸ POC = 0%, actual revenue = 0, actual costs = 1,000, RA calculates:
  ▸ Revenue = 0
  ▸ Cost of sales = 0
  ▸ WIP = 1,000
▸ POC = 40%, actual revenue = 1,200, actual costs = 1,000, RA calculates:
  ▸ Revenue = 1,2000
  ▸ Cost of sales = 800
  ▸ WIP = 200
▸ POC = 100%, actual revenue = 3,000, actual costs = 1,800, RA calculates:
  ▸ Revenue = 3,000
  ▸ Cost of sales = 2,000
  ▸ WIP = 0
  ▸ Reserves for unrealized costs = 200

The RA method you choose depends on your business requirements.

A sales order line item passes through a number of stages that lead to different results in RA. In the standard system there are three relevant system statuses that you maintain with Transaction OKG3, as shown in Figure 2.

Results Analysis with Status	REL	Released
Cancel Inventory w/Status	FNBL	Final billing
Cancel Inventory/Reserves with Status	TECO	Technically completed

« *Figure 2*
Status Dependency of Valuation

The sales order status determines when RA is calculated and when to cancel WIP and reserves. You *must* use RA when the sales order is a cost object and you use nonvaluated customer stock. RA determines sales order COS, revenue, and WIP. You *can* use RA when you use valuated customer stock with high-value sales orders and when you require detailed margin analysis per sales order.

OSS Note 398627 contains a list of OSS notes on results analysis scenarios. ■

Tip 52

Settlement and Processing Types

Manufacturing orders and product cost collectors automatically generate different settlement types for you.

When you create a manufacturing order, the system generally creates a settlement rule containing a 100% distribution rule to the material being produced. By settling a production order to a material, you are instructing the system to access settlement general ledger (G/L) accounts configured in table T030. The distribution rule for a material can only be created automatically.

Settlement transactions allow all processing to occur automatically. If you encounter problems during settlement, the following is how the procedure works.

Solution

You can maintain settlement profiles with Transaction OKO7 or by going to the IMG menu path:

> CONTROLLING • PRODUCT COST CONTROLLING • COST OBJECT CONTROLLING • PRODUCT COST BY ORDER • PERIOD-END CLOSING • SETTLEMENT • CREATE SETTLEMENT PROFILE

Double-click a settlement profile to display the screen in Figure 1.

Material	1 Settlement Optional
Network	1 Settlement Optional
Profit. Segment	2 Settlement Required
	Settlement Not Allowed

« *Figure 1*
Maintain Settlement Profile Valid Receivers

If you set MATERIAL with either SETTLEMENT OPTIONAL or REQUIRED, manufacturing orders are created with the first automatically created distribution rule with 100% distribution to the material as shown in Figure 2.

Cat	Settlement Receiver	Receiver Short Text	%	Equivalence no.	Settlement type
MAT	P-100	Pump PRECISION 100	100.00		FUL

⌃ *Figure 2 Production Order Distribution Rule Created Automatically*

You normally allow production orders to settle 100% of the material. You can also create additional distribution rules and, for example, settle some or all of the costs to a cost center or other valid receiver.

If you set MATERIAL in Figure 1 with the SETTLEMENT NOT ALLOWED option, no distribution rules will be created automatically for the production order and you must enter them manually. If you manually enter a material as a receiver, error message KD063 appears stating a distribution rule for a material can only be created automatically. You cannot settle internal orders to a material.

When you create a product cost collector with Transaction KKF6N, the system automatically creates a settlement rule as shown in Figure 3.

Cat	Settlement Receiver	Receiver Short Text	Methods	Settlement type
MAT	T-SN	Pump (serial numbers)	5	PER

⚑ **Figure 3** *Product Cost Collector Distribution Rule Created Automatically*

You cannot change the distribution rule of a product cost collector with Transaction KKF6N. OSS Note 932683 explains why you shouldn't change distribution rules with Transaction KKF2.

The production order SETTLEMENT TYPE was created automatically as FUL in Figure 2. FUL settlement allows you to settle all costs for an order in the period and also for all periods prior to the settlement not yet settled.

The product cost collector SETTLEMENT TYPE was created automatically as PER in Figure 3. This settlement type only covers costs for the settlement period. PER rules are used first and remaining costs are settled with FUL rules.

You can carry out settlement with Transaction CO88 or via the following menu path:

> ACCOUNTING • CONTROLLING • PRODUCT COST CONTROLLING • COST OBJECT CONTROLLING • PRODUCT COST BY ORDER • PERIOD-END CLOSING • SINGLE FUNCTIONS • SETTLEMENT

The default processing type AUTOMATIC settles order costs as per the settlement type of each order. Setting the processing type to By Period selects orders with settlement type PER. Setting the processing type to FULL SETTLEMENT produces an error message if costs for previous periods occur on a PER order. ∎

Tip (53) Assembly Scrap Basics

Assembly scrap lets you plan how many assemblies will not meet quality standards.

Because no production process is perfect, there is always a percentage of scrap produced. Assemblies or components that do not meet quality standards may either become scrap or require rework. Depending on the problem, cheaper items may become scrap, while more costly assemblies may justify rework.

Let's look at how you plan and work with assembly scrap.

✓ Solution

Scrap quantities are important, because they cause scrap values. Let's follow a simple example of how assembly scrap applied at the assembly level affects lower-level component and activity quantities.

You plan to produce 100 finished printed circuit boards (PCBs). Planned assembly scrap for the finished PCBs increases component and activity quantities by 10% as shown in the QUANTITY COSTED COLUMN in Figure 1.

	Quantity no scrap	Quantity costed	Assembly scrap
Finished PCBs	**100 PC**	**100 PC**	**0 PC**
— Blank PCBs	100 PC	**110 PC**	10 PC
— BIOS	100 PC	**110 PC**	10 PC
— *Operation 1*	*100 h*	***110 h***	*10 h*
— Processor	100 PC	**110 PC**	10 PC
— *Operation 1*	*100 h*	***110 h***	*10 h*

« *Figure 1*
Component and Activity Quantities with Assembly Scrap

Assembly scrap increases the plan cost of producing the finished PCBs by increasing the quantity of components and activities. Material requirements planning (MRP) will propose a production quantity of 110 assemblies, with the expectation that 100 will be delivered to inventory and 10 confirmed as scrap.

You can plan assembly scrap in the material master with Transaction MM02 or via the following menu path:

> LOGISTICS • MATERIALS MANAGEMENT • MATERIAL MASTER • MATERIAL •
> CHANGE • IMMEDIATELY

Navigate to the MRP 1 view to display the screen in Figure 2.

Lot size data			
Lot size	EX	Lot-for-lot order quantity	
Minimum Lot Size	10	Maximum Lot Size	
Fixed lot size		Maximum stock level	
Ordering costs		Storage costs ind.	
Assembly scrap (%)	10.00	Takt time	

« *Figure 2*
Assembly Scrap Field in MRP 1 View

Complete the ASSEMBLY SCRAP (%) field with a flat rate percentage determined by your historical production scrap rate statistics. You should update this field prior to the next costing run if the statistics change during the current year.

Planned assembly scrap costs are included in the standard cost estimate. You can display how assembly scrap affects costs by creating a standard cost estimate with Transaction CK11N or via the following menu path:

> ACCOUNTING • CONTROLLING • PRODUCT COST CONTROLLING • PRODUCT COST
> PLANNING • MATERIAL COSTING • COST ESTIMATE WITH QUANTITY STRUCTURE
> • CREATE

A standard cost estimate, including assembly scrap, is displayed in Figure 3.

Costing structure		Total value	Scrap	Currency	Quantity	Scrap quantity	U...	Resource
▽ 🖩 STANDARD FG	◑	50,880.14	0.00	USD	1,000.000	0.000	EA	1303 100010682
🖩 PRIMER	◑	250.19	22.74	USD	7.700	0.700	GAL	1303 400000691
▷ 🖩 SFG	◑	25,598.54	2,327.14	USD	1,100.000	100.000	EA	1303 300002252
🖩 URETHANE A 16	◑	6,770.69	615.52	USD	6,637.932	603.448	LB	1303 400000693
🖩 MDI ISO B MATERIAL	◑	1,678.07	152.55	USD	1,062.069	96.552	LB	1303 400000694

⌃ **Figure 3** *Cost Estimate with Assembly Scrap*

You can see the value of scrapped components in the SCRAP column and the corresponding quantity in the SCRAP QUANTITY column. While only material cost estimates are displayed in Figure 3, the quantity and value of all other items including activities and overhead are also increased by 10%.

You can analyze plan and actual scrap variances in detailed reports with Transactions PKBC_PKO and PKBC_ORD. ▪

Tip 54 Component and Assembly Scrap

Component scrap lets you plan how many additional components you will issue because some will not meet standard.

Component scrap includes the cost of faulty or lost components in the cost of sales. If component scrap is not planned, all scrap costs post as a variance. Planned component scrap is treated as additional consumption of the relevant component. Let's look at how you plan and work with component scrap.

Solution

Let's follow a simple example of how component scrap applied at the component level affects component quantities, and then look at the master data.

You plan to produce 100 finished printed circuit boards (PCBs). Assembly scrap is calculated first, then component scrap. Assembly scrap applied to the finished PCBs increases all component and activity quantities by 10%, as shown in the QUANTITY COSTED column in Figure 1.

	Quantity no scrap	Quantity costed	Assembly scrap	Component scrap
Finished PCBs	**100 PC**	**100 PC**	**0 PC**	**0 PC**
Blank PCBs	100 PC	**110 PC**	10 PC	0 PC
BIOS	100 PC	**110 PC**	10 PC	0 PC
Operation 1	*100 h*	*110 h*	*10 h*	–
Processor	100 PC	**116 PC**	10 PC	6 PC
Operation 1	*100 h*	*110 h*	*10 h*	–

« *Figure 1*
Component Scrap Increases Component Quantities

If 5% component scrap is applied to the Processor component, the quantity is increased from 110 to 116, as shown in the PROCESSOR row. Because COMPONENT SCRAP is applied after ASSEMBLY SCRAP, the COMPONENT SCRAP is 6 PC (pieces).

Assembly and component scrap increase the plan cost of producing finished PCBs by increasing the plan quantity of components and activities. MRP will propose production of 110 assemblies, with the expectation that 100 will be delivered to inventory and 10 confirmed as scrap. MRP will also propose the consumption of 116 pieces of the Processor component, even though only 100 would be needed without planned scrap.

You can plan component scrap with Transaction MM02 or via the menu path:

LOGISTICS • MATERIALS MANAGEMENT • MATERIAL MASTER • MATERIAL • CHANGE • IMMEDIATELY

Navigate to the MRP 4 view to display the screen in Figure 2.

Selection method		Component scrap (%)	10.00

≫ **Figure 2** *Component Scrap Field in MRP 4 View of Component*

Complete the COMPONENT SCRAP (%) field with a flat rate percentage determined by your historical scrap rate statistics. You should update this field prior to the next costing run if the statistics change during the current year.

You can also plan component scrap in the BASIC DATA tab of the bill of materials (BOM) item. You can maintain BOM items with Transaction CS02 or via the following menu path:

LOGISTICS • PRODUCTION • MASTER DATA • BILLS OF MATERIAL • BILL OF MATE-RIAL • MATERIAL BOM • CHANGE

Double-click a BOM item to display details as shown in Figure 3.

Operation scrap in %		☐ Net ID	Component scrap (%)	5.00

≫ **Figure 3** *Component Scrap Field in BOM Item Details*

A COMPONENT SCRAP entry in the BOM item takes priority over the MRP 4 view field. A cost estimate, including component scrap, is shown in Figure 4.

Costing structure			Total value	Scrap	Currency	Quantity	Scrap quantity	U...	Resource
▽ ▦ STANDARD FG		◑	48,581.82	0.00	USD	1,000.000	0.000	EA	1303 100010682
	▦ PRIMER	◑	227.44	0.00	USD	7.000	0.000	GAL	1303 400000691
▷ ▦ SFG		◑	25,598.54	0.00	USD	1,100.000	0.000	EA	1303 300002252
	▦ URETHANE A 16	◑	6,155.17	0.00	USD	6,034.483	0.000	LB	1303 400000693

≫ **Figure 4** *Cost Estimate with Component Scrap*

The QUANTITY and TOTAL VALUE of SFG are increased by 10%. This is not shown in the SCRAP column because component scrap is an input scrap. ▪

Tip 55 Operation Scrap Basics

Operation scrap lets you plan how many assemblies will not meet quality standards.

Operation scrap can be defined as the percentage of assembly quantity that does not meet production quality standards. For example, planned operation scrap of 20% means that if you start an operation with 125 pieces, you will lose 20% (25 pieces) during the operation. One hundred pieces will be available for the subsequent operation. Operation scrap is an output scrap, because it reduces the planned output quantity in the production process.

Solution

Let's follow an example of how operation scrap applied at the operation level affects component and activity quantities.

Let's say you begin a process with 100 finished printed circuit boards (PCBs). If planned operation scrap of 10% is entered in the first operation and 20% is entered in the second operation in the routing, 72 finished PCBs will be available at the end of the second operation, as shown in Figure 1.

	Routing	BOM	Input quantity	
Plan: **100 PC**		Blank PCBs	100 PC	For output of 100, enter assembly scrap in *finished PCB*
Operation 100 scrap 10% ↓ -10	Operation 1 Install/test	BIOS	100 PC	
	↓ (100 h)			Component scrap 4 % ↑
Operation 90 scrap 20% ↓ -18	Operation 2 Install/test	Processor	104 PC	
	↓ (90 h)		Component quantity needs to be reduced by BOM operation scrap	
	Finished PCBs	**72 PC**		

« *Figure 1 Operation Scrap Decreases Operation Output Quantity*

By decreasing the output quantity of operations, operation scrap increases the cost of producing the finished PCBs. Material requirements planning (MRP) will propose a production quantity of 100 assemblies, with the expectation that 72 will be delivered to inventory and 28 partial assemblies will be confirmed as scrap. No operation scrap is entered in the bill of materials (BOM) item in this example.

You can plan operation scrap with Transaction CA02 or via the following menu path:

LOGISTICS • PRODUCTION • MASTER DATA • ROUTINGS • ROUTINGS • STANDARD ROUTINGS • CHANGE

Double-click an operation to display details as shown in Figure 2.

General data
Scrap in %   10.000

« **Figure 2**
Operation Scrap Field in Operation Details

Complete the SCRAP IN % field with a flat-rate percentage determined by your historical scrap statistics. You should update this field prior to a costing run.

You can also plan operation scrap in the BASIC DATA tab of the BOM item. You can maintain BOM items with Transaction CS02 or via the following menu path:

LOGISTICS • PRODUCTION • MASTER DATA • BILLS OF MATERIAL • BILL OF MATE-RIAL • MATERIAL BOM • CHANGE

Double-click a BOM item to display details as shown in Figure 3.

| Operation scrap in % | 10.00 | ✔ Net ID | Component scrap (%) | |

☆ **Figure 3** *Operation Scrap Field in BOM Item*

You can enter operation scrap in the OPERATION SCRAP IN % field. The NET ID indicator is selected to ignore assembly scrap.

A cost estimate including operation scrap is shown in Figure 4.

Costing structure		Total value	Scrap	Currency	Quantity	Scrap quantity	U...	Resource
▽ ▦ STANDARD FG	●	46,254.68	0.00	USD	900.000	0.000	EA	1303 100010682
▦ PRIMER	●	227.44	22.74	USD	7.000	0.700	GAL	1303 400000691
▷ ▦ SFG	●	23,271.40	2,327.14	USD	1,000.000	100.000	EA	1303 300002252
▦ URETHANE A 16	●	6,155.17	615.52	USD	6,034.483	603.448	LB	1303 400000693
▦ MDI ISO B MATERIAL	●	1,525.52	152.55	USD	965.517	96.552	LB	1303 400000694

☆ **Figure 4** *Cost Estimate with Operation Scrap*

Operation scrap is shown in the SCRAP and SCRAP QUANTITY columns. ◼

Tip (56) Purchase Order Deletion Flag

You may need to set purchase order deletion flags to set production order deletion flags.

As the number of manufacturing orders increases in your system over time, you'll often find period-end processing time increasing. For companies that generate large numbers of orders, period-end processing time can take hours or even days to complete. One way to remove manufacturing orders from period-end processing is to set the deletion flag for each individual production order with Transaction CO02, select FUNCTIONS • DELETION FLAG • SET from the menu bar.

You may receive a lot of different errors messages while attempting to set the deletion flag on production orders. If you use external processing in routing operations you may receive an error message, such as CO434: Order 1000200135: Purchase order 4500087936 still exists. This means before you can set the production order deletion flag, you need to set the purchase order external processing deletion flag. You can set the purchase order deletion flags with one of the following three methods:

▶ Maintain each purchase order individually with Transaction ME22N

▶ Mass maintenance with Transaction MEMASSPO

▶ Archive with Transaction ME98

Let's analyze each of these methods in turn.

Solution

You can manually set a purchase order line item deletion flag with Transaction ME22N or via the following menu path:

> LOGISTICS • MATERIALS MANAGEMENT • PURCHASING • PURCHASE ORDER • CHANGE

Choose the purchase order, select an external processing line item, and click the Trash can icon to display the screen shown in Figure 1.

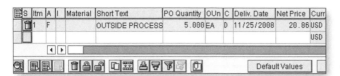

« Figure 1
Purchase Order Line Item with Deletion Flag Set

You can only set the deletion flag if the purchase order line item quantity equals the delivered quantity. When the deletion flag is set for an external processing line item, you can set the production order deletion flag.

The second method for setting purchase order deletion flags is with mass processing Transaction MEMASSPO or via the following menu path:

> LOGISTICS • MATERIALS MANAGEMENT • PURCHASING • PURCHASE ORDER • MASS MAINTENANCE

Select table EKPO in the TABLES tab, select field EKPO-LOEKZ in the FIELDS tab, and click the Execute icon. Type in the purchase order number and click the Execute icon to display the screen shown in Figure 2.

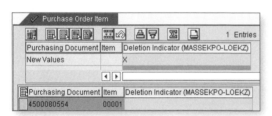

« Figure 2
Purchase Order Mass Maintenance Screen

Type an X in the DELETION INDICATOR field of the NEW VALUES row and click the two horizontal lines and vertical arrows icon to populate the DELETION INDICATOR in all of the PURCHASING DOCUMENT ITEMS selected on the screen. Click the Save icon and the system will carry out the proposed changes in the material masters.

The third method for setting purchase order deletion flags is with archiving Transaction ME98 or via the following menu path:

> LOGISTICS • MATERIALS MANAGEMENT • PURCHASING • PURCHASE ORDER • FOLLOW-ON FUNCTIONS • ARCHIVE

Click the Preprocessing button and create a variant to limit the selection of purchase order line items. You should only use this transaction if you are carrying out an archiving procedure because it's possible to create deletion indicators at the header level that cannot be undone. ∎

Tip 57 Production Order Deletion Flag

Setting the deletion flag on production orders helps you reduce period-end processing time.

You can reduce period-end processing time by setting the deletion flag on older production orders. There are two ways you can set deletion flags:

► Maintain each production order individually with Transaction CO02
► Archive with Transaction ME98

Let's analyze these two methods in detail in the following solution.

 Solution

You can manually set a production order deletion flag with Transaction CO02 or via the following menu path:

> Logistics • Production • Shop Floor Control • Order • Change

Type in a production order number, press $\boxed{\text{Enter}}$, and select FUNCTIONS • DELETION FLAG • SET from the menu bar, as shown in Figure 1.

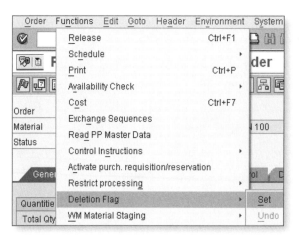

« *Figure 1*
Set Production Order Deletion Flag

The following message is displayed in the status bar at the bottom of the screen if you are successful in setting the deletion flag: DELETION FLAG IS ACTIVE → DISPLAY ONLY.

If you are not successful in setting the deletion flag, select GOTO • LOGS • DELETION FLAG and use the information in the error messages to make any necessary corrections. The deletion flag is revocable, meaning you can manually remove it by selecting UNDO in Figure 1.

The second method available to set production order deletion flags is with archiving Transaction CO78 or via the following menu path:

> LOGISTICS • PRODUCTION • SHOP FLOOR CONTROL • TOOLS • ARCHIVING • ORDERS

Click the DELETION FLAG/DELETION INDICATOR button, type in a variant name, and click the Maintain button to display a selection screen to restrict the number of production orders included in the process. The screen in Figure 2 is displayed.

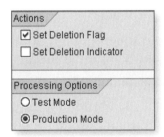

« **Figure 2**
Production Order Archiving Selection Screen

Make sure the SET DELETION FLAG checkbox and PRODUCTION MODE radio button are selected before saving the variant. If you set the DELETION INDICATOR you can still display the production order as normal, however, this status is not revocable, which means you cannot remove the DELETION INDICATOR. If you are not carrying out an actual archiving run, then you only need to set the DELETION FLAG to remove the production order from period-end processing.

After you save the selection variant, click the START DATE and SPOOL PARAMETERS buttons, and then execute the transaction. ■

Product Cost Collector Deletion Flag

Setting the deletion flag on redundant product cost collectors allows you to reduce period-end processing time.

You can improve period-end processing performance by setting the deletion flag on redundant product cost collectors. There are several prerequisites for setting the deletion flag. First, let's look at how to set the deletion flag, and then we'll examine the prerequisites.

 ## Solution

You can manually set a product cost collector deletion flag with Transaction KKF6N or via the following menu path:

> ACCOUNTING • CONTROLLING • PRODUCT COST CONTROLLING • COST OBJECT CONTROLLING • PRODUCT COST BY PERIOD • MASTER DATA • PRODUCT COST COLLECTOR • EDIT

Type in the material number and plant, select a production version checkbox on the left, and press ⌈Enter⌋ to display the screen shown in Figure 1.

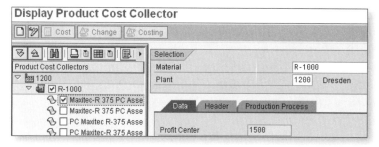

⌃ *Figure 1 Display Product Cost Collector Data*

Click the Pencil and glasses icon to switch to change mode, select EDIT • DELETION FLAG • SET from the menu bar, and click the Save icon. You may receive an error message if you have not met the following prerequisites:

▸ The cutoff period is set to the period, or later, in which the last transactions occurred for production orders attached to the product cost collector. The cutoff period for work in progress (WIP) is set with Transaction KKA0.

▸ The period lock is set for all periods in which transactions occurred for production orders attached to the product cost collector. The period lock for variance calculation is set with Transaction OKP1.

▸ The deletion indicator (status DLT) is set for all production orders linked to the product cost collector. You can analyze relevant production orders with Transaction COOIS while using the With Deletion Flag/indicator checkbox at the lower part of the selection screen.

▸ WIP on the product cost collector has been canceled. If you have difficulty canceling WIP you can try deleting the Results Analysis Key from the product cost collector DATA tab with Transaction KKF6N.

▸ The product cost collector has a balance of zero. To analyze these costs, display the product cost collector with Transaction KKF6N, click the HEADER tab, and then the COSTS button. If you cannot settle the remaining costs because they occur in a previous fiscal year, try changing the settlement profile using the following procedure:

  ▸ Select GOTO • DISPLAY SETTLEMENT RULE from the product cost collector menu bar and GOTO • SETTLEMENT PARAMETERS from the settlement rule menu bar. Note down the settlement profile, run Transaction OKO7, double-click your settlement profile, select the NOT FOR SETTLEMENT radio button, and Save. Set the product cost collector deletion flag and then return to the settlement profile and reselect the TO BE SETTLED IN FULL radio button.

▸ Production versions assigned to the product cost collector have been deleted. You delete production versions with Transaction MM02. Click the Versions button in the material master Costing 1 view, select each production version in turn, and click the Delete button.

Normally, the deletion flag (status DLFL) is revocable (changeable). If you create another product cost collector for the same production process while the deletion flag is set, then you cannot deselect the deletion flag.

Setting the deletion flag is sufficient to remove the product cost collector from period-end processing. You can also set the deletion indicator (status DLT) by selecting EDIT • SET DELETION INDICATOR from the product cost collector menu bar after setting the deletion flag, however it cannot be revoked.

You can obtain additional information about setting the deletion flag in OSS Note 52065. ■

Tip **59**

Allow Movement Types in a Test System

You can allow manual inventory adjustments in a test system while still allowing only controlled adjustments in your production system.

During system implementation, you typically run an initial inventory upload with movement type 561. This movement type lets you adjust inventory quantity without creating a purchase or production order. After go-live, it's a good practice to disallow movement type 561 to make sure that inventory quantity cannot be adjusted manually in an uncontrolled manner. Physical inventory allows you to analyze and correct inventory quantities within a controlled process.

It can be useful to allow postings with movement type 561 in a test system. Let's look at how you enable and disable movement types per transaction code.

 Solution

You can manually add inventory with Transaction MB1C or via the following menu path:

> LOGISTICS • MATERIALS MANAGEMENT • INVENTORY MANAGEMENT • GOODS
> MOVEMENT • GOODS RECEIPT • OTHER

Type in the movement type and plant, and press [Enter] to display the screen shown in Figure 1.

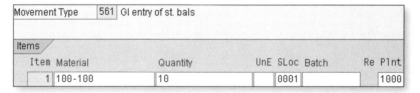

| Movement Type | 561 | GI entry of st. bals | | | | | |

Items						
Item	Material	Quantity	UnE	SLoc	Batch	Re	Plnt
1	100-100	10		0001			1000

⌃ *Figure 1 Manual Goods Receipt with Movement Type 561*

Type in MATERIAL, QUANTITY, and SLOC (storage location), and click the Save icon to post the inventory adjustment.

You can prevent manual goods receipt with Transaction OMJJ or via the following IMG menu path:

MATERIALS MANAGEMENT • INVENTORY MANAGEMENT AND PHYSICAL INVENTORY • MOVEMENT TYPES • COPY, CHANGE MOVEMENT TYPES

Select the Movement Type checkbox, press ⌊Enter⌋, type in Movement Type 561, and press ⌊Enter⌋ again to display the screen shown in Figure 2.

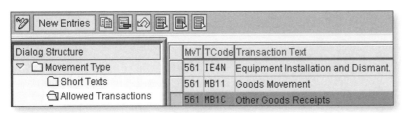

≫ **Figure 2** *Allowed Transactions for Movement Types*

Double-click on the ALLOWED TRANSACTIONS folder on the left to display a list of allowed transactions for movement type 561. Select TCODE (transaction code) MB1C, click the Delete (red minus sign) icon, press ⌊Enter⌋, and save your work.

Now if you attempt to manually adjust an inventory quantity with Transaction MB1C, you'll receive the error message shown in Figure 3.

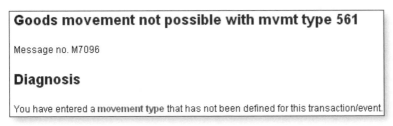

≫ **Figure 3** *Manual Goods Movement Error Message*

To subsequently allow movement type 561 in a test system, click the NEW ENTRIES button in Figure 2, type in the movement type and transaction code, and save your work. ▉

Tip 60 | Subcontracting Process

Subcontracting involves paying a vendor to carry out production processes for you.

Generally speaking, you typically subcontract processes to vendors for specialized operations or because of capacity limitations. You create a subcontract purchase order line item and issue the subcontracted components to the vendor. When you post the goods receipt for the assembled item, the system posts a goods issue from inventory for the components.

The subcontracting process involves sending components to an external vendor where they are assembled. The vendor then returns the completed assembly, and during goods receipt the components are issued from the subcontractor inventory. We'll examine the main processes involved in subcontracting in the following sections.

✓ Solution

The special procurement type field in the material master MRP 2 view determines if a material should be manufactured with a subcontracting process. You can view or change material master views with Transaction MM02 or via the following menu path:

> LOGISTICS • PRODUCTION • MASTER DATA • MATERIAL MASTER • MATERIAL • CHANGE • IMMEDIATELY • VENDOR/SUPPLYING PLANT KNOWN

Select the MRP 2 tab to display the screen shown in Figure 1.

« *Figure 1*
Subcontracting Special Procurement Type

Right-click in the SPECIAL PROCUREMENT field and select POSSIBLE ENTRIES to display a list of special procurement types. This tells MRP to issue a purchase requisition or order to the subcontracting vendor. The system first searches for a subcontractor purchasing info record.

You can create a subcontractor purchase order with Transaction ME21N or via the following the menu path:

> LOGISTICS • MATERIALS MANAGEMENT • PURCHASING • PURCHASE ORDER • CREATE

Enter the subcontractor material purchasing information to display the screen shown in Figure 2.

Itm	A	I	Material	Short Text	PO Quantity	OUn	C	Deliv. Date	Net Price	Curr	Per
10		L	P-100	Pump PRECISION 100	10	PC	D	05/04/2010	100.0000	EUR	1

⌃ **Figure 2** *Subcontract Purchase Order Line Item*

You can indicate that this material is to be procured by subcontracting by entering item category L (third column) when creating the purchase order line item. When you press ⌊Enter⌋, after entering a subcontract item category, two new icons appear in the MATERIAL DATA tab of the item. The details are shown in Figure 3.

⌃ **Figure 3** *Components and Explode BOM in the Material Data Tab*

Click the COMPONENTS icon to display a screen where you can enter the subcontracted components that are sent to the vendor for assembly into finished goods. You can also create a bill of material (BOM) for the subcontracted components that can automatically populate this screen.

You can monitor stock issued to a subcontracted vendor with Transaction ME2O. From this screen you can determine the status of the subcontracted stock. The components that are provided to the subcontractor are managed as stock provided to a vendor. You can issue a transfer posting from unrestricted stock to the stock of material provided to the vendor.

You can post the goods receipt for the end product with a reference to the subcontracted order item. At goods receipt, a consumption posting for the components is also made from the stock of material provided to the vendor. For each goods receipt item, the system copies the components and their quantities as goods issues items. If the vendor (subcontractor) consumed a greater or smaller quantity than was planned in the purchase order, you can adjust the component quantity at goods receipt. ■

Tip 61

Inventory Aging Reports

There are several standard inventory aging reports that are available to you.

Management accountants need to make an allowance each period-end for inventory that may be written off in the future. This is normally stock that is slow or nonmoving, or with an imminent approaching shelf-life expiration date (SLED). Let's look at some standard inventory reports.

 Solution

You can run the standard slow-moving items report with Transaction MC46 or via the following menu path:

> LOGISTICS • MATERIALS MANAGEMENT • INVENTORY MANAGEMENT • ENVIRONMENT • INVENTORY CONTROLLING • ENVIRONMENT • DOCUMENT EVALUATIONS • SLOW-MOVING ITEMS

Enter Sales Organization, Purchasing Organization, or Plant in the selection screen and Execute to display the screen in Figure 1.

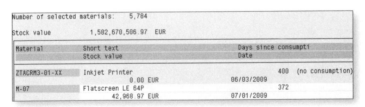

« *Figure 1*
Slow-moving Items Inventory Report

You are presented with the NUMBER OF SELECTED MATERIALS and the total slow-moving STOCK VALUE. If you fine-tune the selection parameters you should be able to insert the stock value directly into your period-end inventory report. You can display STOCK VALUE per MATERIAL by clicking the Double-line button. In the selection screen the PERIOD TO ANALYZE field defaults to 400 Days. The system analyzes days since last goods issue, 372 for MATERIAL M-07 in the example in

Figure 1. If the number of days is more than 400, this is the number displayed, and if there has never been consumption, then no consumption displays.

This analysis enables you to identify materials that are not currently in use. You can determine which stocks are not required and, if necessary, remove them.

There is also a Dead Stock inventory report available. Any period can be selected for analysis. The system suggests 90 days as the period to analyze, calculated from the current date. You run the Dead Stock report with Transaction MC50 or via the following menu path:

> LOGISTICS • MATERIALS MANAGEMENT • INVENTORY MANAGEMENT • ENVIRON-
> MENT • INVENTORY CONTROLLING • ENVIRONMENT • DOCUMENT EVALUATIONS
> • DEAD STOCK

A Dead Stock analysis lets you identify materials with inefficient amounts of stock. Surplus stocks of the material can be viewed and you can check important control parameters, such as safety stock.

For manufacturers such as pharmaceutical companies with limited life components, there is a standard SLED report for selecting batches that may expire before they can be consumed. You can run this report with Transaction MB5M or via the following menu path:

> LOGISTICS • MATERIALS MANAGEMENT • INVENTORY MANAGEMENT • ENVIRON-
> MENT • STOCK • EXPIRATION DATE LIST

Enter the selection screen parameters and Execute to display the screen in Figure 2.

« *Figure 2*
SLED

This report indicates either the number of DAYS since, or until, expiration.

There are many other standard inventory reports available, such as the Inventory Turnover report, which specifies how often average stock has been consumed. Inventory turnover is calculated as the ratio of cumulative usage to average stock level. This report provides a basis for evaluating, for example, how effectively fixed capital has been used. You can locate other inventory reports by browsing the menu paths for the above reports. ■

Tip 62 Inventory — the Lowest Value Principle

You can value inventory at the lowest market price with this useful tip.

Existing inventory is revalued when a new standard price is released with standard price control. This means existing inventory may be valued at a price different from the procurement price. The best way to reduce this effect is to keep inventory stocks low, however, this is not always possible.

There is standard functionality available to value inventory at the lower of the market and procured price. This involves a standard transaction to populate price fields in the material master and standard reporting to determine your inventory value based on these prices. Let's first look at the material master price fields and then see how to update them.

 Solution

You can manually maintain the tax and commercial price fields in the Accounting 2 material master view with Transaction MM02 or via the following menu path:

LOGISTICS • MATERIALS MANAGEMENT • MATERIAL MASTER • MATERIAL • CHANGE • IMMEDIATELY

The screen shown in Figure 1 is displayed.

Determination of lowest value

Tax price 1		Commercial price 1	
Tax price 2		Commercial price 2	
Tax price 3		Commercial price 3	
Devaluation ind.		Price unit	

⌃ *Figure 1 Tax and Commercial Prices in Accounting 2 View*

These price fields are used for alternate inventory values for tax and commercial purposes. This involves valuing inventory as carefully as possible according to the recognition of loss principle. There are several methods available for lowest value determination of inventory.

Let's follow an automatic market price scenario so you can see how the process works, and you can apply it to other inventory valuation scenarios as you like. Run Transaction MRN0 or follow the menu path:

LOGISTICS • MATERIALS MANAGEMENT • VALUATION • BALANCE SHEET VALUATION • DETERMINATION OF LOWEST VALUE • MARKET PRICES

The screen shown in Figure 2 is displayed.

⌃ **Figure 2** *Determine Lowest Value — Market Prices*

The RESTRICTION OF SELECTION section lets you select which materials you will determine market prices for. Enter a MATERIAL range, PLANT, and other parameters to restrict the materials selection.

Click the MARKET PRICE button to display the screen shown in Figure 3.

⤒ *Figure 3 Overview Screen — Selecting Market Price Source*

Selecting a checkbox in the OVERVIEW tab causes a corresponding tab to appear on this screen. For example, if the STANDARD PRICES checkbox is selected, the corresponding tab would appear after the INFO RECORDS tab. The fields behind each tab allow you to select, for example, the lowest purchase order price within the current fiscal year.

Now that you've selected market prices, you can compare them with existing prices. Click the COMPARISON PRICE button shown in Figure 2 to display the screen shown in Figure 4.

Relationship to Market Price	
◉ Lowest Val. Comparisn	
○ Comparisn Prc as Replcmnt Val.	
○ No Comparison Price	

Price Selection: Lowest of...

Phys. Inventory Prices	Valuation Alternatives
☑ Current Material Price	☐ Tax Price 1
☐ Mat. Price Prev. Month	☐ Tax Price 2
☐ Mat. Price Previous Year	☐ Tax Price 3
☐ Current Standard Price	☐ Commercial Price 1
☐ Standard Pr. Prev. Month	☐ Commercial Price 2
☐ Standard Pr. Prev. Year	☐ Commercial Price 3
☐ Current MAP	
☐ MAP Previous Month	
☐ MAP Previous Year	

« *Figure 4*

Comparison Price Selection

The screen in Figure 4 lets you select which prices you'd like to compare with the market prices retrieved from purchase orders in our example. You can run a report displaying the comparison and proposed prices, source, and percentage change. After reviewing the report, you can either run the transaction again with different parameters, or you can update the prices in the fields in the material master. Selecting the DATABASE UPDATE checkbox in Figure 2 causes two additional buttons to appear as shown in Figure 5.

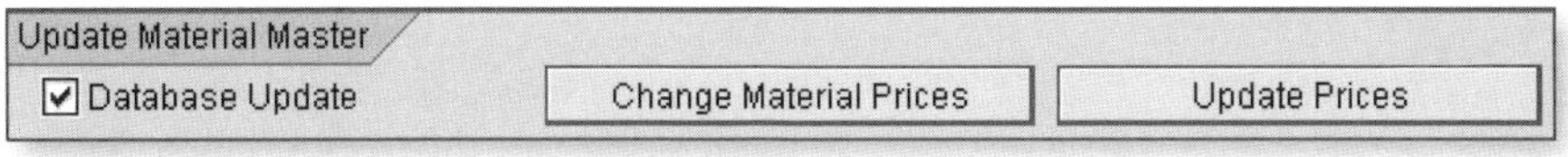

Figure 5 Database Update Checkbox Selected

Click the CHANGE MATERIAL PRICES button to display the screen in Figure 6.

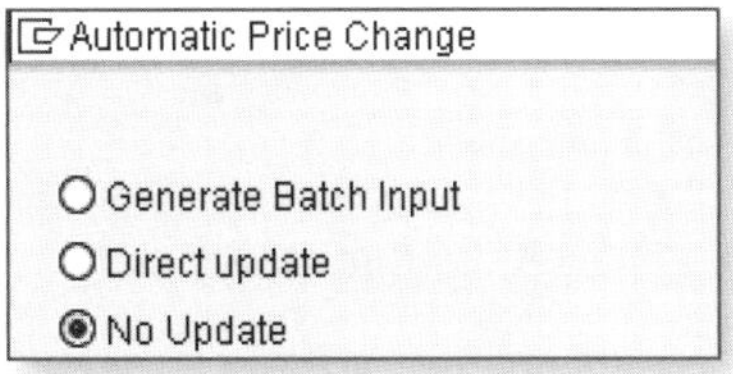

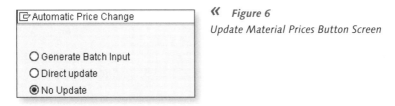

Figure 6 Update Material Prices Button Screen

You'll normally leave the default setting of NO UPDATE selected. You'll still be able to update the tax, commercial, and planned prices in the material master with this default setting. Only select DIRECT UPDATE if you're interested in updating the material standard price.

Selecting DIRECT UPDATE and executing the transaction may result in updating the standard price, resulting in inventory revaluation. Always fully test this setting before using it in your production database.

Press Enter and click the UPDATE PRICES button to display a screen similar to the one shown in Figure 4. Select the material master fields to be updated with the results of the market price valuation. Select RESET to initialize the price in the material master field or to set the value to zero as required.

Tip 63

Change Valuation Class with Inventory

To change valuation class with stock on hand you must transfer the stock and set the deletion flag for open orders.

The valuation class determines which general ledger accounts are updated during inventory movements. You can't change the material valuation class with existing inventory. You must transfer the inventory to another account and flag any open purchase and production orders for deletion. Let's follow an example.

✓ Solution

Maintain valuation class with Transaction MM02 or by following menu path:

> LOGISTICS • MATERIALS MANAGEMENT • MATERIAL MASTER • MATERIAL • CHANGE • IMMEDIATELY

Navigate to the Costing 2 view to display the screen in Figure 1.

« *Figure 1*
Valuation Class Field – Costing 2 View

Right click the VALUATION CLASS field and select POSSIBLE ENTRIES to display a valuation class list restricted by material type. It's good practice to allow only one valuation class per material type since then it will always be correct. You display stock quantity in the Accounting 1 view as shown in Figure 2.

⌃ *Figure 2 Total Stock Field – Accounting 1 View*

The TOTAL STOCK field indicates there are 800 items to be transferred. You can remove this inventory with Transaction MB1A or by following menu path:

> LOGISTICS • MATERIALS MANAGEMENT • INVENTORY MANAGEMENT • GOODS MOVEMENT • GOODS ISSUE

Type in movement type 551 (goods issue for scrapping) and PLANT and press ⌈Enter⌉ to display the screen show in Figure 3.

Item	Material	Quantity	UnE	SLoc	Batch	Re	Plnt
1	100-200	800	PC	0001			1000

《 *Figure 3*

Transfer Inventory to Scrap Temporarily

Type in COST CENTER, MATERIAL, QUANTITY and Storage Location (SLOC) and save to post the goods movement. The next task is to delete all open orders.

You can find all open purchase or production orders with Transaction MMBE or by following the menu path:

> LOGISTICS • MATERIALS MANAGEMENT • INVENTORY MANAGEMENT • ENVIRON-
> MENT • STOCK

Type in the MATERIAL and PLANT, and Execute to display the screen in Figure 4.

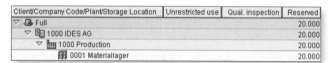

Client/Company Code/Plant/Storage Location	Unrestricted use	Qual. inspection	Reserved
▽ 🗗 Full			20.000
▽ 🗐 1000 IDES AG			20.000
▽ 🏭 1000 Production			20.000
🏢 0001 Materiallager			20.000

《 *Figure 4*

Stock Overview: Basic List

We've removed all Unrestricted stock, however, there are still 20.000 units Reserved for issue to open orders. To view a reservation list, click PLANT 1000 in Figure 4 and select ENVIRONMENT • RESERVATIONS from the menu bar. Determine open production and purchase orders. You set the deletion flag by running:

▶ Transaction CO02 for open production orders: Select FUNCTIONS • DELETION FLAG • SET from the menu bar and save

▶ Transaction ME22N for open purchase order line items: Select the line items, click the Trash can icon, and save

After the deletion flag is set for all open purchase and production orders you can change the valuation class in the Costing 2 view with Transaction MM02.

After the valuation class is changed determine the material document you created when saving the screen in Figure 3 by displaying a list of material documents with Transaction MB51. You reverse the material document with Transaction MB1A. Select GOODS ISSUE • CANCEL WITH REFERENCE • TO MAT. DOCUMENT from the menu bar, type in the document number, press ⌈Enter⌉ and save.

OSS Note 160970 provides more information on changing valuation class. ■

Movement Type Account Determination

Goods movements generally result in account postings that you can predetermine and control.

You can control which general ledger (G/L) accounts and assignments are determined for each movement type. You can also control whether a user can change the default G/L account and account assignments.

 Solution

You can maintain whether the G/L account is available for manual entry during a goods movement with Transaction OMB6 or via the following IMG menu path:

> MATERIALS MANAGEMENT • INVENTORY MANAGEMENT AND PHYSICAL INVENTORY • GOODS ISSUE / TRANSFER POSTINGS • SET MANUAL ACCOUNT ASSIGNMENT

Scroll down to Movement type 551 for GI (goods issue) scrapping, click the Account control field, and press the [F4] key to display the screen in Figure 1.

MvT	Movement Type Text	Acc	Account control	Short Descript.
551	GI scrapping	.		Entry in this field is optional.
552	RE scrapping	.	+	Entry in this field is required.
553	GI scrapping QI	.	-	Field is suppressed.
554	RE scrapping QI	.	.	Entry in this field is optional.

« *Figure 1*
Maintain Manual Account Assignment for Movement Types

In this example, Movement Type (MvT) 551 is configured for the G/L account ENTRY IN THIS FIELD IS OPTIONAL during a goods movement. If you choose the FIELD IS SUPPRESSED option, the automatically determined G/L account can't be changed.

You can maintain whether the cost center field is available for manual entry during a goods movement with Transaction OMBW or via the IMG menu path:

> MATERIALS MANAGEMENT • INVENTORY MANAGEMENT AND PHYSICAL INVENTORY • GOODS ISSUE / TRANSFER POSTINGS • DEFINE SCREEN LAYOUT

Double-click MOVEMENT TYPE 551 and double-click the text Additional account assignments to display the screen in Figure 2.

	Suppress	Req. Entry	Opt. entry
Calculation period (FI only)	◉	○	○
Material number (FI only)	◉	○	○
Cost center	○	○	◉

« *Figure 2*

Maintain Field Status Group for Movement Types

Cost center is set as an Optional entry (OPT. ENTRY). Now that we've maintained the G/L account and other account assignment options, the next step is to maintain the movement type with Transaction OMJJ or by using the following IMG menu path:

> MATERIALS MANAGEMENT • INVENTORY MANAGEMENT AND PHYSICAL INVENTORY • MOVEMENT TYPES • COPY, CHANGE MOVEMENT TYPES

Select the MOVEMENT TYPE checkbox, navigate to Movement Type 551, and double-click the text ACCOUNT GROUPING to display the screen in Figure 3.

MvT	S	Val.Update	Qty update	Mvt	Cns	Val.strng	Cn	TEKey	Acct modif	Check acct.ass.
551		☑	☑			WA01	2	GBB	VNG	☑

⌃ *Figure 3 Maintain Movement Type Account Grouping*

If the Check account assignment (CHECK ACCT.ASS.) checkbox is not selected, the system uses the G/L accounts or account assignments determined automatically. You can select the checkbox to allow users to manually maintain a G/L account or assignment.

The Account modifier (ACCT MODIF), VNG in this example, automatically determines the G/L account. You can maintain automatic G/L account determination with Transaction OBYC. Double-click TRANSACTION GBB and scroll down to account modifier VNG. The G/L accounts you enter for each valuation class determine the G/L accounts automatically determined during goods issue from inventory for scrapping with movement type 551. You can enter different account modifiers and associated G/L accounts for each movement type. You can display table T156X with Transaction SE16N for an overview of movement type settings.

If you assign an expense G/L account to a movement type, you may need to set up automatic account assignments for cost centers with Transaction OKB9. You predetermine all account postings if you do not allow users to change defaults. ∎

Part 6

Material Ledger

Things You'll Learn in this Section

With the material ledger you can carry inventory in up to two additional valuations and also at actual costs, described as follows:

▸ **Carry material prices in multiple currencies and valuations**
Material inventory values are normally carried in only company code currency. The material ledger enables the system to carry inventory values in two additional currencies/valuations. This is achieved by updating all goods movements in the material ledger in up to three currencies or valuations. Currency amounts are translated into foreign currencies at historical exchange rates directly at the time of posting.

▸ **Value inventory at actual costs**
Actual costing valuates all goods movements within a period at the standard price (preliminary valuation). All price and exchange rate differences for the material are collected in the material ledger.

At the end of the period, an actual price is calculated for each material based on the actual costs of the period. This actual price is called the periodic unit price and can be used to revaluate the inventory for the period to be closed. You can use this actual price as the standard price for the next period.

Actual costing determines what portion of the variance is to be debited to the next-highest level using material consumption. The actual bill of materials enables variances to be rolled up over multiple production levels all the way to the finished product. You can choose to have cost center variances also taken into account.

This category of ideas describes how multiple valuations and actual costing work, and the material ledger period-end closing process. It also describes the implementation steps needed during production startup. The actual cost component split and deactivating the material ledger are also explained.

Tip 65 Multiple Valuations with the Material Ledger

The material ledger enables you to valuate your inventory in multiple currencies and is the basis of actual costing.

The material ledger has two basic functions:

- ▶ To carry material prices in multiple currencies and valuations
- ▶ Actual costing

Let's discuss the first bullet point in detail.

Solution

Without the material ledger, inventory valuation is carried in company code currency and legal valuation. The material ledger enables the system to carry inventory in two additional currencies and valuations. In addition, all goods movements are updated in up to three currencies and valuations.

You can activate the material ledger components of multiple inventory valuations and actual costing separately. You should fully test which currencies and valuations you need before activating the material ledger because you cannot change these settings later in a production system. For more information, read OSS Note 53947 — Changing currencies after production startup.

If you use multiple valuation approaches, SAP recommends activating the material ledger in all valuation areas within a company code.

During the material ledger implementation, you can copy additional local currencies from Financial Accounting (FI). It is a good practice to have the same valuation approaches in both FI and the material ledger, so that documents in both modules are comparable. A valuation approach is the combination of currency type and valuation. The first step in introducing the material ledger to multiple valuations is setting up FI local currencies. For more information, read OSS Note 122008 — Activate transfer prices/multiple valuation approaches.

You can maintain additional local currencies in FI with Transaction OB22 or via the following IMG menu path:

FINANCIAL ACCOUNTING • FINANCIAL ACCOUNTING GLOBAL SETTINGS • COMPANY CODE • PARALLEL CURRENCIES • DEFINE ADDITIONAL LOCAL CURRENCIES

The screen shown in Figure 1 is displayed.

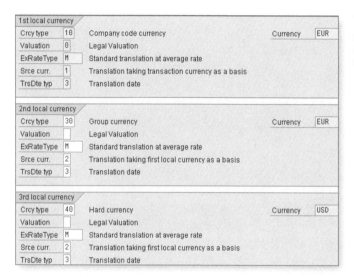

« *Figure 1*

Define Additional Local Currencies for Company Code

It's mandatory to define at least one local currency in FI as shown in the 1ST LOCAL CURRENCY section. This local currency includes COMPANY CODE CURRENCY and LEGAL VALUATION. All first local currency fields are grayed out and cannot be changed.

If you define additional local currencies, every FI document will include the postings in the additional local currencies. You may need to add additional document layout columns to display the additional currencies in FI documents. The material ledger does not have to be activated to define additional local currencies in FI. The material ledger only refers to postings related to inventory transactions, whereas the settings in Figure 1 refer to all FI postings.

If you use transfer prices when moving materials between legal entities, the material ledger allows you to view inventory valuations for both, including transfer pricing (COMPANY CODE CURRENCY and LEGAL VALUATION) for legal reporting, and excluding transfer pricing (GROUP CURRENCY and GROUP VALUATION) for internal management and consolidated reporting requirements. ▪

Tip 66 Actual Costing with the Material Ledger

You can use the material ledger to collect transaction data for materials and use this data to calculate actual prices.

The material ledger has two basic functions:

▶ To carry material prices in multiple currencies and valuations
▶ Actual costing

Let's discuss the second bullet point in detail.

Solution

Actual costing generates a material ledger document for all goods movements within a period at the *standard price* (preliminary valuation). At the end of the period, an actual price is calculated for each material based on the actual costs of the period. This actual price is called the *periodic unit price* and can be used for the following at period-end:

▶ **Revaluate inventory:** The material stock account is debited with the proportional price differences, and the price differences account is credited with the same amount. You can use the actual price as the standard price for the next period.

▶ **Do not revaluate inventory:** Price differences are posted to an accrual account. The amount that would have been posted to the material stock account is posted to another price difference account.

You can decide whether to revalue inventory according to which financial accounts are posted to during automatic account determination with configuration Transaction OBYC. If you want the system to calculate a *periodic unit price* for your materials based on the actual costs incurred in a period, you need to activate actual costing in addition to activating the material ledger.

You can activate actual costing via the following IMG menu path:

> CONTROLLING • PRODUCT COST CONTROLLING • ACTUAL COSTING / MATERIAL
> LEDGER • ACTUAL COSTING • ACTIVATE ACTUAL COSTING

The screen shown in Figure 1 is displayed.

Activate actual costing				Actual activities updated	Short Descript.
Plnt	Name 1	Act. costing	ActAct	0	No activity update
0006	New York	☑	2	1	Activity update not relevant to price determina
0007	Werk Han	☑	2	2	Activity update relevant to price determination

⌃ *Figure 1 Activate Actual Costing*

In this step, you activate actual costing for materials and activity consumption updates in the quantity structure. Here's an explanation of each of the fields:

▶ ACT. COSTING (Activate Actual Costing): If you want to work with multilevel price determination in the Actual Costing component, you must select this checkbox so that the actual quantity structure is updated.

▶ ACTACT (Update of Activity Consumption in the Quantity Structure): Actual costing determines what portion of the variance is to be debited to the next-highest level using material consumption. The actual bill of material (BOM) rolls variances up over multiple production levels all the way to the finished product.

Left-click then right-click the field and select POSSIBLE ENTRIES to display the list on the right in Figure 1. The possible entries are explained as follows:

▶ 0 NO ACTIVITY UPDATE: Update is not active.

▶ 1 ACTIVITY UPDATE NOT RELEVANT TO PRICE DETERMINATION: Update is active but not relevant to price determination. Consumption is updated in the quantity structure but not taken into account upon price determination.

▶ 2 ACTIVITY UPDATE RELEVANT TO PRICE DETERMINATION: Variances between the activity prices/process prices posted during the period and the actual price at the end of the period are adjusted subsequently. In addition, you must set multilevel price determination (option 3) in the material master Accounting 1 view. In this case, you must use standard prices for all materials that you want to use in actual costing.

After you activate actual costing you'll need to carry out an actual costing run each period-end with Transaction CKMLCP. The functionality of the actual costing run screen is similar to the standard cost estimate costing run screen. First, assign plants to the actual costing run, and then follow the rows. ∎

Period-End Closing with the Material Ledger

You can use the material ledger to calculate actual price at period-end.

There are three possibilities for period-end if you've activated the material ledger:

- No period-end processing
- Single-level price determination
- Multilevel price determination

Let's discuss each possibility in detail.

Solution

By activating the material ledger, you may or may not affect your current period-end processing steps as follows:

- **No period-end processing**
  If you've activated the material ledger with only one currency type, and you're not using the actual costing functionality, there is no need for period-end processing. A material ledger document will post for every inventory-related transaction in the legal valuation approach in company code currency.

  Activating the material ledger in this case gives you additional inventory reporting that you can access with Transaction CKM3 or via the following menu path:

  > ACCOUNTING • CONTROLLING • PRODUCT COST CONTROLLING • ACTUAL COSTING/
  > MATERIAL LEDGER • MATERIAL LEDGER • MATERIAL PRICE ANALYSIS

The screen in Figure 1 is displayed.

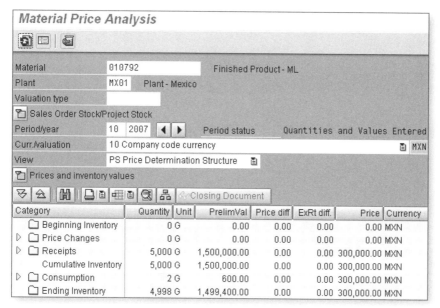

☆ *Figure 1* *Material Price Analysis Screen*

This screen lets you access all material transactions for a period. Transactions are grouped by CATEGORY, which you can progressively expand to display all of the transaction documents within a CATEGORY. Now let's look at the next level of period-end processing.

▶ **Single-level price determination**

Single-level refers to an individual material and its procurement process. A simple example with three levels within the material ledger includes purchased materials, subassemblies, and finished products. When you use actual costing, all materials are valuated with a preliminary periodic unit price that remains constant during a given period. This price can be, for example, a standard price or an actual price from the previous period determined by the material ledger.

During a period, the material ledger posts differences to a price difference account and updates them separately for each material. At the end of a period, you can use single-level price determination to assign the variances for each material. This allows the cumulative price differences to be assigned proportionally to the ending inventory quantity and the material consumption of the period.

To carry out period-end processing in the material ledger, you need to create an actual costing run with Transaction CKMLCP or via the following menu path:

> ACCOUNTING • CONTROLLING • PRODUCT COST CONTROLLING • ACTUAL COSTING/ MATERIAL LEDGER • ACTUAL COSTING • EDIT COSTING RUN

The screen shown in Figure 2 is displayed.

Create Cost Estimate								
Flow step	Authorizn	Parameters	Execute	Log	Status	Successful	Errors	Still open
Selection		▶▢▶		🗔		0	0	0
Determine Sequence		▶▢▶		🗔		0	0	0
Single-Level Pr. Determination	🔓	▶▢▶		🗔		0	0	0
Multilevel Pr. Determination	🔓	▶▢▶		🗔		0	0	0
Revaluation of Consumption		▶▢▶				0	0	0
Post Closing	🔓	▶▢▶		🗔		0	0	0
Mark Material Prices		▶▢▶				0	0	0

⌃ *Figure 2 Edit Actual Costing Run*

The functionality of the actual costing run screen is similar to the standard cost estimate costing run screen you run with Transaction CK40N. You first assign plants to the actual costing run, and then you follow the rows listed in the FLOW STEP column. To carry out single-level price determination, you first carry out the SELECTION and DETERMINE SEQUENCE steps and then the SINGLE-LEVEL PR. DETERMINATION step.

The system calculates periodic unit prices for the period and updates them in all valuation approaches in the material price analysis. The system also updates the price in company code currency in the material master for the period.

▶ **Multilevel price determination**
During multilevel price determination, you assign the differences calculated during single-level price determination progressively to the next-highest levels of the production process using a multilevel actual quantity structure, which is a type of actual bill of material (BOM). For example, purchase price differences for raw materials are rolled up to subassemblies and then to finished products.

The system calculates periodic unit prices for the period and updates them in all valuation approaches in the material price analysis. The system also updates the price in company code currency in the material master for the period.

At period-end, during actual costing, inventory can:

▸ Be revaluated with the actual price of the period (periodic unit price). The material stock account is debited with the proportional price differences, and the price differences account is credited with the same amount.

▸ Remain with the same value and price differences are posted to an accrual account. If you do not revalue inventory with the actual price, the amount that would have been posted to the material stock account is posted to another price difference account.

Price differences allocated to consumption remain on the price difference account at this point. You can decide to revalue inventory or not according to which financial G/L accounts are posted to during automatic account determination with configuration Transaction OBYC. To proceed with multilevel price determination, execute the remaining steps following single-level price determination in Figure 2. ▨

Tip **68** Material Master Conversion during Startup

After selecting the material ledger Activation checkbox, you need to convert material master Accounting 1 view data.

You need to create additional master and transaction data in addition to selecting the material ledger Activation checkbox with Transaction OMX1.

✓ Solution

You can carry out material master conversion per plant or range of plants with Transaction CKMSTART or via the following menu path:

> ACCOUNTING • CONTROLLING • PRODUCT COST CONTROLLING • ACTUAL COSTING/
> MATERIAL LEDGER • ENVIRONMENT • PRODUCTION STARTUP • SET VALUATION
> AREAS AS PRODUCTIVE

The screen shown in Figure 1 is displayed.

Plant   `6000`   to

⌃ *Figure 1 The Material Ledger Conversion Program Selection Screen*

This transaction can perform two conversions: material master data and purchase order history. Let's discuss material master data conversion in detail.

When this program runs it builds extra valuation views by currency type per period for each material master Accounting 1 view. You can display a material master with Transaction MM03 or via the following menu path:

> LOGISTICS • MATERIALS MANAGEMENT • MATERIAL MASTER • MATERIAL •
> DISPLAY • DISPLAY CURRENT

Navigate to the Accounting 1 view to display the screen shown in Figure 2.

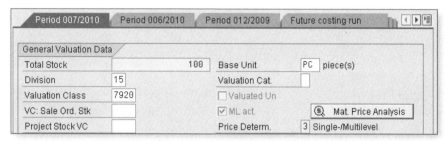

General Valuation Data

Total Stock	100	Base Unit	PC piece(s)
Division	15	Valuation Cat.	
Valuation Class	7920	☐ Valuated Un	
VC: Sale Ord. Stk		☑ ML act.	🔍 Mat. Price Analysis
Project Stock VC		Price Determ.	3 Single-/Multilevel

⌃ *Figure 2 Accounting 1 View Displays Separate Tabs for Each Period*

The material ledger stores material prices separately for each PERIOD after the conversion program is run. Also, up to three valuations are stored for each period as separate columns, as shown in Figure 3.

Prices and values

	MXN	EUR	USD
Currency	Company code currency	Group currency	Hard currency
Standard Price	21.60	2.59	2.59
Per. unit price	21.90	2.59	2.63
Price Unit	1	1	1
Prc. Ctrl	S	S	S
Inventory Value	2,160.00	259.00	259.00

⌃ *Figure 3 Accounting 1 View — Three Currency Types per Period*

If you need to convert large volumes of material master and purchase order history (POH) data, you can enter POH manually in the OK code field when in Transaction CKMSTART selection screen, as shown in Figure 4.

« *Figure 4*
Manually Enter POH in OK Code Field

Press ⌷Enter⌷ to select material master data separately, as shown in Figure 5.

○ Master data + PO hist.(normal)
◉ Master Data Only (Step 1)

« *Figure 5*
Selection of Material Master Only Field Available

Select MASTER DATA ONLY to reduce the runtime of Transaction CKMSTART. ▪

Tip **69** Purchase Order Conversion during Startup

After selecting the material ledger Activation checkbox, you need to convert purchase order history (POH) data.

You need to convert POH transaction data for additional valuations after selecting the Activation checkbox with Transaction OMX1.

 Solution

You can create POH records by currency type per plant or range of plants with Transaction CKMSTART or via the following menu path:

> ACCOUNTING • CONTROLLING • PRODUCT COST CONTROLLING • ACTUAL COSTING/
> MATERIAL LEDGER • ENVIRONMENT • PRODUCTION STARTUP • SET VALUATION
> AREAS AS PRODUCTIVE

The screen shown in Figure 1 is displayed.

⌃ *Figure 1 The Material Ledger Startup Program Selection Screen*

This transaction performs two conversions: material master data and POH. Let's discuss POH conversion in detail.

The program creates extra POH records by currency type. The production startup of the material ledger can run for a long time if it has to translate several million POH history in tables EKBE and EKBZ on an Oracle database. You can improve performance with the following steps:

1. Around 30-60 minutes after the program starts, check to see if there are records in table MLWERE with Transaction SE16N. After the records appear, check the statistics for table MLWERE with Transaction DB20, and re-create statistics if none exist. See OSS Note 384145 for details on re-creating table statistics.

2. Run multiple Transaction CKMSTART batch jobs for a single plant. This ensures the job load is distributed over several application servers.

3. Run Transaction CKMSTART separately for material master data and POH. To do this, type POH in the OK code field as shown in Figure 2.

«   *Figure 2*
Manually Enter POH in OK Code Field

Press ⌜Enter⌝ so the PO HISTORY ONLY (STEP 2) selection option at the bottom of Transaction CKMSTART is available for entry, as shown in Figure 3.

⌃   ***Figure 3*** *Selection of PO History by PO Document Range Available*

First, select MASTER DATA ONLY (STEP 1) and execute the transaction. The material ledger is then active in the selected plants, however, no postings for existing POH records are created for the parallel currencies.

To create the POH records for parallel currencies, start Transaction CKMSTART again and enter the plants and POH in the OK code field. Make sure you only enter plants for which the first step has already been executed. Select PO HISTORY ONLY (STEP 2) and execute. When the transaction is finished, you can make postings without restrictions.

You can also distribute the generation of the POH records over several jobs. Divide up the existing PO document numbers into partial intervals and enter these intervals into the PURCHASING DOCUMENT range shown in Figure 3. First, start the job for the highest PO numbers, because these have the highest chance of still being used. You should ensure that you use the same plant selection used previously. Also, make sure that you process all existing PO numbers and that the partial intervals do not overlap each other. OSS Note 592091 provides further details on performance when converting POH. ▪

Tip 70 Reconciliation during Production Startup

Your material ledger inventory balances should reconcile with financial accounting balances for all valuations.

The material ledger data should be treated as the master repository of inventory balances and reconcile with the Financial Accounting general ledger (FI-GL) account balances. A prerequisite for material ledger reconciliation is that Materials Management (MM) reconciles with FI-GL account balances.

Solution

Let's first discuss MM and FI-GL reconciliation and then the material ledger and FI-GL reconciliation.

▶ **MM and FI-GL Reconciliation**
   You can detect errors between MM and FI-GL balances with report RM07MMFI. Run Transaction SA38 or choose SYSTEM • SERVICES • REPORTING from the menu bar of any screen. Type in RM07MMFI and execute the report, then enter a company code and execute to display a comparison of FI-GL balances and MM values, as shown in Figure 1.

CoCode	Company Name		Period Checked	Period	Start Date	Start Time
G/L acct	Value of materials	Value of G/L account			Variance	Crcy
6000	IDES México, S.A. de C.V.		Current period	07/2010	08/12/2010	15:52:29
300000	334,738.43	0.00			334,738.43-	MXN
300010	0.00	0.00			0.00	MXN

⊼ *Figure 1 MM / FI-GL Balance Comparison*

With this report you compare the value of MM and FI-GL account balances for each general ledger (G/L) account. You can double-click a line to display the MM inventory value per plant. There are several possible reasons for value differences. Because the report does not block materials, differences can result if there are postings while the report is running. You can run the report several times to see if the differences change. Online Service System (OSS) Note 198596 discusses additional possible reasons for differences between MM and FI-GL valuations with report RM07MMFI.

You should investigate and make corrections to remove all inconsistencies between MM and FI-GL valuations in the production client prior to the material ledger conversion. OSS note 520010 discusses several methods for removing inconsistencies, which may include contacting SAP for assistance.

▶ **The Material Ledger and FI-GL Reconciliation**

After you've reconciled MM and FI-GL balances you can then activate the material ledger per plant with Transaction OMX1. During production startup with Transaction CKMSTART, the material stock values for the key date are translated from the first local currency to the parallel currencies. As a result, the totals of the stock values of the parallel currencies in the material subledger may not correspond with the account balances of the stock accounts in FI-GL.

You can adjust the account balances of the parallel currencies to the stock values in the subledger with Transaction CKMADJUST or via the following menu path:

> ACCOUNTING • CONTROLLING • PRODUCT COST CONTROLLING • ACTUAL COSTING/
> MATERIAL LEDGER • ENVIRONMENT • PRODUCTION STARTUP • RECONCILIATION
> WITH BALANCE SHEET ACCOUNTS IN FI

The screen shown in Figure 2 is displayed.

Company Code	6000
Parameters	
Account:Stock Corr.	459000

« *Figure 2*
Reconciliation of Material Subledger and G/L

You carry out reconciliation per COMPANY CODE. If the material ledger has not been set to productive for all plants of a company code, you cannot adjust the parallel currencies in the G/L or subledger because stock values are not managed in parallel currencies in plants without the material ledger.

The FI-GL ACCOUNT:STOCK CORR. (Account for Stock Corrections) in Figure 2 is required for posting small differences. Its purpose is similar to an exchange rate gain/loss account with the postings usually small rounding differences.

This adjustment does not have to take place immediately after production startup. It can still take place if goods movements and invoices have already been posted in the company code. You can even omit the adjustment. In this case, however, the balances of the material stock accounts in the second and third local currencies do not represent the stock values of the materials in these currencies. Transaction MB5L displays inconsistencies in the first local currency. ■

Tip 71 Preparation for Production Startup

You can streamline the material ledger implementation by planning data conversion activities

 Solution

Let's examine, in detail, four of the main steps you need to plan in advance when implementing the material ledger.

1. **Timing**

   SAP documentation advises to activate the material ledger at the start of a period. The display of the material ledger data is based on corresponding entries in the material ledger tables. If goods movements exist for a period prior to setting a plant as productive, the material ledger ending inventory for the prior period differs from the beginning inventory of the current period. OSS Note 201751 discusses recommended timing in more detail.

   In practice, carrying out activation and production startup along with other period-end activities is not advisable. Activation mid-month toward the end of a fiscal year allows you one to two months to work through any issues. The following fiscal year you will then have clean material ledger data. If you convert too early in the fiscal year, users may forget that there is no material ledger data for the start of the fiscal year.

   You should also take into account that from the moment of activation to the end of production startup you cannot perform any goods movements in affected plants and you can't create materials.

   Consider activating actual costing at the start of the following period. From the point of activation, materials movements are then updated in the material ledger quantity structure tool and you can perform multilevel costing.

One of the issues to consider when implementing the material ledger is the timing of the activation and production startup steps. You also need to consider how to deal with existing purchase and production order data.

2. **Purchase Order Volume**

Here are some points to avoid long runtimes during production startup with Transaction CKMSTART:

▸ Use Transaction MR11 to perform account maintenance to clear older purchase order items automatically

▸ Archive purchase order data you no longer need with Transaction ME98 and archiving object MM_EKKO

▸ Enter purchase order history (POH) in the OK code field of Transaction CKMSTART and restrict purchasing document selection by plant and number range

▸ Wait until table MLWERE contains entries during production startup on an Oracle database and then re-create table statistics with Transaction DB20

3. **Production Orders**

Before production startup, consider closing all manufacturing orders and create new orders after. For already existing production orders, there is no connection to the material ledger quantity structure tool during the production startup. These orders are not taken into consideration during multilevel calculations.

Existing production order history is not translated into the parallel currencies at production startup. This can lead to problems when reversing goods movements as the value of goods received is calculated incorrectly in the other currencies.

Problems can also occur when you settle product cost collectors. Close product cost collectors before you activate the material ledger and then re-create them. To create a new product cost collector you must set the deletion flag for the old one because only one valid product cost collector is allowed for each material/plant characteristics combination and production version.

4. **Legacy Data**

Material masters, purchase orders, and POHs from legacy systems or external systems should be transferred before the production startup. If you transfer materials from external systems, make sure that the accounting view is created and that the material type permits the update of quantities and values in all plants.

You can create material masters after activating the material ledger, however, you must use Transaction MM01. You should always transfer purchase orders and purchase order histories before activating the material ledger. This ensures that the system translates the purchase order history in all additional currencies because this is easier than importing parallel valuation data yourself.

OSS Note 596558 contains more information on the material ledger startup. ▪

Tip (72) Post Conversion Activities

Post conversion activities you can consider include updating database statistics, order settlement, and resource usage.

Three post material ledger conversion activities to consider are updating database statistics, improving order settlement performance, and resource usage.

Solution

Let's examine each of these three post conversion activities in detail.

▶ **Update Database Statistics**

By running update statistics regularly you make sure that the database statistics are up to date which improves database performance. This is especially important following installations and upgrades, such as the material ledger. Table MLHD in particular will slow down accounting document selection for all financial accounting transactions if the statistics are not updated.

First, let's look at a typical scenario where you're likely to encounter accounting document selection and then discuss how to update table MLHD statistics.

You can display a list of material documents with Transaction MB51 or via the following menu path:

> LOGISTICS • MATERIALS MANAGEMENT • INVENTORY MANAGEMENT • ENVIRONMENT • LIST DISPLAYS • MATERIAL DOCUMENTS

Enter a material and plant, and Execute to display a list of material documents. Double-click a line to display a material document, select the DOC. INFO tab, and click the FI Documents button, to display the screen shown in Figure 1.

Doc. Number	Object type text	Ld
4900000000	Accounting document	
1000401887	Spec. purpose ledger	
1000000352	Material ledger	

《 *Figure 1*
List of Documents in Accounting Dialog Box

Double-click the Accounting document to display the accounting document associated with the material movement. You can reduce the time for the system to locate the accounting document by updating table MLHD statistics. You can update table statistics with Transaction DB20 or via the following menu path:

Tools • CCMS • DB Administration • Cost-Based Optimizer • Create Statistics

The screen shown in Figure 2 is displayed.

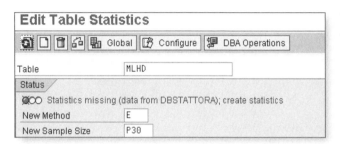

« **Figure 2**
Edit Table Statistics

If you see a red or yellow Status for Table MLHD, you can create new statistics by clicking the New Page icon or choosing Statistics • Create Statistics from the menu bar. Click the Refresh icon to update the displayed statistics. A green status means the table statistics are updated. It is a good idea to update all database statistics following the material ledger production startup.

▶ **Order Settlement and Goods Receipt for Order**
You should check the performance of order settlement and goods receipt for orders following production startup. Release-dependent OSS Notes 498446 and 533119 discuss corrections that can improve performance.

▶ **Resource Usage**
The system updates the material ledger data for current goods movements, invoices, order settlements, and other business transactions. This should have little or no influence on transaction runtimes. Runtimes of a goods movement with or without the material ledger activated will only differ by a few percent.

If you are using the material ledger for actual costing with or without an actual cost component split, period-end closing activities are required, which you start and monitor in the costing cockpit with Transaction CKMLCP. OSS Note 668170 contains detailed information on actual costing resource usage. ◼

Tip 73 · Actual Cost Component Split

The actual cost component split lets you compare plan and actual cost components in Profitability Analysis (CO-PA).

Actual costing with the material ledger allows variances to flow to finished and semifinished products based on the consumption of lower level components. While multilevel price determination lets you see the actual price of all materials at the end of the period, you cannot display price differences rolled up separately from the lowest to highest level materials. You only see price differences assigned from the next lowest level.

You can, however, activate the actual cost component split in actual costing and compare the plan and actual cost components in CO-PA.

✓ Solution

Let's examine the steps required to compare plan and actual cost components. You activate the actual cost component split via the following IMG menu path:

> CONTROLLING • PRODUCT COST CONTROLLING • ACTUAL COSTING/MATERIAL LEDGER • ACTUAL COSTING • ACTIVATE ACTUAL COST COMPONENT SPLIT

The screen in Figure 1 is displayed.

Activate Actual Cost Component Split		
Valuation Area	Company Code	ActCstCmpSplt Active
6000	6000	☑

« *Figure 1*
Activate Actual Cost Component Split

Select the required indicators and save your work to activate the actual cost component split per plant. After activation, you need to create the data for the actual cost component split to ensure that your plant data is consistent.

You can run the report that carries out the productive start for the actual cost component split with Transaction SA38 or by selecting SYSTEM • SERVICES •

REPORTING from the menu bar of any screen. Type in MLCCS_STARTUP and Execute the report. Enter the plants to be converted and Execute.

You can access the actual cost component split by displaying the material master with Transaction MM03 or via the following menu path:

> LOGISTICS • MATERIALS MANAGEMENT • MATERIAL MASTER • MATERIAL • DISPLAY • DISPLAY CURRENT

Navigate to the ACCOUNTING 1 view to display the screen in Figure 2.

| Previous price | 21.90 | |
| Last price change | 05/01/2003 | 🔳 Cost components |

⌃ **Figure 2** *Actual Cost Component Split Button — Accounting 1 View*

Click the COST COMPONENTS button to display the screen in Figure 3.

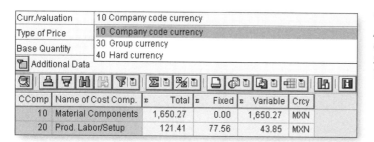

CComp	Name of Cost Comp.	Σ	Total	Σ	Fixed	Σ	Variable	Crcy
10	Material Components		1,650.27		0.00		1,650.27	MXN
20	Prod. Labor/Setup		121.41		77.56		43.85	MXN

Curr./valuation: 10 Company code currency
Type of Price: 10 Company code currency / 30 Group currency / 40 Hard currency
Base Quantity
Additional Data

« **Figure 3**
Actual Cost Component Split Displaying Valuations

You can display the actual cost component split for different valuations. You can map the actual cost component to CO-PA via the IMG menu path:

> CONTROLLING • PROFITABILITY ANALYSIS • MASTER DATA • VALUATION • SET UP VALUATION USING MATERIAL COST ESTIMATE • DEFINE ACCESS TO ACTUAL COSTING/MATERIAL LEDGER

You can then map the actual cost components to value fields with Transaction KE4R or via the following IMG menu path:

> CONTROLLING • PROFITABILITY ANALYSIS • MASTER DATA • VALUATION • SET UP VALUATION USING MATERIAL COST ESTIMATE • ASSIGN VALUE FIELDS

Now you can compare plan and actual cost components in CO-PA reporting. ▪

Tip (74) Deactivating the Material Ledger

You can deactivate the material ledger without having to refresh a test system from the production system.

You can't deactivate the material ledger in a production environment because it would cause inconsistencies in the system. Before activating the material ledger, it's recommended to fully check the functionality in a test environment.

While you can't deactivate the material ledger in a production system, you can in a test environment. This lets you test the functionality multiple times without refreshing the test system from the production system. Let's look at how to activate and deactivate the material ledger.

✓ Solution

You can activate the material ledger with Transaction OMX1 or via the following IMG menu path:

> CONTROLLING • PRODUCT COST CONTROLLING • ACTUAL COSTING/MATERIAL LEDGER • ACTIVATE VALUATION AREAS FOR MATERIAL LEDGER

Double-click the Activate Material Ledger text to display the screen shown in Figure 1.

Valuation Area	Company Code	ML Act.	Price Deter.	Price Det. Binding in Val Area
7100	7000	☐		☐

⩘ *Figure 1* Activate Material Ledger Valuation Area

To activate the material ledger for a VALUATION AREA (plant), select the ML ACT. checkbox and type in either 2 (transaction based) or 3 (single-/multilevel actual costing) in the Price Determination (PRICE DETER.) field. This setting determines the proposed material price determination when creating a new material master. This entry is ignored at production startup. The system automatically sets the indicator to 2 in the material master for all materials present.

After you activate the material ledger, you need to set the valuation areas as productive with Transaction CKMSTART or via the following menu path:

> ACCOUNTING • CONTROLLING • PRODUCT COST CONTROLLING • ACTUAL COSTING/ MATERIAL LEDGER • ENVIRONMENT • PRODUCTION STARTUP • SET VALUATION AREAS AS PRODUCTIVE

The selection screen shown in Figure 2 is displayed.

« *Figure 2*
Set Material Ledger Plant as Productive

Type in the PLANT that you activated in Figure 1, and click the Execute icon. At this point, if you attempt to deselect the checkbox entered in Figure 1, you will receive Error Message OM464, which indicates that the material ledger plant can no longer be deactivated because the plant data has been converted to productive.

In a test system, you can allow the checkbox to be deselected by running the report SAPRCKMJX. You can run this report with Transaction SA38 or via the following menu path:

> SYSTEM • SERVICES • REPORTING

Type in report SAPRCKMJX and click the Execute icon to display the screen shown in Figure 3.

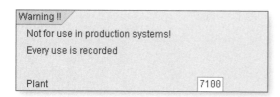

« *Figure 3*
Cancel Material Ledger Production Startup

Type in the PLANT and click the Execute icon to display a list of messages indicating the system steps taken to cancel the production startup. You can now deselect the activation checkbox in Figure 1 and save the setting.

You can find more information on deactivating the material ledger in the OSS Note 108374 — Canceling material ledger production startup. ■

Part 7

Profitability Analysis

Things You'll Learn in this Section

Profitability analysis (CO-PA) lets you analyze the profitability of segments of your market according to products, customers, orders, and other characteristics as well as organizational units such as company codes or business areas. The aim is to provide your sales, marketing, planning, and management organizations with decision-support from a market-oriented viewpoint.

There are two forms of CO-PA:

▶ **Costing-based:** You map costs and revenues to value fields. Costs are posted at the same time as revenue with valuation which accesses the cost components in the standard cost estimate. This guarantees you access at all times to a complete, short-term profitability report.

▶ **Account-based:** With this approach you use accounts for analysis instead of value fields. While you still use characteristics for analysis and reporting, you will always be able to reconcile with financial accounting.

You can use both types of CO-PA at the same time. Unless otherwise mentioned, all scenarios in this book refer to costing-based CO-PA, since this contains the most functionality and flexible analysis capability.

Valuation allows you to map standard cost estimate cost components to value fields in CO-PA. You can use valuation in profitability analysis in both plan and actual. You can use scenario based planning with different versions based on best and worst case sales plans. You can create as many plan versions as you need. You can enter the sales plan into CO-PA and run a complete sales cycle from CO-PA through sales and operations planning, long-term planning, transfer activity quantities to cost center accounting, create standard cost estimates and transfer cost components to CO-PA. You can then determine the profit margin for the particular sales plan version.

You can transfer production variance categories to individual value fields during period-end settlement. This together with period-end assessment of cost center under/over absorption to CO-PA provides you with a complete and detailed view of your actual manufacturing expenses.

Account- versus Costing-Based CO-PA

You can use both account- and costing-based profitability analysis. Both serve a purpose and have their advantages and disadvantages.

Both account- and costing-based profitability analysis (CO-PA) display results by market segments, or characteristics, such as customer and product. Values are organized according to accounts in both account-based CO-PA and Financial Accounting (FI). This means account-based CO-PA can be used in parallel with costing-based CO-PA to reconcile FI and costing-based CO-PA.

While account-based CO-PA makes reconciliation with FI easier because postings occur to both modules at the same time, it's the flexibility of costing-based CO-PA that makes it a more useful reporting tool. Costing-based CO-PA is intended to provide a short-term profit and loss statement for sales management. One of the main functions of costing-based CO-PA is the valuation of planned sales volumes or the actual sales volume transferred from billing or from incoming orders using costing-based values, for example, sales deductions and standard cost of goods manufactured.

The advantage of this procedure is that the data is always up to date. The primary function of the costing-based CO-PA is to offer all of the information required to make decisions in the area of sales and profitability accounting.

Solution

Let's looks at some of the differences between both types of CO-PA in detail:

► **Valuation**
Valuation in costing-based CO-PA lets you post the standard cost estimate and cost components to separate value fields in CO-PA at the time of billing or incoming sales orders. Because these are calculated values that need value fields to post to they cannot post to account-based CO-PA. Yet these calculated postings give you immediate visibility to margin analysis in advance of FI reporting analysis capability.

▶ **Sales Order Receipt**

In costing-based CO-PA, you can transfer sales order receipts to CO-PA so that an early profit forecast can be carried out. This function is not available in account-based CO-PA. Record type A corresponds to incoming sales order data, and record type F to incoming billing data. In both cases, cost of sales are determined by valuation with cost estimate and cost components. The value of goods issued are transferred to costing-based CO-PA with condition type VPRS.

If the goods issue and corresponding billing document occur in separate posting periods, differences can occur between the FI and costing-based CO-PA because the cost of goods manufactured is transferred to account-based CO-PA only when the goods value is transferred during goods issue.

▶ **Cost Center Assessment**

Cost center under/over absorption costs are transferred to costing-based CO-PA value fields, which you specify during assessment cycle maintenance. The update to account-based CO-PA is carried out with an assessment cost element.

▶ **Order and Project Settlement**

You can settle each production variance type to separate value fields, and report on this level of detail in costing-based CO-PA. You define the mapping of variances to value fields in a PA transfer structure with Transaction KEI1. The PA transfer structure is assigned to the manufacturing order settlement profile.

In account-based CO-PA, settlement is carried out under settlement cost elements that are defined in the settlement structure. A PA transfer structure is not required for settlement with account-based CO-PA.

▶ **Sales and Profit Planning**

A main function of sales and profit planning for costing-based CO-PA is the valuation of planning values, such as sales volume, with price lists of sales and distribution and imputed costs and sales deductions.

In account-based CO-PA, amounts and quantities can be entered by cost element for any market segments and user-selectable planning levels.

▶ **Currency**

In costing-based CO-PA, all amounts are stored at a minimum in operating concern currency, as specified in the operating concern attributes. You can also store values in local currency as well, though this has the effect of doubling the stored data transaction.

Account-based CO-PA stores all transactions in three currencies: the transaction currency, the local currency, and the controlling area currency.

OSS Notes 69384 and 421230 provide more information on account- and costing-based CO-PA. ■

Tip 76   Cost of Sales Cost Element

You should create the cost of sales accounts as primary cost elements type 12 — sales deduction.

When setting up the Controlling (CO) module, you create primary cost elements type 1 to expense general ledger accounts. This ensures that all primary expenses are posted to CO and available for analysis. A question often asked is, are the cost of sales (COS) account postings expenses?

 Solution

All analyzable expenses are incurred while manufacturing a product before goods receipt into inventory. COS postings occur when the product is subsequently removed from inventory and shipped to a customer. This is a sales deduction not a controllable expense. COS accounts should not be created as a type 1 primary cost element because a cost center manager has no control over the postings. Sales, marketing, and profit center managers are responsible for COS.

COS accounts should instead be created as primary cost elements type 12 (sales deduction) so that postings can occur to Profitability Analysis (CO-PA) and Profit Center Accounting to allow sales deductions and profitability accounting. Parallel postings to a cost center are not required for cost element type 12.

All revenues, sales deductions, and other values are defined as condition types in Sales and Distribution (SD). General ledger accounts linked to condition types must be created as cost element types 11 (revenue) and 12 (sales deduction) to transfer condition types to CO-PA.

You can map SD condition types to CO-PA value fields with Transaction KE4I or via the following IMG menu path:

> CONTROLLING • PROFITABILITY ANALYSIS • FLOWS OF ACTUAL VALUES • TRANSFER OF BILLING DOCUMENTS • ASSIGN VALUE FIELDS

CTyp	Name	Val. fld	Description	Transfer +/-
VPRS	Cost	VV140	Cost of goods sold	☑

⌃ **Figure 1** *Assign SD Condition Types to CO-PA Value Field*

Standard condition type VPRS retrieves the material master price and maps it to value field VV140 in the example shown in Figure 1.

In a make-to-stock (MTS) scenario, the posting to CO-PA occurs during the release of the billing document to accounting (CO-PA record type F). This ensures CO-PA receives the revenue and cost information at the same time. An MTS scenario involves inventory that is not manufactured for specific sales orders or projects.

In a make-to-order (MTO) scenario, the posting to CO-PA occurs during the settlement of the sales order at month-end (CO-PA record type C). An MTO scenario involves inventory that is manufactured for specific sales orders or projects. You can map the cost elements to value fields in a PA transfer structure that you configure with Transaction KEI1 or via the following IMG menu path:

> CONTROLLING • PROFITABILITY ANALYSIS • FLOWS OF ACTUAL VALUES •
> ORDER AND PROJECT SETTLEMENT • DEFINE PA TRANSFER STRUCTURE

Select a PA transfer structure and double-click Assignment lines. Select an assignment line and double-click Source to display the screen in Figure 2.

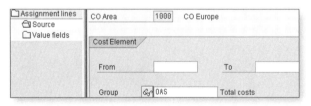

≪ **Figure 2**
PA Transfer Structure Define Source Cost Elements

COST ELEMENTS contained in COST ELEMENT GROUP OAS are mapped to VALUE FIELDS. To display COST ELEMENT GROUP OAS's contents, click the Glasses icon.

To maintain the value fields mapping, double-click VALUE FIELDS on the left in Figure 2 to display the screen shown in Figure 3.

≪ **Figure 3**
PA Transfer Structure Define Value Fields

Cost element group OAS is mapped to CO-PA VALUE FIELD VV370. ■

Tip 77

Statistical Conditions and Profitability Analysis (CO-PA)

Statistical conditions let you calculate and display additional values in CO-PA.

Statistical conditions are defined in the Sales and Distribution (SD) functionality. They're for informational purposes only and do not post to general ledger (G/L) accounts or change the net value of an item. Statistical condition values can be used in SD pricing procedures for functions such as subtotaling.

You can post statistical condition types to value fields in CO-PA for additional reporting without affecting the SD net value. A typical standard supplied statistical condition type is VPRS, which calculates the material standard or moving average price. It allows you to determine expected profit margin without affecting the net value calculation.

Let's look at how you can define statistical condition types and how you can map them to CO-PA value fields.

Solution

You can maintain statistical condition types in SD pricing procedures with Transaction V/08 or via the following IMG menu path:

> SALES AND DISTRIBUTION • BASIC FUNCTIONS • PRICING • PRICING CONTROL • DEFINE AND ASSIGN PRICING PROCEDURES

Double-click the text Maintain pricing procedures, select the system-supplied pricing procedure RVAA01, double-click the text Control data, and scroll down to Step 940 to display the screen in Figure 1.

Step	Counter	CTyp	Description	Fro	To	Manual	Required	Statistics
940	0	VPRS	Cost			☐	☐	☑

《 Figure 1
Statistical Condition Type in Pricing Procedure

The selected STATISTICS checkbox ensures that this value will not be included in the net value calculation. The next step is to map the statistical condition to a CO-PA value field with Transaction KE4I or via the IMG menu path:

> CONTROLLING • PROFITABILITY ANALYSIS • FLOWS OF ACTUAL VALUES • TRANSFER OF INCOMING SALES ORDERS • ASSIGN VALUE FIELDS

Double-click the text Maintain Assignment of SD Conditions to CO-PA Value Fields and scroll down to condition type VPRS to display the screen shown in Figure 2.

CTyp	Name	Val. fld	Description
VPRS	Cost	VV140	Cost of goods sold

« Figure 2
Assignment of SD Conditions to Value Fields

During invoicing, the value of VPRS will be transferred to CO-PA value field VV140 following this configuration step. This condition typically gets its value from the standard price field of the material master and represents the cost of goods sold (COGS). It is set as statistical, so it will not be part of the sales price calculation. In the pricing procedure it allows for easy determination of gross profit. It also allows for an easy data update to CO-PA for the standard COGS.

You can check your customizing settings for mapping condition types to CO-PA value fields with Transaction KEAF or via the following IMG menu path:

> CONTROLLING • PROFITABILITY ANALYSIS • TOOLS • ANALYSIS • CHECK CUSTOMIZING SETTINGS

Double-click the text Value Field Analysis, select the checkbox for Transfer of billing docs / Incoming sales order, and click the Execute icon. Click the SD Conditions button and scroll down to condition type VV140 to display the screen shown in Figure 3.

Value Fiel	Text - Value Field	CstngSheet	Text - Costing Sheet	Condition	Text - Condition	+/-	Accrual Condition	Statistical
VV140	Cost of goods sold	RVAACA	Standard	EK01	Costs			
				PI01	Intercompany Price			X
				VPRS	Cost	X		X

⌃ Figure 3 *Value Field Analysis Details*

In this analysis screen, CONDITION VPRS is assigned to VALUE FIELD VV140 as a STATISTICAL condition as shown in the last column and row.

OSS Notes 20254, 355505, and 62536 provide more information on statistical condition types and CO-PA. ■

Map Manual Account Adjustments

You can map period-end financial manual adjustments to costing-based Profitability Analysis (CO-PA).

Many companies need to manually adjust sales figures in Financial Accounting (FI) at period-end, for example, to reduce revenue for dispatched goods that have not yet reached the customer's warehouse. Let's look at how you map these manual FI postings to costing-based CO-PA.

✓ Solution

You first create a characteristic group with Transaction KEPA or via the following IMG menu path:

> CONTROLLING • PROFITABILITY ANALYSIS • FLOWS OF ACTUAL VALUES • INITIAL STEPS • CHARACTERISTIC GROUPS • MAINTAIN CHARACTERISTIC GROUPS

Click on the New Entries button, enter the name and text of your new group, and press ⟨Enter⟩ to display the screen in Figure 1.

▽ 🗀 Characteristic groups		Characteristic group	Text
🗀 Characteristics		FI	Map Manual Finance Postings to CO-PA

⩗ *Figure 1 Maintain Characteristic Groups*

Select you new CHARACTERISTIC GROUP, double-click CHARACTERISTICS at the left, click the New Entries button, and enter the characteristics that will be available for input during the FI posting as shown in Figure 2.

Field Name	Field description	Entry status
KNDNR	Customer	2 Required entry
ARTNR	Product	1 Field ready for input

« *Figure 2*
Characteristics and Entry Status

Adding characteristics makes them available for entry during the FI posting. Be selective with which characteristics you make as REQUIRED ENTRY because financial corrections are often made at a high level and not all characteristics may be known or needed.

Next, assign the characteristic group to business Transaction RFBU with Transaction code KE4G or via the following IMG menu path:

> CONTROLLING • PROFITABILITY ANALYSIS • FLOWS OF ACTUAL VALUES • INITIAL STEPS • CHARACTERISTIC GROUPS • ASSIGN CHARACTERISTIC GROUPS FOR ASSIGNMENT SCREEN

Make the assignment as shown in Figure 3.

BusTran.	Name	Charact. group	Name
RFBU	FI: Postings	FI	Map Manual Finance Postings to CO-PA

⌃ **Figure 3** *Assign Characteristic Group to Business Transaction*

This entry creates a link between business Transaction RFBU, financial postings, and your characteristic group FI. The next step is to map the general ledger (G/L) accounts for manual financial corrections to value fields. Then, whenever you make an FI posting with the G/L account, the values will flow to CO-PA.

You can map G/L accounts to value fields with a PA transfer structure that you can maintain with Transaction KEI2 or via the following IMG menu path:

> CONTROLLING • PROFITABILITY ANALYSIS • FLOWS OF ACTUAL VALUES • DIRECT POSTING FROM FI/MM • MAINTAIN PA TRANSFER STRUCTURE FOR DIRECT POSTINGS

Select Structure FI, double-click ASSIGNMENT LINES, and click the New Entries button to display the screen shown in Figure 4.

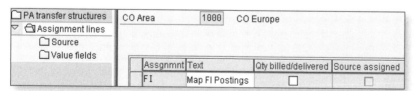

⌃ **Figure 4** *Maintain PA Transfer Structure Assignment Lines*

Next, select your new ASSIGNMENT LINE, double-click SOURCE to enter your manual G/L accounts, and then double-click VALUE FIELDS to map your value fields. ▪

Tip 79 Interface Sign Logic

You can transfer condition values with original signs to Profitability Analysis (CO-PA) to calculate the balance value.

Conditions from the Sales and Distribution (SD) functionality in SAP ERP are updated as positive values in CO-PA. The only exceptions are reverse transactions, such as credit memos and returns. This is because signs are handled differently in different modules. For example, revenues are positive in SD but negative in Financial Accounting (FI). Consequently, CO-PA defines all values as positive and subtracts costs and sales deductions from revenues in reporting.

This means that revenues, sales deductions, and costs all have the same sign in CO-PA.

You therefore need to map revenues, sales deductions, and costs to separate value fields. In reporting, you subtract sales deductions from revenues to get the net revenue, and then subtract costs from net revenue to obtain contribution margins.

This design ensures that even if the same values are stored with different signs in SD and FI, the postings in CO-PA are correct. However, there can be some issues with condition values in the following two scenarios. Let's examine each item in detail and look at some standard solutions.

 Solution

The first scenario often occurs with customer rebates:

▶ **Condition types that can have both negative and positive values**
Many companies offer discounts to their customers in the form of rebates, depending on the total volume of business over a period of time. For such rebate agreements, rebate accruals are generated based on conditions. At the end of the rebate period, during rebate settlement, the rebate conditions are calculated with the opposite sign to balance the final rebate amount. In this scenario, rebate conditions have both positive and negative signs, and you should transfer the signs together with the condition values.

You can transfer the signs and condition values using Transaction KE4I or via the following IMG menu path:

> CONTROLLING • PROFITABILITY ANALYSIS • FLOWS OF ACTUAL VALUES • TRANSFER OF BILLING DOCUMENTS • ASSIGN VALUE FIELDS

Double-click ASSIGNMENT OF SD CONDITIONS to display the screen in Figure 1.

CTyp	Name	Val. fld	Description	Transfer +/-
0B02		VV090	Accrued bonus	☑
0B01	Rebate CRM	VV090	Accrued bonus	☑
0B02	Material Rebate CRM	VV090	Accrued bonus	☑
0PR0		VV010	Revenue	☐
0VPR		VV140	Cost of goods sold	☐

« **Figure 1**
Assignment of SD Conditions to Value Fields

If you select the TRANSFER +/- checkbox, the SD condition value is transferred to CO-PA along with its plus or minus sign. The system calculates a balance of the positive and negative values to ensure that the correct total for that condition type is shown in the corresponding value field.

The second scenario often occurs with customer discounts:

▶ **Condition types that occur more than once in a billing document**
You can use the same configuration when condition types occur more than once in a billing document. The potential problem with this design is when the same discount condition type exists in a billing document more than once but with different signs. Although it isn't common, it can happen if you have multiple condition records with opposite signs. If you use the above configuration step you can have the correct amount but with different signs posted to CO-PA from SD and FI.

To avoid this scenario, you should not select this checkbox and instead post to separate value fields, one for SD to CO-PA and another for FI to CO-PA. The TRANSFER +/- sign checkbox cannot be used to reconcile the sign handling in FI, SD, and CO-PA. In assigning a value field to a condition type, the TRANSFER +/- SIGN checkbox should only be used in rare instances.

The following OSS Notes provide more information on CO-PA sign logic:

▶ 20254 — INFO: Values from SD not transferred to CO-PA

▶ 33178 — INFO: +/- sign logic in CO-PA (SD/FI interface)

▶ 37114 — Incorrect setup/reversal of provision

▶ 52849 — INFO: Transfer of conditions with +/- signs ▪

Tip Valuation

You can map calculated values, such as cost estimate cost components to Profitability Analysis (CO-PA) value fields.

Valuation involves the calculation of values that are mapped to value fields. These are in addition to direct postings, such as revenue and sales deductions. There are several types of valuation available, including specific condition types, costing sheets, and transfer prices. Let's follow an example of valuation by cost estimates.

✓ Solution

There are two ways to calculate cost of sales (COS) in CO-PA. While a retail company only needs to display the total value of goods as COS, a much more detailed breakdown of the costs of goods manufactured is required in a manufacturing company.

It's possible to map each cost component to its own value field, or multiple components to a single value field. It's also possible to map the fixed and variable portions of a component to separate value fields.

Using a costing key, you can determine which cost estimate (costing variant) should be used with which validity date for valuation. You maintain costing keys with Transaction KE40 or via the following IMG menu path:

> CONTROLLING • PROFITABILITY ANALYSIS • MASTER DATA • VALUATION • SET UP VALUATION USING MATERIAL COST ESTIMATE • DEFINE ACCESS TO STANDARD COST ESTIMATES

≪ Figure 1
Maintain Costing Key Details

In this example, the costing key will choose the RELEASED STANDARD COST ESTIMATE at the time of goods issue. The next step is to assign the costing key to a material, material type, or characteristic. You can assign a costing key to a material with Transaction KE4H or via the following IMG menu path:

> CONTROLLING • PROFITABILITY ANALYSIS • MASTER DATA • VALUATION • SET UP VALUATION USING MATERIAL COST ESTIMATE • ASSIGN COSTING KEYS TO PRODUCTS

The screen in Figure 2 is displayed.

PV	RecT.	Plan ver.	Material	Valid to	C.key 1	C.key 2	C.key 3
01	A		DPC4000	12/31/9999	I12		
01	A		HD-1300	12/31/9999	I12		

« *Figure 2*
Assign Costing Key to Product

PV (point of valuation) 01 indicates valuation will happen in real time with actual data, while RECT. (record type) A indicates it will happen during posting of the incoming sales order. By assigning a costing key, you control which cost estimate (standard, modified, or current) should be used depending on the material, material type, or any other combination of characteristics. An entry for the material has priority over an entry for the material type, which in turn has priority over entries defined for other characteristics.

You can assign cost components with Transaction KE4R or via the following IMG menu path:

> CONTROLLING • PROFITABILITY ANALYSIS • MASTER DATA • VALUATION • SET UP VALUATION USING MATERIAL COST ESTIMATE • ASSIGN VALUE FIELDS

The screen in Figure 3 is displayed.

PV	CCo	Name of Cost Comp.	F/V	Fld name 1	Fld name 2
01	10		3	VV150	VV150
01	20	Purchased Parts	3	VV160	VV160

« *Figure 3*
Assign Cost Components to Value Fields

Values of the cost components are transferred by aligning C.KEY (costing key) columns in Figure 2 with six possible value field columns in Figure 3. OSS Note 62536 explains valuation using costing sheets in more detail. ▨

Tip (81) Settle Production Variances to CO-PA

You can maintain the settlement profile and PA transfer structure to settle production variances to CO-PA.

There are two configuration steps required for settling production variances to Profitability Analysis (CO-PA):

▶ Maintain the settlement profile

▶ Maintain the PA transfer structure

Let's look at the details of each step.

✓ Solution

The first step in setting up settlement of production variances to CO-PA is:

▶ **Maintain the settlement profile**
You can configure the settlement profile with Transaction OKO7 or via the following IMG menu path:

> CONTROLLING • PRODUCT COST CONTROLLING • COST OBJECT CONTROLLING • PRODUCT COST BY ORDER • PERIOD-END CLOSING • SETTLEMENT • CREATE SETTLEMENT PROFILE

Double-click a settlement profile to display the screen in Figure 1.

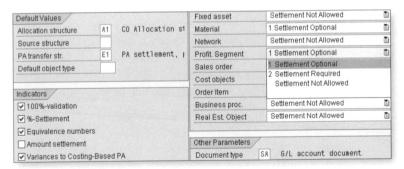

⊼ *Figure 1 Maintain Settlement Profile*

There are three relevant fields in the settlement profile:

▸ PA TRANSFER STR.: Assign a PA transfer structure to map the variance categories to value fields

▸ VARIANCES TO COSTING-BASED PA: Select this checkbox

▸ PROFIT. SEGMENT: Choose either SETTLEMENT OPTIONAL or REQUIRED

After maintaining the settlement profile, the next step required is:

▸ **Maintain PA transfer structure**

You can maintain the PA transfer structure with Transaction KEI1 or via the following IMG menu path:

> CONTROLLING • PRODUCT COST CONTROLLING • COST OBJECT CONTROLLING • PRODUCT COST BY ORDER • PERIOD-END CLOSING • SETTLEMENT • CREATE PA TRANSFER STRUCTURE

Select a PA transfer structure and double-click ASSIGNMENT LINES on the left to display the screen in Figure 2.

Dialog Structure					
▽ ☐ PA transfer structures	PA transfer str	E1	PA settlement, production var.		
▽ ☐ Assignment lines	CO Area	1000	CO Europe		
☐ Source					
☐ Value fields	Assgnmnt	Text	Qty billed/delivered	Source assigned	Value field assign
	20	Price variance	☐	☑	☑
	25	Mixed-price variance	☐	☐	☑
	30	Quantity variances materi	☐	☑	☑

❯ *Figure 2 Maintain PA Transfer Structure Assignment Lines*

You can assign individual production variance categories by creating ASSIGNMENT LINES, and then double-clicking SOURCE to display Figure 3.

Source		VARC	Description
○ Costs / revenue		PRIV	Input Price Variance
		QTYV	Input Quantity Variance
◉ Variances on production orders		RSUV	Resource-Usage Variance
Variance category	PRIV	INPV	Remaining Input Variance
		MXPV	Mixed-Price Variance

« *Figure 3*

Maintain PA Transfer Structure Source Details

The combination of individual variance categories and cost elements defines the SOURCE. If you do not specify a VARIANCE CATEGORY, all of the variances occurring under the cost element are settled to the value field assigned to the cost element. ■

Tip 82 | Data Storage Tables

When creating profitability analysis reports, it helps if you understand the data storage tables.

There are two different types of profitability analysis (CO-PA):

▶ **Costing-based**: Matches revenue and costs, report on margin contribution
▶ **Account-based**: Period accounting, based on profitability segments

Let's discuss the tables used to store both types of CO-PA data.

 Solution

Costing- and account-based CO-PA use the tables displayed in Figure 1.

	Costing based	Account based
Actual line items	CE1XXXX	COEJ
Plan line items	CE2XXXX	COEP
Summary records by profitability segment	CE3XXXX	COSS, COSP
Profitability segment definitions	CE4XXXX	CE4XXXX

⌃ *Figure 1 Costing- and Account-based CO-PA Tables*

In this example, XXXX in the table name represents the operating concern. The PROFITABILITY SEGMENT DEFINITIONS for both types of CO-PA are stored in table CE4XXXX. This includes characteristics for customers, products and sales divisions, and characteristic values. Each unique combination of characteristic values is a profitability segment and is stored in a separate line in this table. You can view the contents of the table with Transaction SE16N. The contents of table CE4IDEA are shown in this example in Figure 2.

Prof. Seg.	SubN	Valid to	Acct-ba.PA	Customer	Product
451	1	12/31/9999		1400	L-40F
452	1	12/31/9999	1		

⌃ **Figure 2** *Profitability Segment Definitions in Table CE4IDEA*

In this example, Profitability Segment (PROF. SEG.) 451 refers to costing-based CO-PA while 452 refers to account-based CO-PA.

▶ **Costing-based CO-PA Tables**

While table CE4IDEA stores profitability segment definitions and is called the segment table, table CE3XXXX in Figure 1 stores summary postings to each profitability segment and is called the segment level table. It contains the revenue and cost data summarized from postings to each profitability segment.

Table CE1XXXX contains detailed line item postings each time a sales order or billing line item is posted, depending on your configuration. Table CE2XXXX contains planning entered by end users.

Costing-based CO-PA stores its transaction data in its own data tables created when activating and generating the operating concern. This means that its data does not affect report performance in another controlling application.

▶ **Account-based CO-PA Tables**

Account-based CO-PA stores transaction data in the tables for overhead cost management. This means that its data can affect the execution speed of reports for other controlling applications that share the same transaction data tables.

Similar to CE3XXXX in Figure 1, the COSS and COSP tables in account-based CO-PA record the key figure data postings in summary form:

▶ COSS stores postings made to Controlling from Financial Accounting entries

▶ COSP stores internal controlling postings, such as cost allocations from a cost center to a profitability segment

Table COEP stores transaction line items for actual data posted to account-based CO-PA profitability segments, while table COEJ stores plan data line items. ■

Tip 83

Summarization Levels and Reporting

You can improve the performance of Profitability Analysis (CO-PA) reports by creating summarization levels.

CO-PA reports can access large amounts of data and take a long time to run. There are several tools available to improve the runtime of CO-PA reports, including summarization levels, summarized data, and frozen data. Let's look at how summarization levels work.

✓ Solution

You can run CO-PA reports with Transaction KE30 or via the following menu path:

> ACCOUNTING • CONTROLLING • PROFITABILITY ANALYSIS • INFORMATION SYSTEM • EXECUTE REPORT

Double-click a report, enter the selection parameters, and Execute. You may see a warning message as shown in Figure 1.

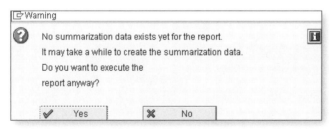

« Figure 1
Summarization Level Warning Message

The message is informing you that the system cannot find a suitable summarization level, which means it may need to access a large volume of detailed line-item data. To improve system performance when selecting reports, you can calculate and store presummarized data. So, when you call up a report, the system no longer needs to read the original detailed data. Instead, it reads the presummarized data, and can take much less time to display the report.

The system can propose summarization levels for you based on user behavior with Transaction KEDVP or via the following IMG menu path:

CONTROLLING • PROFITABILITY ANALYSIS • TOOLS • SUMMARIZATION LEVELS • HAVE PROPOSAL CREATED AUTOMATICALLY

The system displays an overview of the suggested summarization levels and characteristics. The levels are built upon one another and arranged so that the first level produces the best optimization for reports. If you do not wish to use all of the suggested levels, delete the last in the list but not the first.

You can create your own summarization levels with Transaction KEDV or via the following IMG menu path:

CONTROLLING • PROFITABILITY ANALYSIS • TOOLS • SUMMARIZATION LEVELS • DEFINE SUMMARIZATION LEVELS

Select your SUMMARIZATION LEVEL and click the Characteristics button to display the screen in Figure 2.

Summarization level	310	IDES-310	
Field	Name	Characteristic Value	Text
FKART	Billing Type		
GJAHR	Fiscal Year	*	

《 *Figure 2*
Summarization Level Characteristics Values

You have three options for each CHARACTERISTIC VALUE:

▶ **Summarized:** Leave field blank, you cannot report on these values

▶ **Free:** Enter asterisk, you can use these for selection criteria

▶ **Fixed:** Enter single value, for example, one company code

Some characteristics are automatically filled with an asterisk, and must be included with every summarization level. After saving, you then populate your summarization level with Transaction KEDU or via the following menu path:

ACCOUNTING • CONTROLLING • PROFITABILITY ANALYSIS • TOOLS • SUMMARIZATION LEVELS • REFRESH

OSS Notes 67342 and 83204 provide more details on summarization levels. ▣

Customizing Monitor

You can analyze customizing settings for an operating concern.

Postings are mapped to Profitability Analysis (CO-PA) value fields in several configuration transactions. There is an analysis transaction that displays the mapping for you. Let's look at the value field analysis to see how this works.

✓ Solution

You can display CO-PA configuration mapping with Transaction KECM or via the following IMG menu path:

> CONTROLLING • PROFITABILITY ANALYSIS • TOOLS • ANALYSIS • CHECK CUSTOMIZING SETTINGS

Click the Execute icon, type in the operating concern in the dialog box if it appears, press [Enter], and click the VALUE FIELD ANALYSIS text to display the screen in Figure 1.

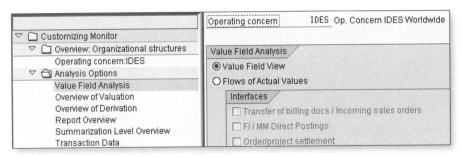

⌃ *Figure 1 Customizing Monitor — Value Field Analysis*

The VALUE FIELD ANALYSIS lets you analyze all of the flows of actual data to CO-PA. You can find inconsistencies by looking at individual value fields. To display a list of all value fields, select the VALUE FIELD VIEW radio button, click Execute, and click the VALUE FIELD VIEW button to display the screen in Figure 2.

Value Field	Text	SD	FI / MM	OPA	IAA	CCA	Ext. Data		ACTUAL	PerVal ACT	PLAN
VV010	Revenue	X(+/-)	X	X				📷	X		X
VV020	Quantity discount	X									X
VV030	Customer discount	X		X					X		X

⌃ *Figure 2* Value Field Analysis Detail

You are presented with a list of all value fields and how each receives postings from other modules. In this example, the FI/MM column indicates direct postings from FI/MM while OPA means order and project settlement. You can click the Legend button for a full explanation of the column headings.

For further details of mappings from other modules, select the FLOWS OF ACTUAL VALUES radio button and all of the checkboxes in Figure 1, and click Execute to display the screen in Figure 3.

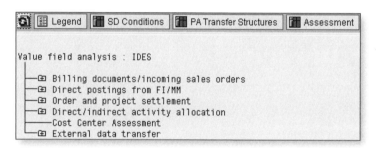

« *Figure 3*
Value Field
Analysis Detail

Click any of the buttons at the top to display the value field mapping details for SD CONDITIONS, PA TRANSFER STRUCTURES, or ASSESSMENT. Expanding the hierarchy nodes in Figure 3 displays more details of condition types and cost elements mapping to value fields. Expand the Order and project settlement hierarchy node in Figure 3 to display the screen in Figure 4.

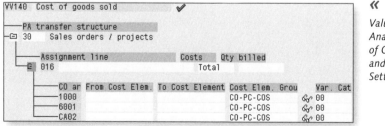

« *Figure 4*
Value Field
Analysis
of Order
and Project
Settlement

In this screen, you can analyze PA TRANSFER STRUCTURES and the mapping of cost element groups to CO-PA. ∎

Part 8

Controlling General

Things You'll Learn in this Section

Controlling (CO) allows you to analyze primary expenses for internal management reporting. You typically post primary expenses as they occur in financial accounting (FI) also to CO. You do this by creating primary cost elements in CO with the same numbering as your primary general ledger (G/L) expense accounts. While postings within FI are for external reporting purposes, in CO you can examine, manipulate, and report on expenses for internal reporting.

Primary overhead costs are posted to cost centers and orders where they are controlled by responsible managers. Cost center managers can examine posted data with standard cost center reports and drill-down to the source documents where necessary to analyze the reasons for the postings.

Overhead costs are allocated with assessments and settlement from cost centers and orders to production cost centers at period-end. All overheads are then allocated to manufacturing orders during activity confirmation during the month and then onto cost of sales when the manufactured goods are placed into inventory.

A controlling area is an organizational unit that represents a closed system used for cost accounting. A controlling area may contain one or more company codes which can operate in different currencies. The company codes within a controlling area must all use the same operational chart of accounts.

In this category of ideas you will find advice on how to initially set up your controlling areas. You will also find shortcuts for quickly navigating the Implantation Guide (IMG) where you set up configuration for your system. There are also ideas on the three main areas where you control posting periods at period-end. You can also read an idea about attaching documents and contracts directly to sales orders.

In this book you'll find many ideas that cross-over with other SAP software, such as the sales order document idea in this category. One of the reasons for the crossover is that most company activities are carried out on orders such as manufacturing, repair, service and quality orders. Almost all orders, even sales orders, can carry costs which you can report on and analyze in CO.

Tip 85

SAP ERP Delivered Controlling Areas

SAP ERP delivered controlling areas are available for reference when creating your own controlling areas.

SAP ERP comes delivered with several example controlling areas such as 0001, CA01, CH01, and SE21. These controlling areas contain customizing data that is necessary to install country-specific information, such as a country's chart of accounts.

Best practice is to copy the standard delivered controlling areas to your own by using a four-digit alphanumeric key, such as JP01 for John's Pharmaceutical, for example. The logic you use for controlling area numbering depends on how many controlling areas your company has or is likely to have. Many companies have one controlling area, which greatly simplifies reporting — especially consolidated reporting. However, if you have a lot of controlling areas in different countries, copying the standard delivered controlling areas with IMG Transaction EC16 is a great starting point for setting up these countries.

Some companies, however, do not copy the standard delivered controlling areas and instead set them up as their own. This causes several problems:

▶ Transaction OKKP2 allows for the deletion of standard delivered controlling areas together with all example master data, transaction data, number ranges, and other controlling area–dependent settings. You must never run this transaction if you are live with controlling area 0001.

▶ You cannot re-import the standard controlling areas from client 000 because you may accidentally overwrite your company's data.

▶ You cannot delete the standard delivered controlling areas to clean up master data and configuration settings as you can if you've correctly copied from them to then create your country-specific controlling areas.

As you can see from the preceding list, there are several disadvantages to using controlling area 0001 as your own controlling area. There are two different transaction codes available for deleting controlling areas. Let's look at both.

Solution

You can delete standard delivered controlling areas with Transaction OKKP2 or via the following IMG menu path:

> CONTROLLING • GENERAL CONTROLLING • ORGANIZATION • MAINTAIN CONTROL-LING AREA • DELETE SAP DELIVERY DATA

You will be presented with a list of standard delivered controlling areas as shown in Figure 1.

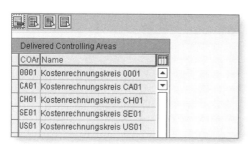

« *Figure 1*
Delete Delivered Controlling Areas

Select the controlling area for deletion and click the highlighted Delete icon to display a dialog box warning that all dependent data will be deleted.

You can delete all controlling areas, including standard delivered controlling areas, with Transaction OKKP or via the following IMG menu path:

> CONTROLLING • GENERAL CONTROLLING • ORGANIZATION • MAINTAIN CONTROL-LING AREA • MAINTAIN CONTROLLING AREA

You will be presented with a list of all controlling areas, as shown in Figure 2.

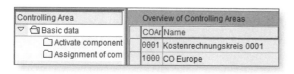

« *Figure 2*
Delete All Controlling Areas

Select a controlling area and click the Delete icon to delete a controlling area. You can't delete a controlling area with this transaction unless all master data, transaction data, and all other dependent data are deleted first.

OSS Note 34879 contains additional information on deleting controlling areas. ■

Open and Close Accounting Periods

You can restrict posting to accounting periods by company code, account type, general ledger account, and user.

Accounting postings are closed for previous periods so that management and legal reports do not change following period-end data analysis, correction, and management sign-off. You can adjust the posting dates allowed per company code for account types such as assets, customers, vendors, general ledger account ranges, and authorized users.

Let's look at how you open and close accounting periods.

Solution

You can open and close accounting periods with Transaction OB52 or by following menu path:

> ACCOUNTING • FINANCIAL ACCOUNTING • GENERAL LEDGER • ENVIRONMENT • CURRENT SETTINGS • OPEN AND CLOSE POSTING PERIODS

The screen shown in Figure 1 is displayed.

Var.	A	From acct	To account	From per.1	Year	To period	Year	From per.2	Year	To period	Year	AuGr
0002	+			3	2011	3	2011					

⌃ *Figure 1 Open and Close Accounting Periods by Company Code*

The first column, VAR. (posting period variant), corresponds to a company code or group of company codes. You must enter at least one company code or group of company codes as a prerequisite for any financial postings. This row must have a + sign (meaning all account types) in column A.

To restrict postings by account type, click the New Entries button to display the screen shown in Figure 2.

Var.	A	A	Short Descript.		Year	To period	Year	From per.2	Year	To period	Year	AuGr
0002	+	+	Valid for all account types		2011	3	2011					
0002	A	A	Assets		2011	3	2011					
0002	D	D	Customers		2011	3	2011					
0002	K	K	Vendors		2011	3	2011					
0002	M	M	Materials		2011	3	2011					
0002	S	S	G/L accounts		2011	3	2011					

⌃ *Figure 2* Open and Close Accounting Periods by Account Type

Left-click a cell in column A (account type), right-click and select POSSIBLE ENTRIES to display the list in Figure 2. To allow manual postings, leave S G/L ACCOUNTS open to the previous period. You can streamline this setting with authorization groups, which we'll cover next.

In Figure 1, there are two posting intervals:

▶ **Interval 1:** FROM PER.1 posting periods indicate the first (FROM PER.1) and last (TO PERIOD) posting periods allowed. If you are using authorization groups, they refer to this interval.

▶ **Interval 2:** FROM PER.2 posting periods are required if you're using authorization groups (last column). Interval 1 posting periods are restricted to users with the authorization group in their user profile. Interval 2 posting periods are available to all users independent of authorization group.

To authorize select users to post manual correction entries in the previous period, make an entry in the AUGR (authorization group) field. The authorization group can only be entered in rows with account type + (second column in Figure 2). An entry in the authorization group field applies to Interval 1 posting periods. Only users with this authorization group in their user profile will be allowed to post to Interval 1 posting periods. All other users will be allowed to post to Interval 2 posting periods, as shown in Figure 3.

Var.	A	From acct	To account	From per.1	Year	To period	Year	From per.2	Year	To period	Year	AuGr
0002	+			2	2011	3	2011	3	2011	3	2011	0001
0002	A		ZZZZZZZZZZ	3	2011	3	2011	3	2011	3	2011	
0002	D		ZZZZZZZZZZ	3	2011	3	2011	3	2011	3	2011	
0002	K		ZZZZZZZZZZ	3	2011	3	2011	3	2011	3	2011	
0002	M		ZZZZZZZZZZ	3	2011	3	2011	3	2011	3	2011	
0002	S		ZZZZZZZZZZ	2	2011	3	2011	3	2011	3	2011	

⌃ *Figure 3* Open and Close Accounting Periods by Authorization Group

In this example, period 2, fiscal year 2011, is available for Postings only to users in authorization group 0001. All users can post to period 3, fiscal year 2011. OSS Note 1483900 contains details of running Transaction OB52. ◾

Tip 87 Controlling Period Lock

You can use the period lock to lock planned and actual transactions for a combination of controlling area, fiscal year, and version.

The Controlling (CO) period lock lets you lock CO transactions that could otherwise cause inconsistencies in reporting CO data across periods. Closing Financial Accounting (FI) and Materials Management (MM) periods prevents financial and inventory postings in closed periods to keep legal and management reporting consistent.

In addition, there are CO transactions that occur independent of FI and MM period controls. Running these transactions after period-end can cause inconsistencies between CO and FI and MM data.

Let's look at how to lock CO transactions.

Solution

You can lock CO business transactions with Transaction OKP1 or via the following menu path:

> ACCOUNTING • CONTROLLING • COST CENTER ACCOUNTING • ENVIRONMENT • PERIOD LOCK • CHANGE

Type in the CO area, fiscal year, and version, and click either the Actual or Plan button to display the screen in Figure 1.

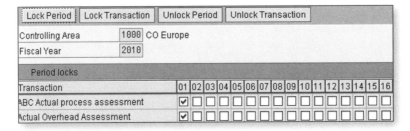

⌃ *Figure 1 CO Period Lock*

You can lock all 39 listed transactions by selecting a PERIOD column and clicking the LOCK PERIOD button. You can lock a transaction for all periods by clicking the TRANSACTION and the LOCK TRANSACTION button. You normally lock CO transactions as part of the accounting period-close process.

An example of a commonly used CO Transaction that requires a PERIOD LOCK is VARIANCE CALCULATION, as shown in Figure 2.

⌃ *Figure 2 Variance Calculation CO Period Lock*

You typically run the VARIANCE CALCULATION and settlement during period-end processing. If you run the variance calculation after final settlement, it may no longer reconcile with the variance posted during settlement to FI and Profitability Analysis.

You need to unlock CO periods if you reverse settlements to make corrections in prior periods. To recalculate a variance, unlock the period, calculate the variance, and then lock the period again.

When setting the deletion flag status for product cost collectors, you need to make sure the period lock is set for all periods in which transactions occurred for production orders attached to the product cost collector.

You can cut off results analysis and work in process by period with Transaction OKG2 or KKA0. The results analysis and work in process calculation data of all previous periods up to and including the cutoff period cannot be changed. OSS Note 190816 contains instructions for setting the cutoff period up to and including Release 4.6B.

By implementing OSS Note 1457107, you can run report RKCOOKP1 and set period locks in the background for several fiscal years in the future if needed. ▪

Closing Materials Management Periods

You close Materials Management each period-end to determine stock balances and valuation data.

Just as you close accounting periods each period-end, you also need to close Materials Management (MM) periods. Stocks and certain valuation data, such as total value, total stock, valuation class, price control indicator, and price unit, are managed by period. In order for values and goods movements to be posted to the correct MM period, the period must be set when a new period starts.

Let's look at how to close an MM period.

✓ Solution

Before closing an MM period you need to determine which period is open. You can determine this with Transaction MMRV or via the following menu path:

> LOGISTICS • MATERIALS MANAGEMENT • MATERIAL MASTER • OTHER • ALLOW POSTING TO PREVIOUS PERIOD

Type in the COMPANY CODE and press ⌷Enter⌷ to display the screen in Figure 1.

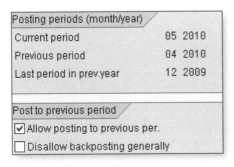

« *Figure 1*
Display MM Current Period

Because the CURRENT PERIOD is 05 2010 in this example, you need to enter the next period, 06 2010, with Transaction MMPV or via the following menu path:

LOGISTICS • MATERIALS MANAGEMENT • MATERIAL MASTER • OTHER • CLOSE PERIOD

The screen shown in Figure 2 is displayed.

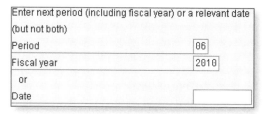

« **Figure 2**
Close Period for MM Records

Type in the next MM PERIOD and FISCAL YEAR, and click the Execute icon to display the screen shown in Figure 3.

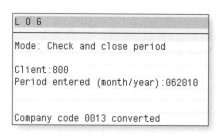

« **Figure 3**
Log Screen Indicating Successful Period Close

When you close an MM period, you normally allow postings to previous periods for several days to allow analysis and correction postings. You can then disable postings to the previous period by deselecting the corresponding checkbox in Figure 1, so the data doesn't change after accounting and controlling reports are run and saved for analysis by management.

You can run batch jobs to automatically close MM periods and also deselect the ALLOW POSTINGS to previous period checkbox. To set up the batch jobs run Transactions MMPV and MMRV and select PROGRAM • EXECUTE IN BACKGROUND from the menu bar. ▉

Add Object Services to Sales Orders

You can attach files to many different documents with object services.

Object services allow you to attach files to documents. These documents include, but are not limited to, the following:

▸ **Purchasing:** Requisition orders, purchasing info records, vendors

▸ **Sales:** Orders, invoices, deliveries, customers, credit management

▸ **Production:** Orders, process orders, work centers, material masters

▸ **Quality:** Inspection lots, equipment, notifications

Let's look at how to activate object services for sales orders and then we'll attach files to the documents listed previously.

Solution

Since SAP R/3 Release 4.7, object services for sales orders are deactivated in the standard system for performance reasons. Object services for sales orders can be reactivated through a setting in your user profile.

You can change your user profile with Transaction SU3 or via the following menu path:

> SYSTEM • USER PROFILE • OWN DATA

Select the PARAMETERS tab to display the screen shown in Figure 1.

Parameter ID	Parameter value	Short Description
SD_SWU_ACTIVE	X	Activate Workflow Box in VA02 & VA03

《 Figure 1
User Profile Parameter ID

Type in Parameter ID SD_SWU_ACTIVE, PARAMETER VALUE X, press Enter, and click the Save icon. Now when you display or edit a sales order, you can access object services. It can be particularly useful to attach documents, such as customer sales contracts, directly to sales orders in the system.

You can display a sales order with Transaction VA03 or via the following menu path:

LOGISTICS • SALES AND DISTRIBUTION • SALES • ORDER • DISPLAY

Click the down-pointing arrow to the right of the Object services icon to display the screen shown in Figure 2.

《 *Figure 2*

Object Services Drop-Down List for Sales Order

The OBJECT SERVICES icon now appears in the top-left corner. The same icon is available by default in all of the other documents listed at the beginning of this tip.

To add files to a sales order, select CREATE ATTACHMENT in Figure 2. After you've attached at least one document, the ATTACHMENT LIST menu item becomes selectable as shown in Figure 3.

《 *Figure 3*

Object Services Selectable Attachment List

Select ATTACHMENT LIST to display the screen shown in Figure 4.

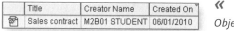

《 *Figure 4*

Object Services Attachment List

Double-click a line to open the attached document. You can find out more information on object services and sales orders from OSS Note 598073. ◾

Tip 90

Implementation Guide Shortcuts

You can use one of three ways to quickly access implementation guide transactions.

The Implementation Guide (IMG) contains thousands of possible menu paths. There are three ways to quickly locate a transaction instead of manually expanding each node:

▶ Run the IMG transaction directly

▶ Search for the IMG transaction text

▶ Navigate to the IMG transaction from technical help

Let's examine each of these IMG navigation shortcuts in detail.

 Solution

Running an IMG transaction directly is not straightforward, because the transaction is sometimes displayed as SPRO instead of the actual transaction. Let's look at an example of defining costing sheets via the following IMG menu path:

> CONTROLLING • PRODUCT COST CONTROLLING • PRODUCT COST PLANNING • BASIC SETTINGS FOR MATERIAL COSTING • OVERHEAD • DEFINE COSTING SHEETS

Choose SYSTEM • STATUS from the menu bar to display the screen shown in Figure 1.

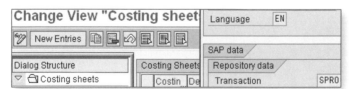

《 Figure 1
Define Costing Sheets IMG Transaction

Transaction SPRO, indicated in the Status dialog box, displays the entire IMG. To discover the actual transaction to define costing sheets chose ADDITIONAL INFORMATION • ADDITIONAL INFORMATION • DISPLAY KEY • IMG ACTIVITY from the IMG menu bar.

The screen shown in Figure 2 is displayed.

« Figure 2

IMG Menu Path with Transaction Code

Running Transaction KZS2, shown in Figure 2, allows you to DEFINE COSTING SHEETS. You can add this transaction to your favorites on the main application screen.

The second option for finding IMG transactions quickly is to click on the Binocular icon at the top of the IMG screen and search for text, such as Costing Sheets.

The third option is with technical help. For example, run Transaction KKAT to display the work in process (WIP) selection screen. Right-click the RA (results analysis) VERSION field and select HELP to display the PERFORMANCE ASSISTANT dialog box shown in Figure 3.

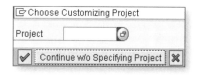

« Figure 3

Technical Help Screen with Customizing Icon

Click the highlighted customizing icon to display the CHOOSE CUSTOMIZING PROJECT dialog box shown in Figure 4.

« Figure 4

Choose Customizing Project Dialog Box

Click the CONTINUE W/O SPECIFYING PROJECT button to display a short list of possible IMG activities. Double-click each activity in turn until you find the correct results analysis IMG transaction. ■

Part 9

Information System

Things You'll Learn in this Section

There is an array of standard reports available to analyze controlling costs. The reporting menu path mirrors the menu path of the system component being reported on. There are three high-level reporting areas within controlling:

▸ Product Cost Planning

▸ Cost Object Controlling

▸ Actual Costing / Material Ledger

Within each component you will find the same menu path structure based on the following report categories:

▸ **Summarized Analysis:** These reports are based on structured hierarchies with data transferred from orders to top-level reporting nodes. You first need to run a data collection program before running the report for recent information. You can, for example, display all manufacturing costs and variances for a plant, and then expand the reporting hierarchy to view lower-level details on individual orders and source documents.

▸ **Object List:** In this report category you generate lists of orders with selection criteria, for example, order type or plant. You can expand the initial order selection screen, which has only a couple of selection fields, to display several screens of selection fields. Orders are listed in rows in the results screen, with key figures appearing as columns.

▸ **Detailed Reports:** Detailed reports contain cost element level data for individual orders. This is most useful if you know the manufacturing order number or product cost collector material number. Detailed reports are useful during variance analysis because they provide cost element details by row, and target, actual, and variance by column. The cost element rows can be grouped together by similar business transactions, such as confirmations, goods issues, and goods receipts.

▸ **Object Comparisons:** You can compare, for example, two different cost estimates or two different manufacturing orders.

▸ **More Reports:** This category includes other reports not assigned to any other category such as line item reports.

This part of the book provides you with techniques to leverage standard reporting.

In this section of the book, you will find techniques to leverage standard reporting.

Tip 91 Line Item Reports

Line item reports let you make a detailed analysis of values posted by posting date.

You often drill down to line item reports for an individual object from summarized analysis and detailed reports. This is useful because there can be a lot of line items. Just as summarization reports group production orders together by characteristics for management reporting, detailed reports group line items together by cost element. Analyzing a detailed report for a production order and drilling down on the cost element with the largest variance is a more efficient method of variance analysis than searching through a lot of line items directly. However, if you are in a situation where you need to display line items directly, the procedure is as follows.

✓ Solution

You can display line item reports with Transaction KOB1 or via the following menu path:

> ACCOUNTING • CONTROLLING • PRODUCT COST CONTROLLING • COST OBJECT CONTROLLING • PRODUCT COST BY ORDER • INFORMATION SYSTEM • REPORTS FOR PRODUCT COST BY ORDER • LINE ITEMS • ACTUAL

A selection screen is displayed as shown in Figure 1.

⌃ Figure 1 Line Item Report Selection Screen

When displaying line items directly, it's important to restrict the posting date range sufficiently to avoid long runtimes, because there can be large numbers of line items. It's usually best to tightly restrict the posting date range initially, and then gradually expand it, if required.

Complete the fields and Execute to display the screen shown in Figure 2.

Document Number	Cost Element	Cost element name	Val.in rep.cur.	Quantity
200178173	890000	Cons.semifin.product	885.30	10
200178173	890000	Cons.semifin.product	468.30	10

☆ *Figure 2 Actual Cost Line Items for Orders*

You typically sort line item lists by VAL.IN REP.CUR. (value in reporting currency) or QUANTITY and analyze the lines with the largest and smallest values by double-clicking to the source documents, such as:

▶ **Confirmation line items:** Source documents are activity confirmations

▶ **Inventory movement line items:** Source documents are material documents

You can access the source documents by either double-clicking the line items shown in Figure 2, or by selecting ENVIRONMENT • SOURCE DOCUMENT from the menu bar as shown in Figure 3.

☆ *Figure 3 Line Item Menu Bar Source Document*

For production orders, you can navigate directly to the accounting documents by selecting ENVIRONMENT • ACCOUNTING DOCUMENTS from the menu bar. You can also select ENVIRONMENT • RELATIONSHIP BROWSER from the menu bar to display linked documents, as shown in Figure 4.

▽ Controlling Document	1000 0900061219
▽ Prod. order conf.	0000109090 00000001
▷ Production order	000060003748
Accounting document	1000 0100000089 2010
Profit Center Doc.	1000 0000397622 2010 A

☆ *Figure 4 Document Relationship Browser*

Double-click any line to navigate to the original document. ∎

Tip 92 Detailed Reports

You can use detailed reports to provide analysis by cost element.

If you use summarized analyses, you'll often drill down to detailed reports. You can also display detailed reports directly from the material or manufacturing order to be analyzed. You typically run a detailed report directly if you identify a material with large variances during variance analysis. Because you can't drill down to line item details from the variance calculation output screen, you need to take note of the material number and run the detailed report to drill down to line item reports and source documents.

Detailed reports are useful during variance analysis because they provide cost element details by row, and target, actual, and variance details by column for an individual product cost collector or manufacturing order. You can display the costs for one or more periods, or cumulatively (all periods). The cost element rows can be grouped together by similar business transactions, such as confirmations, goods issues, and goods receipts.

This style of report is particularly useful when analyzing variance for an order. You search for the cost element with the largest variance and drill down to the line item details by double-clicking the line. You then sort the line item list and double-click the line item with the largest value to display the source document. The source document contains all of the information needed to find the cause of the largest variances.

Solution

You can display and analyze target versus actual costs in detailed production order reports with Transaction KKBC_ORD or via the following menu path:

> ACCOUNTING • CONTROLLING • PRODUCT COST CONTROLLING • COST OBJECT CONTROLLING • PRODUCT COST BY ORDER • INFORMATION SYSTEM • REPORTS FOR PRODUCT COST BY ORDER • DETAILED REPORTS • FOR ORDERS

A selection screen is displayed as shown in Figure 1.

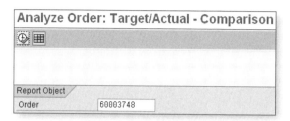

Analyze Order: Target/Actual - Comparison

Report Object
| Order | 60003748 |

« *Figure 1*

Analyze Order Selection Screen

You can display the costs for one period, a range of periods, or all periods. Complete the fields and Execute to display the screen shown in Figure 2.

BusTran.	Origin	Origin (Text)	Σ Total tgt	Σ Ttl actual
Confirmations	1650/RUN	Sewing / Run Time	4,706.44	15,127.19
	1650/SET	Sewing / Set Time	47.41	218.71
	1650/REW...	Sewing / Rework	0.00	14.41
	1660/RUN	Painting / Run Time	46.02	0.00
	1660/SET	Painting / Set Time	15.34	0.00

« *Figure 2*

Analyze Order Result Screen

This is a detailed report with cost elements as rows and TOTAL TGT (Total target) and TTL ACTUAL (Total actual) as columns. Sort a column in descending order and double-click the row containing the largest value to display the line item details, as shown in Figure 3.

Cost Elem.	CElem.name	Σ Val.in RC	Quantity	PUM	Off.acct	Offst.acct
690010	Labour	266.60	449.717	MIN		
690010	Labour	266.31	449.233	MIN		
690010	Labour	266.21	449.050	MIN		
690010	Labour	265.49	447.833	MIN		
690010	Labour	264.85	446.750	MIN		
690010	Labour	264.75	446.600	MIN		

« *Figure 3*

Confirmation Line Items

The QUANTITY column is sorted in descending order. This highlights confirmations with the largest time bookings. By double-clicking a line you can drill down to individual activity confirmations and analyze the reasons for confirmations with the largest QUANTITY. ■

Order Summarization

Order summarization hierarchies allow you to set up and display your own summarized view of manufacturing data.

Order summarization reports are a standard tool for reporting on an overview of manufacturing costs. While product drill-down reports offer summarized reporting based on a system-supplied hierarchy, summarized reports give you the flexibility to create your own reporting hierarchies.

A summarization hierarchy groups together manufacturing orders or product cost collectors at the lowest level summarization nodes, which in turn are grouped together at higher level nodes, to create a pyramid structure. Let's look at how you can create and report on your own summarization hierarchies.

  Solution

You can maintain summarization hierarchies with Transaction KKR0 or via the following menu path:

> ACCOUNTING • CONTROLLING • PRODUCT COST CONTROLLING • COST OBJECT CONTROLLING • PRODUCT COST BY ORDER • INFORMATION SYSTEM • TOOLS • SUMMARIZED ANALYSIS: PREPARATION • CREATE SUMMARIZATION HIERARCHY

Click the New Entries button, enter the name and description of your hierarchy, and double-click the text Data scope to display the screen in Figure 1.

Summarization hierarchy			
▽ 🗀 Summarization hierarchy	Z001	Internal Orders	☐
🗀 Data scope (object types)	Z001	Maintenance/Service Orders	☐
🗀 Data Scope (Totals Records Tables)	Z001	Prod. Orders, QM Orders, Prod. Cost Coll	☑
🗀 Hierarchy levels	Z001	Projects	☐

⌃ *Figure 1 Change Data Scope Object Types Overview*

Select the checkbox next to the order type you'd like to summarize, double-click HIERARCHY LEVELS on the left, and click the New Entries button to display the screen in Figure 2.

Hierarchy	Level	Hierarchy Field	Name	Tot. length
Z001	2	WERKS	Plant	4
Z001	3	AUART	Order Type	4

⋩ *Figure 2* *Change Hierarchy Levels Overview*

In this screen, you can specify the summarization HIERARCHY FIELDS. Once you've defined your hierarchy, the next step is to carry out data collection with Transaction KKRC or via the following menu path:

ACCOUNTING • CONTROLLING • PRODUCT COST CONTROLLING • COST OBJECT CONTROLLING • PRODUCT COST BY ORDER • INFORMATION SYSTEM • TOOLS • DATA COLLECTION

The screen shown in Figure 3 is displayed.

Parameters			
◉ Summarization run			
From Fiscal Year	2011	From Period	001
To Fiscal Year	2011	To Period	002

⋩ *Figure 3* *Data Collection for Summarization Reports*

You normally run data collection following period-end closing for the current and previous period, because data on orders can change within open financial periods. If data collection has already been run, the system resets and recalculates all data within the summarization time frame of the new data collection run. Data outside the time frame is retained. Execute and a data collection results screen appears indicating the number of records read.

Following the data collection you can run summarization reports with Transaction KKBC_HOE or via the following menu path:

ACCOUNTING • CONTROLLING • PRODUCT COST CONTROLLING • COST OBJECT CONTROLLING • PRODUCT COST BY ORDER • INFORMATION SYSTEM • REPORTS FOR PRODUCT COST BY ORDER • SUMMARIZED ANALYSIS • WITH DEFINED SUM-MARIZATION HIERARCHY

You can run the report with a wide period range, or you can restrict the period range if you only need to report on one period. ▪

Tip 94 Variance Analysis in Prior Periods

You can display variance analysis for prior periods with drill-down reports without unlocking variance calculation.

Variance analysis in the current or previous period is a standard period-end procedure. After period-end processing is finished you can lock period-end transactions for prior periods so the data cannot be changed after it is reported to management. While you can display work in process results for previous periods, you do not have this option for variance calculation.

Let's first look at how to lock and unlock transactions for previous periods, and then investigate an option for displaying variance analysis for previous periods without unlocking variance calculation.

Solution

You can close financial accounting periods with Transaction OB52 and material master periods with Transaction MMPV. You also have a third option to close controlling periods with Transaction OKP1 or by following menu path:

> ACCOUNTING • CONTROLLING • COST CENTER ACCOUNTING • ENVIRONMENT • PERIOD LOCK • CHANGE

Type in the controlling area and fiscal year, click the Actual button and scroll down to display the screen shown in Figure 1.

Transaction	01	02	03	04	05	06
Variance calculation		✓	✓	✓	☐	☐	☐

« *Figure 1*
Controlling Period Lock Screen

The first couple of days of period 04, and following completion of period-end processing, period 03 transactions including VARIANCE CALCULATION should be locked. This prevents you from carrying out variance analysis in previous periods. You have two options to analyze production variances in prior periods:

▶ Remove the controlling period lock, carry out variance analysis in the prior period and then replace the controlling period lock. Data may change.

▶ Carry out data collection to gather historical information and run product drill-down variance analysis reports on prior periods.

Product drilldown reports access data which you first populate during a data collection run. You run data collection for product drilldown reports with Transaction KKRV or by following menu path (which brings you to Figure 2):

> ACCOUNTING • CONTROLLING • PRODUCT COST CONTROLLING • COST OBJECT CONTROLLING • PRODUCT COST BY PERIOD • INFORMATION SYSTEM • TOOLS • DATA COLLECTION • FOR PRODUCT DRILLDOWN

| From Fiscal Yr | 2011 | From Period | 3 |
| To Fiscal Year | 2011 | To Period | 4 |

☐ Delete Values Outside Time Period

《 Figure 2
Data Collection for Product Drilldown Reports

You normally run data collection following period-end closing for the current and previous period, since data on orders can change within open periods. The system resets and recalculates all data. Data outside the time frame is retained, unless you select the DELETE VALUES OUTSIDE TIME PERIOD checkbox.

Complete the fields and click the Execute icon.

Following data collection, you can run product drilldown reports with Transaction S_ALR_87013139 or by following the menu path:

> ACCOUNTING • CONTROLLING • PRODUCT COST CONTROLLING • COST OBJECT CONTROLLING • PRODUCT COST BY PERIOD • INFORMATION SYSTEM • REPORTS FOR PRODUCT COST BY PERIOD • SUMMARIZED ANALYSIS • WITH PRODUCT DRILLDOWN • VARIANCE ANALYSIS • VARIANCE CATEGORIES • PERIODIC

Type in selection data and execute to display the report shown in Figure 3.

Navigation	Material		InpPrcVar.--April 2010	Qty var.--April 2010	ResUsgVar--April 2010
Material	MBCS10 SEAT TR...		7,467.63	1,638.22-	0.00
Cost Component	MBCS10 SEAT G...		0.00	0.00	32.73-
Product group	MBCS10 FABRIC S..		7,312.59-	9,092.94-	0.00

≪ Figure 3 *Product Drilldown Report Results Screen*

Each line represents a material and the columns variance categories. Scroll to the right to display the eight variance categories as columns for each period. ■

Tip 95 Origin Groups Provide Detailed Reporting

Origin groups can provide you with a more detailed level of cost component reporting than cost elements.

Cost components group similar cost types together by cost element. Typical examples of cost components are materials, labor, and overhead. You usually choose the simplest possible cost component solution to achieve your required level of reporting detail.

Sometimes you need cost components at a more detailed level than what can be provided by cost elements. For example, you may have one cost element indentifying raw materials. In the pharmaceutical industry, an active pharmaceutical ingredient (API) is the substance in a drug that is pharmaceutically active and by far the highest cost ingredient. To report this component separately from inactive raw materials, you can create a corresponding origin group, assign the origin group to its own cost component, and populate relevant material masters with the origin group. Let's follow an example to demonstrate how this works.

 Solution

You can create an origin group with Transaction OKZ1 or via the following IMG menu path:

> CONTROLLING • PRODUCT COST CONTROLLING • PRODUCT COST PLANNING • BASIC SETTINGS FOR MATERIAL COSTING • DEFINE ORIGIN GROUPS

Enter the controlling area in the pop-up dialog box, press [Enter], and then click the New Entries button to display the screen shown in Figure 1.

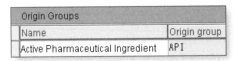

Origin Groups	
Name	Origin group
Active Pharmaceutical Ingredient	API

⌃ *Figure 1 Create Origin Group Screen*

Type in the NAME and key of the new ORIGIN GROUP and click the Save icon.

The next step is to assign the origin group to its own cost component. You can access cost component structure settings with Transaction OKTZ or via the following IMG menu path:

CONTROLLING • PRODUCT COST CONTROLLING • PRODUCT COST PLANNING • BASIC SETTINGS FOR MATERIAL COSTING • DEFINE COST COMPONENT STRUCTURE

Unselect the ACTIVE checkbox, select the relevant cost component structure, and double-click on the COST COMPONENTS WITH ATTRIBUTES folder on the left to display the screen shown in Figure 2.

Dialog Structure	Cost Comp. Str.	Cost Component	Name of Cost Comp.
▽ ☐ Cost Component Structure	01	10	Raw Materials
▽ ☐ Cost Components with Attributes	01	20	Purchased Parts
☐ Assignment: Cost Component - Cost Element Interval	01	25	Freight Costs

New Entries

Figure 2 *Cost Components with Attributes Overview*

This overview screen lists current cost components on the right. You need to create a new cost component for API materials so that you can report them separately to RAW MATERIALS. To create a new cost component for API materials, click the NEW ENTRIES button; type in the cost component structure, cost component, and description; double-click ASSIGNMENT: COST COMPONENT - COST ELEMENT INTERVAL at the left, and click the NEW ENTRIES button to display the screen shown in Figure 3.

Cost Comp. Str.	Chart of Accts	From cost el.	Origin group	To cost elem.	Cost Component	Name of Cost Comp.
01	INT	400000	API	410000	15	API

Figure 3 *Create New Cost Component — Including Origin Group*

Type in the details of the new API cost component, press ⌷Enter⌷, double-click COST COMPONENT STRUCTURE on the left (shown in Figure 2), reactivate the cost component structure, and save your work.

The next step is to populate origin group API in the Costing 2 view of all API materials. You can do this with mass processing Transaction MM17 for table MBEW and field HRKFT. The last step is to create a costing run that will populate the new cost component in all new cost estimates for API materials. ▪

Tip 96

Cost Component Groups Improve Reporting

You can add cost components to standard cost estimate list and multilevel costed bill of material (BOM) reports with cost component groups.

Cost components are not available as columns in standard cost estimate list reports. Cost components available as columns can be useful when analyzing production or purchasing performance across a range of products. You can add cost components to standard cost estimate list reports and costed multilevel BOM reports by creating cost component groups and assigning them to cost components.

 Solution

You first need to create cost component groups, assign them to existing cost components, and then add the columns to layouts in reports. You create cost component groups with Transaction OKTZ or via the following IMG menu path:

> CONTROLLING • PRODUCT COST CONTROLLING • PRODUCT COST PLANNING • BASIC SETTINGS FOR MATERIAL COSTING • DEFINE COST COMPONENT STRUCTURE

Double-click the COST COMPONENT GROUPS on the left, click the New Entries button, type in your COST COMPONENT GROUPS, and press ⎡Enter⎤ to display the screen shown in Figure 1.

It's easier to follow the order of the cost component groups listed if you create all of your cost component groups with two digits. In Figure 1, COST COMPONENT GROUPS 11 through 19 correspond to unique individual cost components. Cost component groups 21, 22, and 23 correspond to groups of cost components for summarized cost component reporting.

Dialog Structure
▽ ☐ Cost Component Structure
▽ ☐ Cost Components with Attributes
☐ Assignment: Cost Component -
☐ Update of Additive Costs
☐ Transfer Structure
☐ Cost Component Views
☐ Assignment: Organiz. Units - Cost Com
⌷ Cost Component Groups

Cost comp. grp	Name
11	Semi-finished goods
12	Set-Up
13	Labour
14	Machine
15	Component materials
16	Material Overhead
17	Labor Overhead
18	Quality Overhead
19	External Processing
21	Total Material
22	Total Labor
23	Total Overhead

⌃ **Figure 1** *Cost Component Groups Overview*

Now that you've created cost component groups, you need to assign them to cost components. To do this, double-click Cost Components with Attributes on the left, and then double-click the first cost component on the right. Enter the appropriate Cost Component Groups and press [Enter] to display the screen shown in 2.

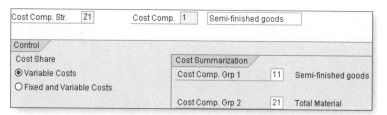

⌃ **Figure 2** *Cost Component Attribute Details — Cost Summarization*

In the Cost Summarization section, you can assign two cost component groups to each cost component. In this example, the second group is a summarization level, so you would add the Total Material group to all material cost components.

The final step for reporting on cost component groups is to assign cost component groups to report columns. Cost component groups can be added as columns in standard reports listing cost estimates, such as Transaction S_P99_41000111. Click on the Change Layout icon and move the required Cost Component columns from the right side of the screen to the left. Press [Enter] and the required cost components will appear in the cost estimate list report. ▪

Tip 97

Display a List of Product Cost Collectors

You can easily display a list of product cost collectors with a standard order selection transaction.

While you can easily display a list of production orders with Transaction COOIS and process orders with Transaction COOISPI, it is not so obvious as to how you can display product cost collectors. Let's look at how you easily display a list of product cost collectors.

✓ Solution

You can display a list of product cost collectors with Transaction S_ALR_87013127 or via the following menu path:

> ACCOUNTING • CONTROLLING • PRODUCT COST CONTROLLING • COST OBJECT CONTROLLING • PRODUCT COST BY PERIOD • INFORMATION SYSTEM • REPORTS FOR PRODUCT COST BY PERIOD • OBJECT LIST • ORDER SELECTION

The screen in Figure 1 is displayed.

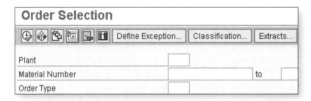

« *Figure 1*
Order Selection Initial Screen

There are many more selection fields available than shown in this first screen. Click the Plus sign icon to display all of the selection fields as shown in Figure 2.

Plant									
Material Number									
Order Type		**Order category**	**Short Descript.**						
Order		01	Internal Order (Controlling)						
External order no.		02	Accrual Calculation Order (Controlling)						
Description		03	Model Order (Controlling)						
Order category	05	04	CO Production Order						
		05	Product Cost Collector						

⌃ *Figure 2 Order Selection All Fields*

By selecting orders with ORDER CATEGORY 05, you restrict the results screen to PRODUCT COST COLLECTORS. You can further restrict the results screen by ORDER TYPE. After you enter ORDER CATEGORY 05, the possible entries for ORDER TYPE on this selection screen are restricted to order types for product cost collectors. You can then enter the order type in the first selection screen shown in Figure 1 without expanding the selection list, you can also save this as a variant.

Limiting the reporting time frame specifies the periods key figures can be read from, but does not affect the order selection.

Click the Execute icon to display the results screen shown in Figure 3.

Order	Material Number	Plan cost debit	Actual cost debit	Crcy	Plan qty	Actual qty	OUM
702626	R-F101	0.00	5,074.75	EUR	0	5	PC

⌃ *Figure 3 Order Selection Results List*

From this report you can:

▶ Display a product cost collector directly by clicking an ORDER and selecting EXTRAS • MASTER DATA from the menu bar

▶ Display a target/actual cost comparison report with cost element detail by double-clicking an ORDER number

▶ Continue drilling down through the cost element report to line item and source document details

You can also change the way the report displays by clicking the:

▶ Currency icon to change from controlling area to company code currency

▶ Time frame icon to change time periods of the displayed report

▶ Valuation view icon to display legal, group, and profit center valuation

▶ Valuation base icon to toggle between absolute and per unit value base

You can sort any of the columns in Figure 3 to help you with variance analysis. ▪

Tip 98 Display Data Directly with Data Browser

You can view data in tables directly with the Data Browser.

The Data Browser lets you access information in tables directly without writing a custom report. It's a powerful standard reporting tool for managers, power users, and consultants.

Two transactions are available for running the Data Browser. Transaction SE16N is a more recent version of Transaction SE16, and while it is more user friendly, both transactions work well. Let's look at each in turn.

✓ Solution

You can run the Data Browser with Transaction SE16 or via the following menu path:

TOOLS • ABAP WORKBENCH • OVERVIEW • DATA BROWSER

Type in the table name and press Enter to display the screen in Figure 1.

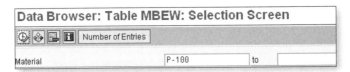

Data Browser: Table MBEW: Selection Screen

| Number of Entries |
| Material | P-100 | to |

⌃ *Figure 1 SE16 Selection Screen*

This selection screen allows you to enter parameters that restrict the data in the following results screen. Select SETTINGS • FIELDS FOR SELECTION from the menu bar to maintain the available selection fields.

Click the NUMBER OF ENTRIES button to display the number of entries that meet the selection criteria. Select SETTINGS • USER PARAMETERS from the menu bar to display the screen in Figure 2.

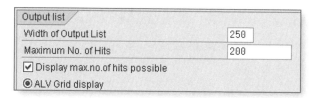

« *Figure 2*
SE16 User Parameters
Dialog Box

Select the ALV GRID DISPLAY radio button to display a user-friendly results screen with the ALV (ABAP List Viewer) grid. The WIDTH OF OUTPUT LIST field isn't relevant in this case because all possible columns are displayed.

The MAXIMUM NO. OF HITS field limits the number of rows displayed in the results screen. The system remembers your entry in this field unless it is blank. In this case, the next time you run the transaction it will default to 500.

You also need to ensure the Field Label radio button (not shown) is selected so the column headings are user-friendly descriptions and not technical names.

You can only run Transaction SE16N by transaction code. The screen in Figure 3 is displayed.

Selection Criteria						
Fld name	Option	Fr.Value	To value	More	Output	Technical name
Client						MANDT
Material	◈◈	P-100		⇨	✔	MATNR

« *Figure 3*
SE16N
Selection
Screen

This selection screen lists all of the possible selection fields by default. Select EXTRAS • CHANGE SETTINGS from the menu bar to display a list of user parameters with more options available than with Transaction SE16 in Figure 2. Type in your selection criteria and Execute to display the screen in Figure 4.

Material	ValA	Val. Type	VTy	Total Stock	Total Value	Pr.	MvAvgPrice	Std price	per	ValCl
P-100	1000			9,989.000	6,896,105.93	S	4,755.50	6,903.70	10	7920
P-100	1300			0.000	0.00	S	683.51	593.32	1	7920

⌃ *Figure 4 SE16N Results Screen*

The ALV grid is displayed by default. This screen lets you easily sort, filter, sum, subtotal, hide and move columns, and export data to Excel. You can find out more about ALV reports by selecting HELP • SAP LIBRARY from the menu bar of any screen and clicking GETTING STARTED – USING SAP SOFTWARE then WORKING WITH LISTS. OSS notes can improve the performance of SE16N. ▪

Drill-Down to Display Table Content

You can use the drill-down functionality to display table content for master data fields without having to start a separate session.

Most users know how to display table content by using field-specific help, accessing the Technical Information dialog box to obtain the table and field name, and then running the Data Browser with Transaction SE16N.

However, what you may not know is that you can drill down to display table content quickly without having to branch to a separate session. Instead, you can drill down to display table content in the same session, which we will discuss in the following example.

✓ Solution

To find table content, you usually first display the master data to determine the table and field names. For example, in the case of VALUATION CLASS, you can display the Costing 2 view of the material master with Transaction MM03 or via the following the menu path:

LOGISTICS • MATERIALS MANAGEMENT • MATERIAL MASTER • MATERIAL • DISPLAY • DISPLAY CURRENT

Left-click the VALUATION CLASS field and press the F1 key to display the help dialog box, shown in Figure 1.

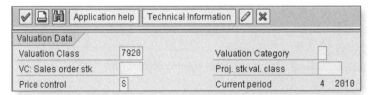

⌃ *Figure 1* *Field-Specific Help — Technical Information Button*

To find the table and field names for VALUATION CLASS, click the Technical Information button (or the fifth icon from the top left depending on your HELP • SETTINGS) to display the dialog box, shown in Figure 2.

Field Data	
Table Name	MBEW
Table category	Transparent table
Field Name	BKLAS
Data Element	BKLAS
DE Supplement	0

⌃   *Figure 2 Technical Information Dialog Box*

In this example, the TABLE NAME is MBEW and the FIELD NAME is BKLAS. To display the table content, you would typically run the Data Browser in a separate session with Transaction SE16N, type in the Table Name, press ⌑Enter⌑ to display a selection screen for certain fields in the table, and then click the Execute icon.

To display the table data without branching to another session, double-click the text in the TABLE NAME field (MBEW). You are then presented with the DATA DICTIONARY view, which defines the field length, type, and description of each field in the table. Select UTILITIES • TABLE CONTENTS from the menu bar in this view to directly display the DATA BROWSER field selection screen. You do not need to first enter the table name as you do when running Transaction SE16N on a separate screen. The table is already selected and you only have to select your required fields and click the Execute icon to display the table contents.

If you see DISPLAY STRUCTURE instead of DISPLAY TABLE when you double-click the TABLE NAME text field in Figure 2, then you can't select UTILITIES • TABLE CONTENT from the menu bar. Data in a structure is not stored in a table and is instead gathered temporarily for each transaction. In this case double-click DATA ELEMENT BKLAS in Figure 2 and click the where-used list icon to find the table. ■

Tip 100   Wildcard Search Options

Wildcard characters are available for you to restrict searches.

Wildcard characters give you flexibility when searching for data in tables. You can use * to replace any string of characters and + to replace any single character. Let's see how this works by looking at some examples.

Solution

You can run the Data Browser with Transaction SE16N or via the following menu path:

> TOOLS • ABAP WORKBENCH • OVERVIEW • DATA BROWSER

Type in table MARC and press `Enter` to display the screen in Figure 1.

Fld name	Option	Fr.Value	To value	More	Output	Technical name
Client						MANDT
Material	◈			⇨	☑	MATNR
Plant	◈	*		⇨	☑	WERKS

« Figure 1
Data Browser Selection Screen

Entering an asterisk symbol or leaving the field blank usually has the same result during wildcard searches. Type an asterisk in the PLANT field in Figure 1 to display the screen in Figure 2.

Material	Plant	Maint. status	Pl	ValCat
647	3100	L	X	
647	3200	L	X	
647	SG01	L	X	

« Figure 2
*Data Browser Results Screen with * as Plant*

The search lists all plants in the results screen. Now let's restrict the results screen by typing *00 in the PLANT field, to display the screen in Figure 3.

Material	Plant	Maint. status	PI	ValCat
647	3100	L	X	
647	3200	L	X	
648	1000	L		

« *Figure 3*

*Data Browser Results Screen with *00 as Plant*

The search has restricted the results screen to only those Plants ending in 00, excluding PLANT SG01. You can use the + sign as a wildcard for one character. Type +000 in the PLANT field and press ⌈Enter⌋ to display the screen in Figure 4.

Material	Plant	Maint. status	PI	ValCat
647	1000	L	X	
647	3000	L	X	
648	1000	L		

« *Figure 4*

Data Browser Results Screen with +000 as Plant

The search has restricted the results screen to only those Plants ending in 000, excluding plants 3100 and 3200 from the results.

You can see from these examples how wildcards can be useful in restricting the results screen to just the data you want to report on.

One common question is, how do you report on table entries that include the wildcard symbols? The answer is you insert the # symbol before the wildcard characters * and + to free them from their special function as wildcards. This is necessary if you want to find data records that contain the * or + characters as literals. You can also use the # escape character to free itself from its special function. It only affects the immediately subsequent special character. However, if the escape character is prefixed on a character that does not have a special function, for example, #A, it is ignored.

Another option available for restricting the results screen is to click the OPTION icon in Figure 1. A dialog box appears as shown in Figure 5.

=	Select: Equal to
][	Select: Exclude range
≠	Select: Not equal to

« *Figure 5*

Option Dialog Box

A list of 14 Boolean logic operators is available to restrict the data selection. ■

Glossary

Accrual Order An accrual order enables you to monitor period-related accrual calculation between expenses posted in financial accounting and controlling.

Active Pharmaceutical Ingredient An active pharmaceutical ingredient (API) is the substance in a drug that is pharmaceutically active, and is by far the highest cost ingredient in pharmaceutical products. One way to identify these costs is with a separate cost component by creating an API origin group and assigning it to API material masters with Transaction MM02, and an API cost component in the cost component structure with Transaction OKTZ.

Activity Based Costing While you typically allocate overhead costs during activity type confirmations or with costing sheets, templates offer an alternative with more flexibility. Although there is more complexity when setting up templates, they are set out logically and are worth considering as a flexible alternative for overhead costs.

Activity Input Planning Just as cost centers can provide planned output services based on activity quantities with Transaction KP26, you can plan cost center activity input quantities from other cost centers with activity input planning using Transaction KP06.

Activity Type An activity type identifies activities provided by a cost center to manufacturing orders. The secondary cost element associated with an activity type identifies the activity costs on cost center and detailed reports.

Actual Costing Actual costing determines what portion of the variance is debited

to the next-highest level using material consumption. All purchasing and manufacturing difference postings are allocated upward through the bill of material to assemblies and finished goods. Variances can be rolled up over multiple production levels to the finished product.

Actual Costs Actual costs debit a product cost collector or manufacturing order during business transactions such as general ledger account postings, inventory goods movements, internal activity allocations, and overhead calculation.

Additive Cost Estimate This is a material cost estimate in which you can enter costs manually in the form of a unit cost estimate (spreadsheet format) so that manual costs can be added to an automatic cost estimate with quantity structure.

Allocation Structure An allocation structure allocates the costs incurred on a sender by cost element or cost element group. The allocation structure is used for settlement and assessment. An assignment maps a source cost element group to a settlement cost element.

Alternative Bill of Material There can be multiple methods of manufacturing an assembly, and many possible bills of material (BOM). The alternative BOM allows you to identify one BOM in a BOM group.

Alternative Hierarchy While there can only be one cost center standard hierarchy, you can create as many alternative hierarchies as you like. You create an alternative hierarchy by creating cost center groups.

Alternative Unit of Measure This is a unit of measure defined in addition to the base unit of measure. Examples of alternative units of measure are order unit (purchasing), sales unit, and unit of issue.

Apportionment Method An apportionment method distributes the total costs of a joint production process to the primary products. The costs of the individual primary products may vary. They are apportioned by means of an apportionment structure.

Apportionment Structure An apportionment structure defines how costs are distributed to co-products. The system uses the apportionment structure to create a settlement rule that distributes costs from an order header to the co-products. For each co-product, the system generates a further settlement rule that assigns the costs distributed to the order item to stock.

Assembly Scrap Assembly scrap is the percentage of assembly quantity that does not meet required quality standards. The plan quantity of the assembly is increased. Assembly scrap is an output scrap, since it affects the planned output quantity of items in the production process. You plan assembly scrap in the MRP 1 view and the Net ID indicator in the basic data tab of a bill of material item.

Automatic Account Assignment Automatic account assignment allows you to enter a default cost center per cost element within a plant.

Auxiliary Cost Component Split Only the main cost component split can update the results of the standard cost estimate to the material master. A second cost component split, called the auxiliary cost component split, is used for statistical information purposes and can be used in parallel to the main cost component split.
You define an auxiliary cost component split by assigning cost component structures to organizational units with Transaction OKTZ.

Backflush Backflushing is the automatic posting of a goods issue for components after their actual physical issue for use in an order. The goods issue posting of backflushed components is carried out automatically during confirmation. Backflushing is used to reduce the amount of work in warehouse management, especially for low value parts. The material components from the BOM required in the operation should be assigned to the operations in the routing.

Base Quantity All component quantities in a BOM relate to the base quantity. You increase the accuracy of component quantities by increasing the base quantity, similar in concept to the price unit.

Base Planning Object This is a simple reference object that can be used for the development of new products before any master data exists.

Base Unit of Measure Material stocks are managed in the base unit of measure. The system converts all quantities you enter in other units of measure (alternative units of measure) to the base unit of measure.

Bill of Material A bill of material (BOM) is a structured hierarchy of components necessary to build an assembly. BOM's together with purchasing info records provide cost estimates with the information necessary to calculate material costs of assemblies.

BOM Application BOM application is a component within a costing variant representing a process for automatic determination of alternative BOMs in the organizational areas within a company.

BOM Item Component Quantity This is the quantity of a bill of material item which is entered in relation to the base quantity of the product.

BOM Item Status These six indicators, such as costing relevancy, are contained in the status/long text tab of a BOM item.

BOM Group A BOM group is a collection of bill of materials for a product or number of similar products.

BOM Status This controls the current processing status of the bill of material (BOM). For example, a BOM may have a default status of *not active* when initially created, which then may be changed to *active* when the BOM is available for use in material requirements planning and released for planned orders.

BOM Usage This determines a section of your company, such as production, engineering or costing. You can define which item statuses can be used in each BOM usage. For example, all items in BOMs with a certain usage may be relevant to production.

Bulk Material Bulk materials are not relevant for costing in a cost estimate and are expensed directly to a cost center. The bulk material indicator is maintained in the MRP 2 view, and also in the bill of material (BOM) item. If a material is always used as a bulk material set the indicator in the material master. If a material is only used as a bulk material in individual cases, set the indicator in the BOM item which has a higher priority.

Business Area A business area is an organizational unit of financial accounting that represents a separate area of operations or responsibilities within an organization. You can create financial statements for business areas and you can use these statements for internal reporting purposes.

Calculation Base A calculation base is a group of cost elements to which overhead is applied. The calculation base is a component of a costing sheet which summarizes the rules for allocating overhead.

Capacity Category Capacity category enables you to differentiate between machine and labor capacity. Machine capacity is the availability of a machine based on planned and unplanned outages and maintenance requirements. Labor capacity is the number of workers who can operate a machine at the same time.

Chart of Accounts A chart of accounts is a group of general ledger accounts and is assigned to each company code. This chart of accounts is the operative chart of accounts and is used in both financial and cost accounting. All companies within the one controlling area must have the same operative chart of accounts. Other charts of accounts include the country specific chart of accounts required by individual country legal requirements and the group chart of accounts required by consolidation reporting.

Co-Product You select the co-product indicator located in the MRP 2 and Costing 1 views if a material is a valuated product that is produced simultaneously with one or more other products. Setting this indicator allows you to assign the proportion of costs this material will receive in relation to other co-products within an apportionment structure.

Company Code A company code is the smallest organizational unit of financial accounting for which a complete self-contained chart of accounts can be drawn up for external reporting.

Component Scrap Component scrap is the percentage of component quantity that does not meet required quality standards before being inserted in the production process. The plan quantity of components is increased. Component scrap is an input scrap, since it is detected before use in the production process. You can plan component scrap in the MRP 4 view and the basic data tab of the bill of material (BOM) item. An entry in the BOM item field takes priority over an entry in the material master MRP 4 view.

Condition Conditions are stipulations agreed with vendors such as prices, discounts, surcharges, freight, duty and insurance. You maintain purchasing conditions in quotations, purchasing info records, outline agreements and purchase orders.

Condition Type A condition type is a key that identifies a condition. The condition type indicates, for example, whether during pricing the system applies a price, a discount, a surcharge, or other pricing such as freight costs and sales taxes.

Confirmation A confirmation documents the processing status of orders, operations and individual capacities. With a confirmation you specify the operation yield, scrap and rework quantity produced, the activity quantity consumed, work center, and who carried out the operation.

Consignment Material Consignment is a form of business in which a vendor maintains a stock of materials at a customer site. The vendor retains ownership of the materials until they are withdrawn from the consignment stores.

Controlling Level The controlling level determines the level of detail of procurement alternatives. The standard setting of controlling level is determined by the characteristics material/plant. You specify which characteristics are updated for the production process by the controlling level.

Currency Type This identifies the role of the currency such as local or global.

Current Cost Estimate A current cost estimate is based on the current quantity structure and current prices, and is used for the costing of materials during the fiscal year to analyze cost changes and developments.

Cost Component A cost component identifies costs of similar types, such as material, labor and overhead by grouping together cost elements in the cost component structure.

Cost Component Group Cost component groups allow you to display cost components in standard cost estimate list reports. In the simplest implementation you create a cost component group for each cost component, and assign each group to each corresponding cost component. You can assign cost component groups as columns in cost estimate list reports and costed multilevel BOMs.

Cost Component Split The cost component split is the combination of cost components that makes up the total cost of a material. For example if you need to view three cost components (material, labor and overhead) for your reporting requirements, the combination of these three cost components represents the cost component split.

Cost Component Structure You define which cost components make up a cost component split by assigning them to a cost component structure. Within the cost component structure you also assign cost elements and origin groups to cost components.

Cost Component View Each cost component is assigned to a cost component view. When you display a cost estimate you can choose a cost component view which filters the cost components you see in the cost estimate.

Cost Center A cost center is master data which identifies *where* the cost occurred. A responsible person is assigned to the cost center that analyzes and explains cost center variances at period-end.

Cost Element A cost element is master data which identifies *what* the cost is. Primary cost elements correspond to financial accounting general ledger accounts, and identify external costs. Secondary cost elements identify costs allocated within Controlling, such as activity allocations from cost centers to manufacturing orders.

Cost Estimate   A cost estimate calculates the plan cost to manufacture a product or purchase a component. It determines material costs by multiplying bill of material quantities by the standard price, labor costs by multiplying operation standard quantities by plan activity price, and overhead by costing sheet configuration.

Costed Multilevel BOM   A hierarchical overview of the values of all items of a costed material according to the material's costed quantity structure (BOM and routing). A costed multilevel BOM is displayed on the left when you view a cost estimate. You can also display a costed multilevel BOM directly with Transaction CK86_99.

Costing BOM   Costing BOMs are assigned a BOM usage of costing and are usually copied from BOMs with a usage of Production at the start of each fiscal year before the main costing run. You can make adjustments to Costing BOMs if you require them to be different from Production BOMs. With system supplied settings standard cost estimates search for costing BOMs before production BOMs.

Costing Lot Size   The costing lot size in the Costing 1 view determines the quantity cost estimate calculations are based on. The costing lot size should be set as close as possible to actual purchase and production quantities to reduce lot size variance.

Costing Run   A costing run is a collective processing of cost estimates. You create and maintain costing runs with transaction CK40N.

Costing Sheet   A costing sheet summarizes the rules for allocating overhead from cost centers to cost estimates, product cost collectors and manufacturing orders. The

components of a costing sheet include the calculation base (group of cost elements), overhead rate (percentage rate applied to base), and credit key (cost center receiving credit).

Costing Type   The costing type is a component of the costing variant, and determines if the cost estimate is able to update the standard price in the material master.

Costing Variant   The costing variant contains information on how a cost estimate calculates the standard price. For example, it determines if the purchasing info record price is used for purchased materials, or an estimated price manually entered in the Planned price 1 field of the material master Costing 2 view.

Demand Management   This involves the planning of requirement quantities and dates for assemblies and definition of the strategy for planning and producing or procuring a finished product.

Demand Planning   Demand planning is a component in advanced planner and optimizer (APO) that allows you to forecast market demand for a company's products and produce a demand plan. APO supply network planning (SNP) can be integrated with planning modules in SAP such as sales and operations planning (SOP).

Dependent Requirements   Dependent requirements are planned material requirements caused by higher-level dependent and independent requirements when running material requirements planning. Independent requirements, generally created by sales orders or manually planned independent requirement entries in demand management, determine lower-level dependent material requirements.

Detailed Reports   Detailed reports display cost element details of manufacturing orders and product cost collectors. You can drill-down on cost elements to display line item reports during variance analysis.

Distribution Rule You maintain distribution rules in settlement rules in cost objects such as manufacturing orders and product cost collectors.

Environment Environments determine the columns available in the template.

External Processing External processing of a manufacturing order operation is performed by an external vendor. This is distinct from subcontracting which involves sending material parts to an external vendor who manufactures the complete assembly via a purchase order.

Functional Area A functional area allows you to create a profit and loss account in financial accounting using cost-of-sales accounting, which compares the sales revenue for a given accounting period with the manufacturing costs of the activity. Expenses are allocated to the functional areas e.g. production, sales and distribution, and administration.

Group Counter A group counter identifies a unique routing within a task list (routing) group.

Initial Cost Split The initial cost split is based on a cost component structure for raw materials which contains separate cost components for all procurement costs such as purchase price, freight charges, insurance contributions and administrative costs.
With an additive cost estimate you can enter a cost component split for costs such as freight and insurance for a material. These costs are added to the price from the material master.

Input Price Variance Input price variance occurs as a result of component price changes after the higher-level cost estimate is released.

Input Quantity Variance Input quantity variance occurs as a result of a difference between plan and actual quantities of materials and activities consumed.

Input Variance Variances on the input side are based on goods issues, internal activity allocations, overhead allocation, and general ledger account postings. The four input variances are: input price, resource-usage, input quantity and remaining input variance.

Internal Order An internal order monitors costs and revenue of an organization for short- to medium-term jobs. You can carry out planning at a cost element and detailed level and budgeting at an overall level with availability control.

Inventory Cost Estimate An inventory cost estimate accesses tax-based and commercial prices in the Accounting 2 view for purchased parts, uses these prices for valuation, and then updates the costing results for finished and semi-finished products in the same fields. You can enter values such as the determination of lowest value in the tax-based and commercial price fields of purchased parts.

Investment Order An investment order monitors investment costs to be capitalized and settled to fixed assets.

Itemization Itemization provides detailed cost estimate data about the resources necessary to produce a product. The costing information for each item includes details such as the quantity, unit of measure and value.

Line Item Reports Line item reports display a list of postings to a cost object within a time frame. You can sort the value or quantity columns to find the largest postings during variance analysis.

Long-Term Planning Long-term planning allows you to enter medium- to longer-term production plans, and simulate future production requirements with long-term material requirements planning. You can determine future purchasing requirements for vendor requests for quotations and update purchasing info records prior to a costing run, and also transfer planned activity requirements to cost center accounting.

Lot Size Variance   Lot size variance occurs if a manufacturing order lot size is different from the standard cost estimate costing lot size.

Main Cost Component Split   The main cost component split is the principal cost component split used by a standard cost estimate to update the standard price. You define the main cost component split when assigning cost component structures to organizational units with Transaction OKTZ.

Mark Standard Cost Estimate   After a standard cost estimate is saved without errors it can be marked, which moves the cost estimate value into the future column in the Costing 2 view. You can create and mark standard cost estimates many times before release. Within the same fiscal period new standard cost estimates overwrite existing marked cost estimates.

Manufacturing Order   Manufacturing order is an umbrella term for production and process orders.

Master Data   Master data is information that stays relatively constant over long periods of time. For example, purchasing info records contain vendor information such as business name, which usually doesn't change.

Material Assignment   You use material assignment to determine which material is to be produced with a routing. On the basis of this assignment, the routing can be used for sales and operations planning, material requirements planning, creating production orders and cost estimates for this material.

Material Ledger   The material ledger consists of the following two parts. Inventory can be carried in up to three valuation approaches. Actual costing determines what portion of variance is debited to the next-highest level using material consumption. All purchasing and manufacturing differences are allocated upwards through the actual bill of material to assemblies and finished goods.

Material Master   A material master contains all the information required to manage a material. Information is stored in views, each corresponding to a department or area of business responsibility. Views conveniently group information together for users in different departments e.g. sales and purchasing.

Material Origin   The material origin indicator in the Costing 1 view determines if the material number is displayed in detailed reports. This is one of the single most important indicators in providing visibility to the causes of variances. If you have already created material master records without the material origin indicator selected, you can use report RKHKMAT0 to select the indicator.

Material Type   A material type groups together materials with the same basic attributes such as raw materials, semi-finished products, or finished products. Material types also determine whether materials are quantity and/or valuation relevant per plant with configuration Transaction OMS2.

Material Price Determination   Material price determination is displayed in the Accounting 1 view and is only applicable if the material ledger is active. Activity-based material price determination (indicator 2) allows price control to be set at either moving average price (V) or standard price (S). This is the setting you use if you are using multiple currencies and/or valuation approaches for transfer pricing, but not the actual costing functionality. In a typical scenario you are interested in reporting on global inventory valuation with and without mark up i.e. internal company profit. Single-/multi-level price determination (indicator 3) is only available for materials with standard price control (S) which remains unchanged during a period. A periodic unit price is updated for information during the period, and used for material valuation in a closed period.

Material Requirements Planning Material requirements planning guarantees material availability by monitoring stocks and generating planned orders for purchasing and production.

Milestone Confirmation The system automatically confirms all preceding operations up to the preceding milestone operation during confirmation of a milestone operation. An operation is marked as a milestone operation in the confirmations field of its control key.
If several operations are marked as milestones, they must be confirmed in the order in which they appear in the processing sequence.

Mixed Costing A costing method that uses multiple cost estimates to calculate a mixed price for a material. An equivalent number is applied to each cost estimate based on a procurement alternative. The result is a mixed cost estimate that can be used to update the standard price.

Mixed-Price Variance Mixed-price variance occurs when inventory is valuated using a mixed cost estimate for the material.

Modified Standard Cost Estimate A modified cost estimate is based on the latest quantity structure and planned prices, and is used for the costing of materials during the fiscal year in order to analyze developments.

Movement Type This is a key indicating the type of material movement such

as goods receipt, goods issue and physical stock transfer.
The movement type enables the system to find predefined posting rules determining how the stock and consumption general ledger accounts post and how the stock fields in the material master record are updated.

Moving Average Price The moving average price in the material master Costing 2 view determines the inventory valuation price if price control is set at moving average and is updated during goods receipt.

Multiple BOM A group of bill of materials that lets you record different combinations of materials (alternatives) for the same product.

Operation An operation is a work-step in a planned or manufacturing order.

Operation Scrap Operation scrap is the percentage of assembly quantity that does not meet required quality standards. Operation scrap is an output scrap, since it reduces the planned output quantity in the production process. You can plan operation scrap in the routing operation details view, and the basic data tab of the BOM item.

Order Type An order type categorizes orders according to their purpose and allows you to allocate number ranges and settlement profiles.

Organizational Unit This represents an organizational structure such as a sales organization in sales and distribution, company code in financial accounting and asset accounting, and plant in materials management and sales and distribution.

Origin Group An origin group enables you to separately identify materials assigned to the same cost element, allowing them to be assigned to separate cost components. The origin group can also be used to determine the calculation base for overhead in costing sheets.

Outline Agreement   This is a longer-term arrangement between a purchasing organization and a vendor for the supply of materials or provision of services over a certain period. The two types of outline purchase agreements are contracts and scheduling agreements.

Output Variance   Variances on the output side result from too little or too much planned order quantity being delivered, or because the delivered quantity was valuated differently. Output variances are divided into the following categories during variance calculation: mixed price, output price, lot size, and remaining variance.

Output Price Variance   Output price variance can occur in three situations. First, it occurs if the standard price is changed after delivery to inventory and before variance calculation. Second, it occurs if the material is valuated at moving average price and is not delivered to inventory at standard price during target value calculation. Third it can occur if you don't select the mixed-price variance indicator in the variance variant.

Overhead Group   An overhead group is used to apply different overhead percentages to individual materials, or groups of materials. You assign an overhead to an overhead key with Transaction OKZ2.

Overhead Key   An overhead key is used to apply overhead percentages to individual orders, or groups of orders. You assign the overhead key in the overhead rate component of a costing sheet.

Overhead Order   Used for short to medium-term monitoring of overhead costs such as marketing campaigns. You can monitor internal orders throughout their life cycle from creation, through the planning and posting of actual costs, to settlement and archiving.

PA Transfer Structure   A PA transfer structure allows you to assign costs and

revenues from other modules to value and quantity fields in profitability analysis.

Phantom Assembly   A phantom assembly is a logical assembly created for efficient maintenance of a single bill of material which is part of many higher-level assemblies. It is neither a physical assembly nor an inventory item. A phantom assembly is not included in a costing run however you can create an individual cost estimate.

Pipeline Material   Pipeline materials, such as oil or water, flow directly into the production process. Stock quantities are not changed during withdrawal.

Plan Reconciliation   This allows you to compare and overwrite the plan *activity quantity* manually entered in the second column of Transaction KP26, with the *scheduled activity* quantity automatically entered in the second last column. Scheduled activity quantities are transferred from sales and operations planning, material requirement planning or long-term planning with Transaction KSPP.
You carry out plan reconciliation with Transaction KPSI. You can select the *plan quantity set* indicator in an activity type to default as selected when planning activity prices and quantities with Transaction KP26. This ensures an activity quantity manually planned will not be overwritten during plan reconciliation.

Planned Order   Planned orders are created automatically by material requirements planning when a material shortage is encountered. A planned order may also be created manually by a planner. Planned orders are converted into production orders for in-house production and purchase requisitions or orders.

Planned Independent Requirements   Planned independent requirements are either created by sales orders or manually by entering quantities and dates in demand management. You may need to make manual entries to generate requirements for purchased components or assemblies with long delivery times in order to satisfy demand by sales orders which you expect, but are not yet entered in the system. An example of this is long-term government defense contracts which can specify several years before the first planned delivery to the customer.

Planned Price 1, 2 and 3   You can manually enter prices in these fields in the Costing 2 view. These are generally used to estimate the purchase price of components early in the lifecycle of a new or modified product.

Planning Plant   This is the plant in which the goods receipt takes place for the manufactured material. If the planning plant and production plant are identical then you need not enter the planning plant as well. The production plant is copied automatically.

Planning Variance   Planning variance is a type of variance calculation based on the difference between costs on the preliminary cost estimate for the order and target costs based on the standard cost estimate and planned order quantity. You calculate planning variances with target cost version 2. Planning variances are for information only, and are not relevant for settlement.

Preliminary Cost Estimate   A preliminary cost estimate calculates the planned costs for a manufacturing order or product cost collector. There can be a preliminary cost estimate for every order or production version, while there can only be one released standard cost estimate for each material. The preliminary cost estimate can be used to valuate scrap and work in process in a WIP at target scenario.

Preliminary Costing   Preliminary costing is carried out when you create a cost estimate for a manufacturing order or product cost collector. It is generally based on a

quantity structure which consists of a bill of material and routing.

Price Control   The price control field in the Costing 2 view determines whether inventory is valuated at standard or moving average price.

Price Indicator   The price indicator field in an activity type determines how the system automatically calculates the price of an activity for a cost center.

Price Unit   The price unit is the number of units to which the price refers. You can increase the accuracy of the price by increasing the price unit. To determine the unit price divide the price by the price unit.

Primary Cost Component Split   The primary cost component split provides an alternative view of cost components based on cost center primary costs. This allows you to more readily analyze changes to your more significant primary costs such as wages, energy and depreciation primary costs by displaying each as a cost component. These costs would normally be divided between cost components as activities are consumed during manufacturing.
This functionality is only normally required if you have significant primary costs that you need to analyze separately from the manufacturing process. To set this up you need to create a primary cost component split in cost center accounting when calculating the activity price. You can only use the primary cost component split to determine your activity costs into components if you automatically calculate the activity price.

Process Order   A process order is a manufacturing order used in process industries. A master recipe and materials list are copied from master data to the order. A process order contains operations which are divided into phases. A phase is a self-

contained work step that defines the detail of one part of the production process using the primary resource of the operation.
In process manufacturing only phases are costed, not operations. A phase is assigned to a subordinate operation and contains standard values for activities which are used to determine dates, capacity requirements, and costs.

Procurement Alternative A procurement alternative represents one of a number of different ways of procuring a material. You can control the level of detail in which the procurement alternatives are represented through the controlling level. Depending on the processing category, there are single-level and multilevel procurement alternatives. For example, a purchase order is single-level procurement, while production is multilevel procurement.

Procurement Type The procurement type defines the material as assembled in-house, purchased externally or both.
An in-house production entry (E) in the procurement type field in the MRP 2 view means a cost estimate will search for a bill of material and routing.
An external procurement type (F) results in the system searching for a purchasing info record price.
A procurement type of both (X) means a planned order can be converted into either a production or purchase order.

Product Cost Collector A product cost collector collects target and actual costs during the manufacture of an assembly. Product cost collectors are necessary for repetitive manufacturing, and optional for order-related manufacturing.

Product Drilldown Reports Product drilldown reports allow you to slice and dice data based on characteristics such as product group, material, plant, cost component and period. Product drilldown reports are based on predefined summarization levels.

Production Line A production line is used in repetitive manufacturing, and typically consists of one or more work centers.

Production Order A production order is used for discrete manufacturing. A bill of material and routing are copied from master data to the order. A sequence of operations is supplied by the routing which describes how to carry out work steps. An operation can refer to a work center at which it is to be performed. An operation contains planned activities required to carry out the operation. Costs are based on the material components and activity price multiplied by a standard value.

Production Process From SAP R/3 release 4.5A on, product cost collectors are created with reference to a production process which describes the way a material is produced i.e. quantity structure used. The quantity structure is taken from the production version, which is noted during the production process. The production process is determined by the following characteristics: material, production plant and production version. One production process can be created for each production version.

Production Resource/Tool A moveable operating resource used in production or plant maintenance.

Production Variance Production variance is a type of variance calculation based on the difference between net actual costs debited to the order and target costs based on the preliminary cost estimate and quantity delivered to inventory. You calculate production variance with target cost version 1. Production variances are for information only, and are not relevant for settlement.

Production Version A production version describes the types of production techniques that can be used for a material in a plant. It is a unique combination of bill of material, routing and production line and is maintained in the MRP 4, Work scheduling and Costing 1 views of the material master.

Profit Center   A profit center receives postings made in parallel to cost centers and other master data such as orders. Profit center accounting is a separate ledger which enables reporting from a profit center point of view. You normally create profit centers based on areas in a company that generate revenue and have a responsible manager assigned.

If profit center accounting is active, you will receive a warning message if you do not specify a profit center, and all unassigned postings are made to a dummy profit center. You activate profit center accounting with configuration Transaction OKKP which maintains the controlling area.

Profitability Analysis   Profitability analysis enables you to evaluate market segments, which can be classified according to products, customers, orders or any combination of these, or strategic business units, such as sales organizations or business areas, with respect to your company's profit or contribution margin.

Purchase Price Variance   When raw materials are valued at standard price, a purchase price variance will post during goods receipt if the goods receipt or invoice price is different to the material standard price.

Purchase Requisition   A purchase requisition is a request or instruction to purchasing to procure a quantity of a material or service so that it is available at a certain point in time. There is no legal requirement to carry out the purchase until a purchase order is created. You can record the purchase requisition in commitment management since it may lead to actual expenditure in the future.

Purchasing Info Record   A purchasing info record stores all the information relevant to the procurement of a material from a vendor. It contains the purchase price field, which the standard cost estimate usually searches for when determining the purchase price.

Purchasing Organization   A purchasing organization procures materials and services, and negotiates conditions of purchase with vendors.

Quantity Structure   A quantity structure consists of a bill of material and a routing. In the process industries a master recipe is used instead of a routing, and in repetitive manufacturing a rate routing is used instead of a routing. A quantity structure is used by a standard cost estimate to determine component and activity quantity.

Quantity Structure Control   Quantity structure control is a costing variant component which automatically searches for alternatives if multiple BOMs and/or routings exist for a material when a cost estimate is created.

Quantity Structure Date   The quantity structure date determines which BOM and routing are selected when initially creating a cost estimate. Since these can change over time, it is useful to be able to select a particular BOM or routing by date when developing new products, or changing existing products.

Reference Variant   A reference variant is a costing variant component which allows you to create material cost estimates or costing runs based on the same quantity structure for the purpose of improving performance or making reliable comparisons.

Release Standard Cost Estimate   When you release a material standard cost estimate the results of the cost estimate are written to the Costing 2 view as the current planned price and current standard price. Inventory is revalued during this process and accounting documents are posted. A standard cost estimate must be marked before it can be released and can be released only once per fiscal period.

Remaining Variance   Remaining variance occurs if variances cannot be assigned to any other variance category.

Remaining Input Variance   Remaining input variance occurs when input variances cannot be assigned to any other variance.

Repetitive Manufacturing   Repetitive manufacturing eliminates the need for production or process orders in manufacturing environments with production lines and long production runs. It reduces the work involved in production control and simplifies confirmations and goods receipt postings.

Request for Quotation   A request for quotation refers to the request made to a vendor to submit a quotation for materials or services.

Requirement   This is the quantity of material needed in a plant at a certain point in time.

Resource-Usage Variance   Resource-usage variance occurs as a result of substituting components. This could occur if a component is not available and another component with a different material number is used instead. The costs for both components are reported as resource-usage variances.

Results Analysis Key   Each product cost collector or order for which you want to create work in process (WIP) must contain a results analysis key. The presence of a results analysis key means that the product cost collector or order is included in WIP calculation during period-end closing. You define results analysis keys with configuration Transaction OKG1.

Rework   Assemblies or components that do not meet quality standards may either become scrap, or require rework. Depending on the problem, cheaper items may become scrap, while more costly assemblies may justify rework.

Routing   A routing is a list of tasks containing standard activity times required to perform operations to build an assembly. Routings, together with planned activity prices, provide cost estimates with the information necessary to calculate labor and activity costs of products.

Routing Header   A routing header contains data that is valid for the entire routing. Select DETAILS • HEADER from the menu bar when displaying a routing to display the routing header.

Sales and Operations Planning   This allows you to enter a sales plan, convert it to a production plan, and transfer the plan to long-term planning.

Sales Order   A sales order is a customer request to your company for delivery of goods or services at a certain time. A sales order line item can be a real cost object if you are using non valuated inventory.

Scale   A scale represents vendor quotations containing reduced prices for greater purchase quantities. Scales are entered when maintaining purchasing info record conditions with Transaction ME12.

Scheduled Activity   Scheduled activity quantities are transferred from sales and operations planning, MRP or long-term planning with Transaction KSPP to cost center/activity type planning. The scheduled activity quantity appears in the second last column when planning activity prices and quantities with Transaction KP26. You can compare and overwrite a manual plan activity quantity with the scheduled activity quantity during plan reconciliation.

Scheduling   During scheduling the system determines the start and finish dates of orders or of operations in an order. Scheduling is performed in material requirements planning, capacity planning and networks.

Scheduling Agreement   A scheduling agreement is a longer-term purchase arrangement with a vendor covering the supply of materials according to predetermined conditions. These apply for a predefined period and a predefined total purchase quantity.

Selection Method   The selection method field in the material master MRP 4 view determines the method of selecting an alternate BOM.

Settlement   Work in process and variances are transferred to financial accounting, profit center accounting and profitability analysis during settlement. Variance categories can also be transferred to value fields in profitability analysis.

Settlement Profile   A settlement profile contains the parameters necessary to create a settlement rule for manufacturing orders and product cost collectors, and is contained in the order type.

Settlement Rule   A settlement rule determines which portions of a sender's costs are allocated to which receivers. A settlement rule is contained in a manufacturing order or product cost collector header data.

Simultaneous Costing   The process of recording actual costs for cost objects such as manufacturing orders and product cost collectors in cost object controlling is called simultaneous costing. Costs incurred typically include goods issues, and receipts to and from an order, activity confirmations and external service costs.

You compare actual costs on cost objects incurred during simultaneous costing and period-end processing with planned costs on cost objects calculated during cost estimate creation during variance analysis.

Source Cost Element   Source cost elements identify costs which debit objects such as manufacturing orders and product cost collectors.

Source List   A list of available sources of supply for a material, indicating the periods during which procurement from such sources is possible. Usually a source list is a list of quotations for a material from different vendors.

You can specify a preferred vendor by selecting a fixed source of supply indicator. If you do not select this indicator for any source, a cost estimate will choose the lowest cost source as the cost of the component. You can also indicate which sources are relevant to material requirements planning.

Source Structure   You define source structures when settling and costing joint products. A source structure contains several source assignments, each of which contains the individual cost elements or cost element intervals to be settled using the same distribution rules. You need a source structure for investment orders.

Special Procurement Type   The special procurement type field found immediately below procurement type in the MRP 2 view is used to more closely define the procurement type. For example, it may indicate if the item is produced in another plant and transferred to the plant you are analyzing.

Special Procurement Type for Costing
If you enter a special procurement type in the Costing 1 view, it will be used by costing. If no entry is made in this field, the system will use the special procurement type in the MRP 2 view.

Splitting Rule   A splitting rule determines how a splitting structure distributes the cost center costs of an individual cost element, range or group over an activity type, range or group.

Splitting Structure   You can allocate activity independent cost center plan costs to activity types either with equivalence numbers or with a splitting structure. A splitting structure contains one or more assignments for which you assign splitting rules for corresponding cost elements and the activity types over which the costs are split. The plan price calculation splits the activity independent costs automatically based on equivalence numbers or a splitting structure if assigned. You can also split the plan costs manually to see how the plan costs are distributed to the activity types.

A splitting structure can also be used to view all cost center costs at the cost center/ activity type level during cost center plan/ target/actual comparison.

Standard Cost Estimate   This is a material cost estimate used to calculate the standard price of a material. The cost estimate must be executed with a costing variant that updates the material master, and the cost estimate must be released. A standard cost estimate can be released only once per period, and is typically created for each product at the beginning of a fiscal year or new season.

Standard Hierarchy   A standard hierarchy represents your company structure. A standard hierarchy is guaranteed to contain all cost centers or profit centers since a mandatory field in cost and profit center master data is standard hierarchy node.

Standard Text   You can use standard texts as templates to create texts for operations, phases, or secondary resources. The standard text associated with the standard text key defaults from the work center to the operation in a routing.

Standard Price   The standard price in the material master Costing 2 view determines the inventory valuation price if price control is set at standard (S). The standard price is updated when a standard cost estimate is released. You normally value manufactured goods at standard price.

Standard Value   This is the planned value for executing an operation in a routing. For example you may define that it normally takes five minutes to drill a hole in a metal plate, or that it takes one hour setup time to prepare to manufacture a batch of pharmaceuticals. The standard value is multiplied by the planned activity rate to determine the value of activities in cost estimates.

Standard Value Key   The standard value key in the basic data tab of an operation defines and gives a dimension (for example, time or area) to one of up to six standard values available in an operation.

Statistical Key Figure   Statistical key figures define values describing cost centers, profit centers and overhead orders such as number of employees or minutes of long-distance phone calls. You can use statistical key figures as the tracing factor for periodic transactions such as cost center distribution or assessment. You can post both plan and actual statistical key figures.

Subcontracting   In subcontracting you supply component parts to an external vendor who manufactures the complete assembly. The vendor has previously supplied a quotation which is entered in a purchasing info record with a category of subcontracting.

Summarization Hierarchy Reports   Summarization reports are based on data collected at the levels and nodes of a summarization hierarchy. A summarization hierarchy groups together manufacturing orders or product cost collectors at the lowest-level summarization nodes, which in turn are grouped together at higher-level nodes, to create a pyramid structure. You can create your own multiple hierarchies with Transaction KKR0.

Target Cost Version   The target cost version determines the basis for the calculation of target costs. Target cost version 0 calculates total variance and is used to explain the difference between actual debits and credits on an order. It is the only target cost version that can be settled to financial accounting, profit center accounting and profitability analysis.

Task List   A task list (routing) is a list of tasks containing standard activity times required to perform operations to build an assembly. Task lists, together with planned activity prices, provide cost estimates with the information necessary to calculate labor costs of products.

Task List Group   A task list group indentifies routings that have different production steps for the one material.

Task List Type   A task list type classifies task lists according to their function. Typical task list types include routing, reference operation set, rate routing and standard rate routing.

Template   A template allows you assign senders and receivers, calculate what is to be sent based on nearly any field available in orders and master data, and determine when the line is activated.
A template exists within an environment which defines columns available in the template.

Tracing Factor   Tracing factors determine the cost portions received by each receiver from senders during periodic allocations such as assessments and distributions.

Transfer Control   Transfer control is a costing variant component that requires a higher-level cost estimate to use recently created standard cost estimates for all lower-level materials. Preliminary cost estimates for product cost collectors use transfer control.

Transfer Price   This is the price charged for transfer of a material or product from one business unit (company code or profit center) to another. The amount of price mark up is generally determined by tax authorities in each country involved in the transfer, and is the basis of legal inventory valuation.
Global companies are also interested in global inventory group valuation excluding transfer pricing in consolidations reporting. This provides a view of inventory valuation based on actual cost of purchase and manufacture for internal reporting and analysis.

Total Variance   Total variance is a type of variance calculation based on the difference between actual costs debited to the order and credits from deliveries to inventory. You calculate total variance with target cost version 0, which determines the basis for calculation of target costs.

Under/Over Absorption   Cost center balance, otherwise known as under/over absorption, represents the difference between cost center debits and credits during a period or range of periods. Cost center under/over absorption occurs due to differences between plan and actual debits, and plan and actual credits.

Unit Costing   Unit costing is a method of costing that does not use bills of material or routings, typically when developing new products. You create a preliminary structure of materials and activities in a view similar to a spreadsheet.

User Exit   A user exit is a point in the standard program where you can call your own program. In contrast to customer exits, user exits allow developers to access and modify program components and data objects in the standard system.

Valuation Approach   A valuation approach describes the values that are stored in accounting as a combination of a currency type (such as the group currency) and a valuation view (such as the profit center valuation view). The combination of various valuation approaches is known as a currency and valuation profile.

Valuation Category   The valuation category located in the material master Accounting 1 and Costing 2 views determines which criteria are used to group partial stocks of a material in order to value them separately. The valuation category is part of the split valuation functionality. Normally you will have only one price per material per plant. Split valuation allows you to valuate, for example, batches separately. Moving average price (V) is the only price control setting available if you activate split valuation and enter a valuation category. You assign valuation types to valuation categories, and valuation categories to plants in Transaction OMWC.

Valuation Class   The valuation class in the material master Costing 2 view determines which general ledger accounts are updated as a result of inventory movement or settlement.

Valuation Date   The valuation date determines which material and activity prices are selected when initially creating a cost estimate. Purchasing info records can contain different vendor-quoted prices for different dates. Different plan activity rates can be entered per fiscal period.

Valuation Grouping Code   The valuation grouping code allows you to assign the same general ledger account assignments across several plants with Transaction OMWD to minimize your work. The grouping code can represent one or a group of plants.

Valuation Type   You use valuation types in the split valuation process which enables the same material in a plant to have different valuations based on criteria such as batch.

You assign valuation types to each valuation category, which specify which individual characteristics exist for that valuation category. For example, you can valuate stocks of a material produced in-house separately from stocks of the same material purchased externally from vendors. Then you select Procurement type as the valuation category and internal and external as the valuation types.

Valuation Variant   The valuation variant is a costing variant component that allows different search strategies for materials, activity types, subcontracting and external processing. For example, the search strategy for purchased and raw materials typically searches first for a price from the purchasing info record.

Valuation Variant for Scrap and WIP This valuation variant allows a choice of cost estimates to valuate scrap and work in process (WIP) in a WIP at target scenario. If the structure of a routing is changed after a costing run, WIP can still be valued with the valuation variant for scrap and WIP resulting in a more accurate WIP valuation.

Valuation View   In the context of multiple valuation and transfer prices, you can define the following views:
Legal valuation view
Group valuation view
Profit center valuation view
Together with a currency type and a currency, the valuation view creates what is called a valuation approach. You can maintain up to three different valuation approaches in financial accounting, controlling and the material ledger.

Value Field   In costing-based profitability analysis, value fields store the base quantities and amounts for reporting. Value fields can either be highly summarized (representing a summary of cost element balances, for example) or highly detailed (representing just one part of a single cost element balance).

Variance Calculation   Variance calculation provides information to assist you during analysis of how the order balance occurred. In other words, it helps you determine the reason for the difference between order debits and credits. It does this by analyzing variance causes and assigning categories. The three main types of variance calculation are: total, production and planning.

Variance Categories   During variance calculation, the order balance is divided into categories on the input and output sides. Variance categories provide reasons for the cause of the variance, which you can use when deciding what corrective action to take.

Variance Key   Variances are only calculated on manufacturing orders or product cost collectors containing a variance key. This key is defaulted from the Costing 1 view when manufacturing orders or product cost collectors are created. The variance key also determines if the value of scrap is subtracted from actual costs before variances are determined.

Variance Variant   The variance variant (Transaction OKVG) determines which variance categories are calculated. If a variance category is not selected, variances of that category are assigned to remaining variances. Scrap variances are the only exception to this rule. If scrap variance is not selected, these variances enter all other variances on the input side.

Version   Versions, formerly known as plan versions, enable you to have independent sets of planning and actual data.

WBS Element   See work breakdown structure.

Wildcard   Wildcard characters allow you flexibility when searching for data in tables. You can use * to replace any string of characters and + to replace any single character.

WIP at Actual   Work in process (WIP) at actual is valuated based on actual debits to a manufacturing order or product cost collector.

WIP at Target   Work in process at target is valuated based on a cost estimate.

Work Breakdown Structure   A work breakdown structure (WBS) exists within Project System as part of a project hierarchy. A WBS consists of WBS elements which describe tasks in a project to perform within a defined time period. A WBS element is a cost object.

Work Center   Operations are carried out at work centers representing, for example, machines, production lines or employees. Work center master data contains a mandatory cost center field. A work center can only be linked to one cost center, while a cost center can be linked to many work centers.

Work in Process   Work in process (WIP) represents production costs of incomplete assemblies. For balance sheet accounts to accurately reflect company assets at period-end, WIP costs are moved temporarily to WIP balance sheet and profit and loss accounts. WIP postings are canceled during period-end processing following delivery of associated assemblies to inventory.

Workflow   Workflow is a method of automating communications between people and processes in the system. For example you can automatically send an email to a user when the status of an item changes.

Bibliography

Andrea Anderson: *Quick Tip: Understanding CO-PA Reporting Table Types*. Financials Expert, Volume 1, Issue 6, June 2002.

Gary Fullmer: *Ask the FI/CO Expert: "How Can You Segregate the Expected Inbound Freight Costs in Manufactured Goods' Standard Cost Estimates?"* Financials Expert, Volume 1, Issue 5, May 2002.

John Jordan: *Product Cost Controlling with SAP*. SAP PRESS, December 2008.

John Jordan: *Production Variance Analysis in SAP Controlling*. SAP PRESS Essentials, December 2006.

Mitresh Kundalia: *3 Hidden Secrets to Help Fine-Tune the CO-PA Ledger*. WIS Financials, Las Vegas, March 2007.

Mitresh Kundalia: *The Good and the Bad of CO-PA's Transfer +/- Option*. Financials Expert, Volume 3, Issue 5, May 2004.

Rohana Gunawardena: *Hassle-Free Material Ledger Conversion*. WIS Financials, Las Vegas, March 2007.

SAP Training Course Guide: *AC412-Cost Center Accounting-Advanced Functions-Release 470*. April 11, 2006.

SAP Training Course Guide: AC415-Overhead Cost Orders-Release 470. April 11, 2006.

SAP Training Course Guide: *AC505-Product Cost Planning-Release 470*. April 11, 2006.

SAP Training Course Guide: *AC510-Cost Object Controlling for Products-Release 470*. April 11, 2006.

SAP Training Course Guide: *AC515-Cost Object Controlling for Sales Orders-Release 470*. April 11, 2006.

SAP Training Course Guide: *AC530-Actual Costing/Material Ledger-Release 470*. April 11, 2006.

SAP Training Course Guide: *AC605-Profitability Analysis-Release 470*. April 11, 2006.

SAP Training Course Guide: *AC610-Profit Center Accounting*-Release 46C. April 26, 2001.

Stef G.M. Cornelissen: *Quick Tip: Manually Adjust Postings from FI to CO-PA.* Financials Expert, Volume 6, Issue 5, May 2007.

Sydnie McConnell: *Summarize Your Cost Estimate Analysis View for More Flexible Reporting.* Financials Expert, Volume 6, Issue 8, September 2007.

Additional Resources

SAP PRESS Books

Two closely related books available for further reading are:

▶ *Product Cost Controlling with SAP*

▶ *Production Variance Analysis in SAP*

Each book discusses different areas in Controlling in SAP ERP and can be found at *www.sap-press.com*. You can use this book to reference the others.

OSS Note Search

OSS notes are corrections made available in advance to their release in a support package. Support packages are identified by release levels and are corrective OSS notes grouped together in packages and applied the system together. When you read an OSS note you should always check the affected releases and the support package it was delivered in mentioned at the end of the note.

The SAP Support Portal allows you to search the SAP knowledgebase for OSS notes relevant to issues you're investigating. You enter key words and search the knowledgebase for relevant notes. There are many OSS notes categories such as consulting, customizing, and program errors. Many OSS notes offer advice in areas where the system behavior isn't obvious, in addition to corrections for program errors.

One useful search technique involves searching for a system message number. Many OSS notes are related to system messages generated when you're having system difficulties. Message numbers are contained in OSS notes so you can locate them during a search containing the message number.

You access the SAP Service Marketplace with web address: *http://service.sap.com/*

You access the SAP Support Portal with web address: *http://service.sap.com/support/*

You'll need a user ID to logon to the Service Marketplace and Support Portal, which you can obtain by asking your manager or basis team.

Internet Search

The quickest and easiest way to look for information when researching an issue is an Internet search on a major search engine such as Google or Bing. Type in SAP and key words such a message number. Within the first results page you should find some useful links.

SAP Online Documentation

You'll find extensive documentation at the SAP Help Portal: *http://help.sap.com/*

Navigation through the menu paths can take some practice. The advantage of this search strategy is you can browse through nearby menu items to find related functionality. The help menu paths generally mirror the application menu paths.

You often encounter links to SAP online documentation on the results screen of an Internet search. While this can be the quickest way to navigate directly to online documentation, searching manually through the menu path structure can uncover useful related information that doesn't necessarily contain the search keywords.

Financials Expert Online

This website provides an extensive knowledgebase of finance related articles: *http://www.financialsexpertonline.com/*

The articles are well written by experienced SAP professionals. All articles go through a professional editing process. You can enter keywords and search for related articles. There's also a link to a schedule of upcoming financial conferences on the homepage.

While there is a subscription fee to read the full version of knowledgebase articles, it's a source of professionally written articles generally not readily available through any other source.

SAP Conferences

There are two organizers of major SAP conferences and events:

▶ Wellesley Information Services (WIS) is a leading provider of information to SAP professionals. WIS organizes annual financial conferences in several countries with typically thousands of attendees: *http://www.wispubs.com/sap/*

▶ Americas' SAP Users' Group (ASUG) is the largest community of SAP professionals. There are SAP user groups in most other countries. On the homepage you can access a calendar of events including large annual and smaller regional conferences: *http://www.asug.com/*

Conferences are a great way to expand your area of expertise in SAP by providing you the opportunity to attend sessions on other SAP modules. They also provide a great way to network with professional business users who work with the same issues that you deal with on a day to day basis.

ERP Corp Website

My company website offers information on assisting you with your SAP Controlling implementation, maintenance and upgrades, and details of consulting and training services. There are articles available for download, and a user forum you can post issues for comments by other site users. You can also become a member for discounts on downloads and receive a regular newsletter with tips and SAP news: *http://www.erpcorp.com/*

OSS Customer Message

When all else fails, you can create an OSS customer message. You create a customer message when you consider there is a program error. Be sure to fully research the issue with any or all of the above techniques before contacting SAP support directly. If your initial support contact considers the problem is that you don't fully understand the standard program you'll receive a short response advising the SAP consulting service is available for a fee.

OSS note 67739 provides detailed information on setting customer message priority. Web address: *http://service.sap.com/support/*

John Jordan is Founder and Principal Consultant at ERP Corp. Specializing in Controlling and all associated integration areas, he assists companies gain transparency of production costs, resulting in increased efficiency and profitability. He regularly speaks at conferences and publishes articles, and is the author of *Production Variance Analysis in SAP* (2006) and *Product Cost Controlling with SAP* (2008), both of which are SAP PRESS bestsellers. He is considered one of the leading experts in ERP Controlling Component by clients and peers.

You can reach John at *jjordan@erpcorp.com*.

Index

D

Includes insightful, ready-to-use tips and workarounds

Provides a visually-oriented, uniform design making the tips easy to use

Helps you save time and improve efficiency

Ajay Jain Bhutoria, Cameron Lewis

100 Things You Should Know About SAP ERP HCM

Have you ever spent days trying to figure out how to generate a personnel report in SAP ERP HCM only to find out you just needed to click a few buttons? If so, you'll be delighted with this book — it unlocks the secrets of SAP ERP HCM. It provides users and super-users with 100 tips and workarounds you can use to increase productivity, save time, and improve the overall ease-of-use of SAP ERP HCM. The tips have been carefully selected to provide a collection of the best, most useful, and rarest information.

approx. 300 pp., 49,95 Euro / US$ 49.95
ISBN 978-1-59229-361-2, Oct 2010

>> www.sap-press.com

Provides guidance for design, customization, and implementation of the SAP General Ledger

Includes details on new ledger definitions, Document Splitting, Profit Center Accounting, and parallel accounting

Features a complete chapter on parallel valuation for IFRS reporting

Eric Bauer, Jörg Siebert

The SAP General Ledger

This book gives you complete overview of the SAP General Ledger, including all of the new features like Document Splitting, Profit Center Accounting, parallel accounting, and Balanced Scorecard. It also includes a complete chapter on the SAP General Ledger's role in reporting for IFRS, including parallel valuation. A must-have for all finance professionals who have migrated or are migrating to the SAP General Ledger, this book is a resource that can be used in both daily work and at the implementation level.

505 pp., 2. edition 2010, 79,95 Euro / US$ 79.95
ISBN 978-1-59229-350-6

>> www.sap-press.com

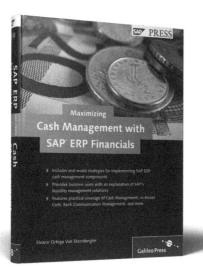

Includes real-world strategies for implementing and integrating SAP ERP Cash Management components

Provides business users with an overview of SAP's liquidity management solutions

Features practical coverage of Cash Management, In-House Cash, SWIFT integration, and more

Eleazar Ortega

Maximizing Cash Management with SAP ERP Financials

This book provides an overview of the functionality for all key cash management components, including best practices, real-world business scenarios, and key configuration and master data information. It explains how all the components can be integrated, and how both the individual components and the integrated solution can be maximized for optimal performance. Topics covered include SAP ERP Cash Management, Electronic Banking, Liquidity Planner, In-House Cash, Bank Communications Management, and integration with SAP ERP Financials and other components.

362 pp., 79,95 Euro / US$ 79.95
ISBN 978-1-59229-324-7

>> www.sap-press.com

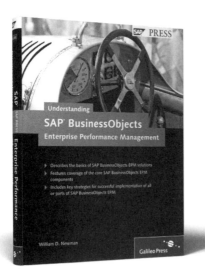

Provides key stakeholders and decision-makers with a practical functional overview of SAP BusinessObjects EPM solutions

Features coverage of the core EPM components, including BPC, FIM, SM, and SPM

Includes key strategies for successful implementation of all or parts of EPM

William D. Newman

Understanding SAP BusinessObjects Enterprise Performance Management

This book provides decision-makers with guidance on implementing and using the SAP BusinessObjects Enterprise Performance Management solutions, including Strategy Management, Financial Information Management, Spend Analytics, XBRL and more. Readers will benefit from the strategic, high-level overviews of the various products in the EPM application, and develop an understanding of the best practices for implementation, integration, and use. The scenario-based approach should appeal to a broad range of stakeholders, from executives to functional department heads and managers.

282 pp., 2010, 69,95 Euro / US$ 69.95
ISBN 978-1-59229-348-3

>> www.sap-press.com

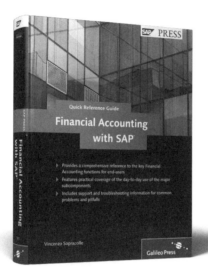

Provides a comprehensive reference to the key Financial

Accounting functions for end-users

Features practical coverage of the day-to-day use of the major sub-components

Includes support and troubleshooting information for common problems and pitfalls

Vincenzo Sopracolle

Quick Reference Guide: Financial Accounting with SAP

If you use SAP ERP Financials on a daily basis, this definitive, comprehensive guide is a must-have resource. You'll find practical, detailed guidance to all of the key functions of the Financial Accounting component, including troubleshooting and problem-solving information. You'll find easy-to-use answers to frequently asked questions in the core areas of the SAP General Ledger, Asset Accounting (AA), Accounts Payable (AP), Accounts Receivable (AR), Banking (BK), and Special Purpose Ledger (SPL). In addition, the book includes quick-reference material such as lists of transaction codes, tables, and menu paths.

665 pp., 2010, 69,95 Euro / US$ 69.95
ISBN 978-1-59229-313-1

>> www.sap-press.com

Interested in reading more?

Please visit our Web site for all
new book releases from SAP PRESS.

www.sap-press.com